Dark Oasis

© 2017 Jasun Horsley. All rights reserved.

Published by Auticulture Press.

Cover design: Jasun Horsley. From original artwork by William Blake.

Library of Congress Cataloguing-in-Publication Data

Horsley, Jasun, 1967—
    Dark Oasis: A Self-Made Messiah Unveiled, first edition

ISBN: 978-1-7751590-1-8 (pbk original)

1. Sociology, cults. 2. Spirituality. 3. Psychology, religious. 4. Memoir. 5. Biography.

http://auticulture.com

Dark Oasis

A Self-Made Messiah Unveiled

Jasun Horsley

Also by Jasun Horsley:

Paper Tiger: A Mythic Narrative
Seen and Not Seen: Confessions of a Movie Autist
Prisoner of Infinity: UFOs, Social Engineering, and the Psychology of Fragmentation (2018)
The Vice of Kings: Occultism, Social Control, Abuse Culture (2018)

"The greatest power one human being can exert over others is to control their perceptions of reality."
—Phillip K. Dick

"Don't ever buy nothing from a man named truth."
—Monsters of Folk, "Man Named Truth"

Contents

Introduction: Is Any of This True?   1

Part One: Snake in the Garden

- Beyond Anything You Could Imagine   8
- My Introduction to Gurus   10
- The Lion & the Lamb   16
- The Dying Portal   22
- When in Rome   29
- The Garden   32
- Into the Fire   36
- The Good King   39

Part Two: Intervention

- The Black Glove   46
- Word from God   49
- An Empire of Self-Interest: The Document that Overturned the Rock   53
- A Living Paradox   67
- Enter Joyce   72

Part Three: The Evolution of a Guru

- Early Years & "Awakening"   76
- Unconditional Surrender or Blind Submission?   83
- Early Christian Influences: Finney and Murray   88
- A Seasoned Warrior   92

- Silence is Golden: JDR, Game Player? 98
- The Key to Satan's Masterpiece 104
- The Demon-Carrier 110
- "I Am That": A Man After God's Own Heart 115
- Who Am I This Time—Myshkin or Machiavelli? 125
- Unveiling de Ruiter/Weaning Joyce 133
- A Ruse by Any Other Name 141
- Edging Towards the Dark Side 150
- John's Secret Id-Entity? 156

Part Four: The Shadow of Truth

- Injured Other 166
- The Bully of Light? 169
- Re-Writing Reality: Using Language for Spiritual Indoctrination 174
- Creating Dependency (A College without Graduates) 180
- A Golden Bubble: Spiritual Bypassing & "Okayness" as the Seeker's Opiate 190
- Individuation & the "Dark" Side of Spirituality 199
- Enter the Dragon: Archetypal Possession 207

Part Five: Don't Ever Buy Nothing from a Man Named Truth

- Off to See the Wizard 219
- Render Unto Caesar 228
- Candy's Story 232

- A Thorn in His Side   238

Part Six: Coming into the Now

- Meeting Machiavelli (2013 update)   244
- Wounded Anina (2015 Update)   248
- Ignorance is Strength: Oasis 2017   269
- Historical Precedents for Spiritual Power Abuse   280
- Casualties of "Truth"   287

Part Seven: End-Times at Oasis?

- A Wounded Choir/Injured Others   304
- The Perils of Matching "Perfection"   321
- Father & Son   333
- Reaching Out to Nicolas   344
- Oasis Strikes Back   350
- An Open Letter to Nicolas   358
- Selling Sand: Guru Worship, Reality Distortion & the Question of Harm   367

Appendix One: The Things Bob Had to Swallow   377

Appendix Two: The Bully Type   382

Appendix Three: Man of Sorrows: Hidden Christian Roots   386

Appendix Four: Ministered by Truth: Cult Mechanics in Action   394

Appendix Five: How to Spot a Cult   403

About the Author   407

Introduction: Is Any of This True?

"Who doesn't desire his father's death?"
—Fyodor Dostoyevsky

There are two things you need to know about cults. First, as a general rule, no one who belongs to a cult thinks they are in a cult. Second, the sort of people who join cults are not, generally speaking, cult-like people. They are not less but *more* intelligent than average, not less but *more* independent-thinker types. Most people who participate in something they eventually discover to have been a cult, do so because they are trying to get free from the, mostly unacknowledged, cult-like nature of greater society. They know enough to want to get clear of the mind control programs of culture, but not enough to recognize the danger signs as they leave the reservation. Desperate for orientation, now the cultural map no longer works for them, they fall prey to the first charismatic leader they come across. Or rather, the first charismatic leader who meets and matches their own needs, whose teeth fit their wound.

What follows is my own story of how I found the right guru-teeth to match my wounds and reenacted the original betrayal trauma. It is a cautionary tale that begins with the brightest of hope and ends in a deep, dark swamp of deception, manipulation, exploitation, and abuse. But, long and painful as it has been, this has also been a deeply illuminating journey, and it continues to be so. By the end of this rainbow, the pot of gold is looking to be where I might have least expected to find it: in the recognition that the only way to drain the swamp—is by entering all the way into it.

This book begins as an autobiographical account and it ends that way. This is all autobiographical, finally, because whatever drew me to this spiritual teacher in the first place, whatever caused me to fall "under his spell," is the same thing that drove me to deconstruct his story and find my way through the maze of projections and illusions, back to the truth of myself. The truth of "John de Ruiter" is something only he can ever fully know.

Based on my own brush with guru worship and cult mentality, the function and appeal (but also the *trap*) of gurus is that they help us to recreate a primary arrangement. When we follow a guru we experience ourselves as fundamentally inferior, at least insofar as we experience our guru as *superior to us* (and they would hardly be much of a guru if we didn't see them as our superior). This is a similar gulf to the one a child experiences between itself and its parents (and adults in general), just as if they belonged to a different species, a different *genus*. As children, we try to please our parents with good behavior; as we mature, we try to match *their* behavior as a way to bridge the gulf and become adults.

A child grows up (becomes socialized) *through a combination of obedience and imitation*, and this is more or less how "spiritual seekers" relate to gurus. That's the social overlay, anyhow. At a more primal level, a child's growth is a biological inevitability, and any child who grows to be an adult supplants its parents in the evolutionary chain, not merely by becoming their equal but by *surpassing* them. This is where the parallel with gurus and followers begins to fail, because it's extremely rare for a disciple to surpass their guru in stature. What's considered more common, on the other hand, is when, at some point, the guru is "exposed" in all his humanness and, through the resulting disillusionment, the follower "graduates"—or at least quits being a disciple.

This is more or less the process this book recounts, the standard coming of age ritual. To fully embody the role of father surrogate, a guru has finally to be recognized as a *false* authority. It's not enough for me to say, at the end of my experience, that I don't need a guru; first of all, the part of me that *did* need a guru has to be identified and integrated.

All of this is underneath my drive to analyze John de Ruiter and to work out the rights and the wrongs of his behavior and teachings. At the same time, as the narrative unfolds, it also presents an opportunity for me to enact the denied coming of age ritual of confronting *my own father*. Since my father was long dead by the time I met de Ruiter, de Ruiter became a surrogate, a stand-in for that lost ritual. I needed to look him in the eye and reject his jurisdiction over my life. While writing this book, my goal has been to weave my own experiences with what I hoped—with all the audacity of rebellious youth—would be a decent facsimile of de Ruiter's experience. If I judged him (and I did), it was only because I was judging *myself*. The apple of knowledge never falls far from the tree.

The personal history that makes up the bulk of this book is meant to present events and inner experiences as a written portrait of John de Ruiter. It is primarily inspired by the author's need to get stuff "off his chest," to get the psychic detritus of a failed discipleship cleared out, as if emptying an attic to turn it into a living space. While it is a true account, it's also a work of fiction because the mere act of writing things down turns them into fiction. If I am going to write about de Ruiter effectively, then, the first thing to admit is that this was never going to be an "objective" analysis. There's really no such thing as an objective anything; there are degrees of subjectivity, and one thing I want to avoid is a subjective interpretation that pretends to be objective. Hopefully, all of the personal history will make it clear just how personal, how *subjective*, my analysis of John de Ruiter is going to be.

Finding out that de Ruiter might not be the impeccable man of knowledge or living embodiment of Truth I once took him for caused a major upheaval in my psyche. To keep on with the living space metaphor, the experience was akin to discovering that the foundations of my house had termites in them. There wasn't anything to do at that point but to go down into the basement and see if it was possible to save my home.

The difficulty in writing this first part of the story was in staying accurate to the experiences I had *at the time*, while keeping my current perspective intact. Imagine if you wrote an account of a glorious love affair that lasted for a couple of years and then ended horribly. Everything you remember about that person from the early days was experienced through senses colored by passionate love and desire. But when you go back over the time, you will find yourself re-seeing it through the eyes of disillusionment.

I don't necessarily feel like John de Ruiter betrayed me. I certainly don't feel like he ruined my life. I think that, just as when we fall in love, I *allowed* myself to be fooled, even deceived—and that, to a large degree, I fooled and deceived myself. But I also think that this was easily as valuable an experience—perhaps considerably more so—than it would have been if no "betrayal" had occurred. In a certain sense, we cannot be "wrong" about being in love (the feelings we have are as real as we experience them to be). We can only be wrong about the degree to which we attribute those feelings to another person. Because all such feelings can only be sourced in ourselves.

Postscript, 2017.
I finished this book in early 2011. I sat on it for two years before returning to it and writing the first version of this introduction. I chose not to publish it during that period because I didn't trust my motives for writing it, much less releasing it. In

2013, I wrote that my primary motive was that this is a compelling story with the potential to serve as a cautionary tale for others and that, while I knew the appeal might be limited, I suspected there were readers out there who would find themselves in here. I never did publish in 2013, for reasons that are unclear to me now; presumably it was after going over the MS and feeling it still wasn't "right." I also reasoned that enough people by then knew the book existed, so if there was a clear reason to make it public, I would hear from at least one or two of them. I didn't hear from anyone.

Then, in May of 2015, I received an email from one of my sources, an ex-John-ite, informing me about a disturbing incident involving one of de Ruiter's followers, named Anina, who had gone missing in the forests of Alberta in 2014 and whose body was found a month or so later. Her death was ruled a suicide. Shortly after she disappeared, her parents allegedly received a call from John de Ruiter, in an alarmed state, insisting that Anina's death was not a suicide but definitely a crime! (They didn't even know she was dead at that point.)

Anina's journals (parts of which her parents made public in 2015) described her sexual awakening with de Ruiter; they included the phrase "John taught me how to make love," as well as: "I wondered how John can make love to many women while being married to one." The official position of Oasis, de Ruiter's organization, was that she was speaking of visions but *not of an actual physical relationship.* In 2015 De Ruiter categorically denied that any physical sexual interaction ever occurred between them. Anina's parents went public with passages from Anina's private journals. De Ruiter expressed public sympathy for their plight while privately he pursued legal action against them.

As a result of this disturbing development, I decided, once again, to publish the book. My reasoning was that, whatever possible distortions I witnessed around de Ruiter and his organization, and whatever harm his teachings may or may not have done to others, the collateral damage of his empire appeared to be getting worse. At the very least, there were surely a growing number of people who had followed de Ruiter and his teachings who were becoming increasingly divided internally, confused about whether or not they were doing the right thing. I felt that my own testimony could help them to reach a deeper understanding.

Yet somehow, I *still* didn't release the book. This time it was partially, though not entirely, out of a rational concern that de Ruiter might pursue legal action against me if I did so. It was also out of a general sense that it would be better to err on the side of patience and forbearance than of recklessness and zeal (which in the past had always been my tendency). Ironically, this is a philosophy I partially adopted from John himself, that the only thing to do is nothing.

Then, in March 2017, there were further developments at Camp Oasis, developments that finally and irrevocably confirmed the long-circulating rumors of John's sexual involvement with his participants and the existence of an "inner circle" (and practices) unknown to the larger community. Perhaps more arguably, the evidence of the harm wrought by this (probably decades-long) hidden arrangement of power, and the corresponding misuse, was also becoming indisputable. Even so, my primary aim in publishing this work is not to cast judgment on John de Ruiter or on any of his followers but to help facilitate a deeper understanding of what is, at base, an all-too-human problem. This is the problem at the heart, not only of spiritual groups but of all social groupings: the imbalance and abuse of power which no adult is either immune to or entirely innocent of.

Jasun Horsley, 2017

Part One
Snake in the Garden

"What you must realize is that God cannot turn out to be anything other than you."
—Joseph Chilton Pearce, *Evolution's End*

Beyond Anything You Could Imagine

"The best lack all conviction, while the worst
Are full of passionate intensity.
Surely some revelation is at hand;
Surely the Second Coming is at hand."
—W.B. Yeats, "The Second Coming"

I first heard of John de Ruiter from the woman who became my wife. We hadn't met in the flesh yet. She told me about John on the telephone.

"He is beyond anything you can imagine," she said.

"I can imagine quite a lot," I replied, testily. I was thinking of Carlos Castaneda's sorcerer teacher, don Juan, at the time. It was a bit presumptuous of me, since I didn't imagine him (Castaneda did).

"Well, OK. He is beyond anything *I* could imagine," she said.

She said something about John being like "the Second Coming." I was appalled. This was not a person given to hyperbole or absurd claims, nor was she the credulous type (she wasn't a Christian either). I fancied I'd had my own experiences and/or encounters with "Christ consciousness." I'd even believed, at times in my life, that I might be "the One." So I suspended judgment, both about my future wife's sanity and John de Ruiter's messianic qualities.

That night, I had a dream.

Flashback.

A few months before the conversation with my wife-to-be, before our paths had crossed at all, I was walking on Hampstead Heath, London, with an acquaintance called Gifford. I'd met Gifford a few weeks before through the intervention of my mother, who had given him a book I'd written in 2002 called *Matrix Warrior*. The book was a "handbook for unplugging" inspired by the famous sci-fi movie and sparked by my growing belief, or quasi-belief, that I might be The One. While Gifford and I were talking about it, he mentioned a guru he used to work for (doing sound recording) who had taken his followers to see the movie. I made a mental note of the guru's name and intended to do an online search. I then forgot all about it.

End flashback.

The night after my wife-to-be told me about John de Ruiter, while I was asleep and dreaming, I woke up and realized I was no longer in my bed. I was naked, lying on a table that was raised up at an angle so that I was almost vertical. On my right was John de Ruiter. In front of me, without using my eyes, I could see a row of people, all naked, watching me. They seemed to have angels' wings, which I took as an indication of benevolence and superhuman power. In other ways, they appeared quite ordinary.

I kept my eyes closed, embarrassed by my nakedness. I didn't know where I was or how I had got there; I resolved to pretend I was asleep until I woke up. There was another man on my left, whispering in my ear. At first it seemed like gibberish, then slowly I recognized it as a foreign tongue. I was being cleaned all over my body, with particular attention to my penis. A piece of wood was being used on my teeth, and someone, possibly John, was holding a sharp instrument, like scissors, near my groin. For a moment I was afraid I was going to be circumcised.

I had a dim recall of how I'd arrived there. The previous dream—from which I had "awakened"—was of being transported in the back of van, at night, through some eastern European country. There was intrigue involving Nosferatu-type characters, all unclear. In contrast to that, there was nothing dreamlike about the present experience.

John, or someone, said my name. "Jason." (I later changed the spelling to Jasun.) I replied with the affirmative, thereby letting them know I was awake. There was a feeling of excitement or anticipation among the gathering. It was similar to when Thomas Anderson is unplugged in *The Matrix*, when his naked body is brought into the Nebuchadnezzar and cleaned and reconstituted for his new existence. I was undergoing an initiation.

I was questioned about my father's business. The questions seemed nonsensical at the time, and even more so when I woke. Waking from the dream was like changing locations, or moving from one body to another. In the blink of an eye I returned to my previous existence, with memory of another, separate reality in which I had seemingly been "initiated."

The dream—or whatever it was—convinced me to look further into John de Ruiter.

My Introduction to Gurus

"So long as man remains free he strives for nothing so incessantly and so painfully as to find someone to worship."
—Dostoyevsky, *The Brothers Karamazov*

Until I met John de Ruiter I had no interest in gurus. I grew up as an atheist, mostly because of my father. My stepfather, a spiritual seeker, came along several years before my father left. His years teaching in India left him with aspirations to guru-hood, and he loved to counsel troubled souls (especially female ones). He practiced Yoga every day, and though he never tried to indoctrinate us, we were aware of his spiritual philosophy. As an adolescent, I saw him use my mother's money (having no other means of support) to fly to Oregon and attend a retreat with the Rajneesh community. He returned wearing dark red clothes with a picture of the Bagwan (Osho) around his neck. He was notably slower moving than before, more docile, and his eyes were glassy. My mother was not happy, even less so when he stopped having sex with her and continued to spend her money on return trips to Oregon.

This experience, combined with my ingrained religious skepticism, gave me a strong feeling of distrust and distaste for gurus and spiritual teachers. When Osho was imprisoned, it confirmed my belief that he was no more than a clever conman.[*] My perspective took a radical turn when, at the age of twenty, I discovered Carlos Castaneda and immersed myself in tales of sorcery. Don Juan became my imaginal guru. I read Aleister Crowley and became a student, though not a practitioner, of the occult arts. I learnt Spanish and spent two years in Mexico, "on the trail of don Juan." My two goals in life at that time were: 1) to meet a soul mate and fall in love; and 2) to find a man of knowledge and become a sorcerer. If I had been forced to choose between the two, I would have been hard-pressed, but would have probably picked the second.

Fitting, then, that meeting the woman who would become my wife (twenty years later) and finding a "man of knowledge" in the form of a Canadian citizen of Dutch descent named John de Ruiter, occurred almost simultaneously. In fact, one led directly

---

[*] Later, I discovered there was more to the story than that. As well as armed guards protecting the compound, there were claims that the food was drugged (which might explain why my stepfather seemed like a zombie when he came back). It has even been speculated that the entire community was, as also rumored about Jonestown, an intelligence operation, or at least heavily infiltrated by government agents, whose presence would have converted the community into something far from an authentic spiritual movement.

to the other. Until I met de Ruiter, a man of knowledge and a guru were two very different things to me. The "spiritual path" held no interest compared to the warrior's way and the world of sorcery (I read and re-read Castaneda's books over the years, until the teachings were ingrained in me). Perhaps because of my stepfather's folly, gurus, unlike sorcerers and magicians, were not something I took seriously.

The first time I met John de Ruiter, it was at the Center Point building, located in a sort of nameless space between Tottenham Court Road and Charing Cross Road, in central London. The building has a history to it, both personal and occult. The personal is that, as an adolescent, I used to travel from Yorkshire to London to buy Marvel comics at The Forbidden Planet on Denmark Street; seeing the Center Point building as I emerged from the London Underground signified that my quest for power was nearing its final destination, and filled me with a sense of great excitement. The occult history is something I only found out about while writing this book. Madeline Montalban, a witch, lived in an apartment at the site where Center Point now stands, and in November of 1949, her abode was the location of an occult ritual. The ritual was attended by Kenneth Grant, head of the British branch of the OTO (I corresponded regularly with Grant between 2001 and 2003), his wife Steffi, and Gerald Gardner ("the father of Wicca"). The aim of the ritual was to raise "a current of magical energy with the purpose of contacting certain extraterrestrial intelligences" by dancing around a large sigil inscribed on parchment, designed by the artist and magician Austin Osman Spare. The rite was interrupted, however—so the story has it—before the invocation could be completed.

Center Point was one of the first skyscrapers in London and construction finished around 1967 (reports vary), the year I was born. The building gained an increasingly notorious reputation as it remained empty for many years (between nine and fifteen, depending on the source); as late as 2005, several floors were still unused. Modern folklore attributes this to the uncompleted occult ritual, the as-yet unrealized summoning of extraterrestrial forces. Whatever the case, my first meeting with John de Ruiter was the first time I had set foot inside the Center Point building. I didn't know anything about its association with extraterrestrial intelligences or occult rituals at that time, but it was with a sense of excitement that I mounted the steps and entered the building.

The room consisted of a small stage with around sixty chairs arranged in front. It was almost full, and the people varied in age between mid-twenties and seventies, most in their thirties and forties. There was a PA to one side with a couple of technicians standing next to it. I went and spoke to them. I was told that, if no one asked a question, de Ruiter would simply sit in silence and that he might even leave. That struck me as a bit odd after everyone had paid fifteen pounds to get in. I hadn't paid (I had walked in without paying); but even so I was determined to make the trip worthwhile. After filling in some basic details and signing the form (giving them permission to use the recording), I sat in one of two chairs in front of the stage where de Ruiter would be sitting. There was a microphone, which we were shown exactly how to hold. I was both nervous and excited.

Presently, de Ruiter came into the room. He was easy to recognize because I had seen a YouTube video and some pictures at his website. He was tall and slim in a light-colored linen suit; his beard and hair were white-blonde and well-groomed. He moved in a graceful, slightly robotic fashion. He sat down and placed a thin microphone attachment around his ear. On the table next to him was a vase of flowers and a glass of water. He sat completely still for a time, staring straight ahead. His eyes slowly moved around the room, as if taking in everyone present. In order to see the people at the edges of the room, he moved his head slowly to the side, but besides this he made no visible movement. His stillness was impressive. He had enormous presence; without saying a word, he held the room.

I felt tense. My name was written at the top of a sheet of paper, but another man took the microphone before I did. He asked a question, I forget what it was, and after a long silence, de Ruiter began to speak. He spoke in an extremely slow, soft, and deep tone of voice. His sentences were broken by long pauses, sometimes as much as thirty seconds between phrases. What he said seemed extremely vague, bordering on meaningless. I was already familiar with de Ruiter's tempo and phrasing from the YouTube material and several audios which my wife-to-be had sent me. I had found them inconclusive, and despite my dream I hadn't made up my mind about him. I didn't understand why he felt the need to speak so slowly, or why he had to be so solemn the whole time. Couldn't he crack a joke once in a while? Or at least pick up the pace a bit? A lot of the time, as on this occasion, what he was saying really didn't mean much; it was a stream of spaced out (literally), poetic, simple-minded platitudes. I told myself that the questioner might be getting something from the words which I wasn't picking up on. De Ruiter was directing his communication at him and not at me, and I did my best to suppress my skepticism and suspend judgment until I had my own experience.

I had been told to wait until John looked at me before speaking, but when the time came I couldn't tell if he was looking at me or not. I am slightly short-sighted, and he seemed to be looking through me more than at me. Finally, he must have realized I wasn't ever going to speak.

"What can I do for you?" he said.*

I asked my question. De Ruiter spent several minutes gazing at me. Every now and then he opened his mouth or smacked his lips faintly, as if readying to speak, then became still again. Finally, he began to speak. With the first words out of his mouth, he zeroed in on something quite specific I had been working through with my wife-to-be. Just like that, with those first few words, I was a believer. We spoke for around twenty minutes and I did most of the talking. My experience was one of being led—by de Ruiter's words and perhaps other methods which I couldn't observe—to a deeper knowledge and understanding of myself. De Ruiter appeared to do this without ever addressing my intellect directly. Intellectually, his words were unimpressive and at times simplistic. My impression, after this first encounter, was that de Ruiter was bypassing my intellect and speaking *directly to my body*.

I went back to see him again the following night. This time, instead of listening, as a way to reduce my irritation with the endlessly asinine questions, I focused my gaze on de Ruiter and "tuned into" his physical presence. For the duration of the meet, I kept as statue-still as he was. By the end, my body felt both lighter and more solid. I experienced a feeling of peace and, at the same time, empowerment. Was this what it felt like to be John de Ruiter, I wondered? If so, it felt really, really *good*.

---

* After that time, I listened to countless tapes and went to many meetings, and never heard de Ruiter invite the questioner to speak, much less ask what he could do for them. This became a bit of a feather in my cap later.

The Lion & the Lamb

"Is it not possible to eat me without insisting that I sing praises of my devourer?"
—Fyodor Dostoyevsky, *The Idiot*

As it had been for my wife, John's impact proved life-changing for me. This wasn't just a philosophy or a system of belief; it was a way of being, and the proof was in the living. There didn't seem to be any possible downside, and I had no compunctions at all about spreading the gospel, any way I could, as far and wide as my media skills allowed. My position was as an anti-guru personality who had found a genuine guru. At the time, I thought I was the *last* person to be brainwashed or duped into worshipping another human being. I saw myself as an Apostle of John. The first time I was interviewed about de Ruiter (on Diet Soap podcast, with Doug Lain), the show aired on November 11th, 2009—John's 50th birthday! Naturally I saw it as a sign, and I sent him a birthday email via Oasis. I never received a response.

Some people questioned my admiration of de Ruiter, insisting he was just another corrupt guru. The most damning evidence they cited was de Ruiter's messy break up with his wife, Joyce, in late 1999, the result of his affair with Benita and Katrina von Sass, two sisters born in Canada of German descent. Though de Ruiter spoke repeatedly of "core-splitting honesty," apparently he had neglected to mention to Joyce his new "bond of being" with the two sisters. His wife (a Christian, as John had also been before his awakening) was understandably upset and accused him of adultery. John's explanation was that he had not told her about the affair because it had been "a movement of being" and he had only been doing what he knew in his heart to be true. I understood from this that he had neglected to mention it out of innocence rather than duplicity. If he hadn't denied it when Joyce accused him of adultery, it was because, to him, it *wasn't* adultery. To most people this was a dubious, not to say puny, excuse. But by then de Ruiter was such an exceptional being to me that I accepted his version over his wife's unquestioningly. Like many of his other followers at the time, I considered him beyond ordinary moral (or even human) judgment.

For myself, I *knew* that his philosophy of "okayness" worked. Letting go of the endless drive to achieve or self-improve, the ceaseless discipline of the warrior's way or spiritual path, was a profound breakthrough for me. It was the truth I had been waiting my whole life to hear, that it was okay to be an ordinary person, that there really was nothing to do, because "no one can do 'to be.'" Essential to de Ruiter's teachings was the idea that we, as persons, are "wonderfully worth nothing." De Ruiter taught that the self we are accustomed to is a constructed, false self that has usurped the throne of our true being. Its only value and function is in giving over that space to our "being" and letting it live our lives for us. Like Thomas Anderson's life in the matrix, our ordinary selves were expendable. Deep down inside, I knew the truth of it. It was how I had always felt myself to be: worthless. Hearing that "nothing works but surrender" was music to my battle-weary ears.

*

When I had first seen John at Centre Point, I had come away with the impression that he was a mostly *yin* being, passive, like a baby. I had felt a desire to take care of him. I distrusted the apparatus that had formed around him, the Oasis community, and I suspected it was a result of his passivity, of his being so surrendered that he didn't have any interest in what grew up around him, like barnacles on a rock. I had heard (from my wife to be) that he let himself be groomed and dressed by the von Sass sisters, hence there was a dramatic change in his image around 2000 (when he first started out, he looked more like a redneck Jesus).*

The other main impression I got of de Ruiter was that he seemed to be lacking an obvious dark side. His apparent absence of *yang* energy, of a dynamic, provocative, challenging presence, his baby-like placidity, all begged the question of where his other side was hiding. He had an unmistakably Christ-like persona—but where was the other guy? Where, and what, was de Ruiter's shadow? I wondered if it had to do with his having attained enlightenment before he had fully integrated that shadow? (According to his website bio—which is a bit vague—he was only nineteen or twenty when he had his second awakening.) I didn't take my speculation much further, and I didn't question what might become of an enlightened being's shadow. The idea that de Ruiter might be in any way corrupt or untrustworthy (due to this apparent lack in him) didn't occur to me. What did occur to me was that he seemed somehow incomplete.

The second time I saw de Ruiter was in the UK, in April of 2010, around twenty months after our first meeting and a week after my 43rd birthday. Before the first meeting, one of the Oasis group told my wife and I that John had been married the year before. We were both surprised: we hadn't even heard about his break-up with the von Sass sisters! I experienced a moment of cynicism, and made a quip about John being "unlucky in love." What bothered me was the clear evidence that, for all his truth-

---

* Actually, John's look begun to transform before the von Sasses came along. According to one of my sources: "One lady who worked in the visual media industry called Jeanne Parr suggested to him that if he wore those clothes and had his hair down people would not take him seriously."

embodying, de Ruiter didn't have much of a track record with relationships. Though I took my doubts with me into the first meeting, they dissolved into nothingness as I gazed at him on stage. His form seemed to shift and change as I stared at it and he appeared to be filled with light. His face seemed to be looking in several directions at once, and I hallucinated that he was sitting, standing, and levitating, all at the same time. As he sat in his leather chair, he emanated power, presence, charisma. His stillness and silence inspired awe. His voice sounded like it came from underwater, flowing like honey or nectar, soothing as it entered me, filling me with sweetness, nourishing my being.

At the second meeting of the first day (April 15th 2010), I took "the Chair." I told John I didn't know what I was there for, since the only thing I wanted was pain relief and I knew there wouldn't be any of that. I talked about my absent father and how he had left "a big hole in my life." I said that I had finally found someone big enough to fill that hole. I told him that he had come to me in my dreams and that I felt like I was "his." I wondered if he could ask me a question, since I trusted him "more than myself" to come up with the right question. Five minutes passed in silence while we gazed at each other and I got lost in all sorts of visual hallucinations.

Finally, he spoke. "You have been awakened," he said. The words gave me a thrill. "Awakened to the profound reality within. It moves you, by your own awareness in it—it apprehends you. You know it's bigger than all of the self that you're accustomed to. More than your self, it's more than your person and your life. You've been awakened to greater reality within. Once awakened to that, you are also called to that."

I felt validated, vindicated. De Ruiter was acknowledging my awakened nature, and letting everyone else there know it too. He was giving me confirmation of my calling.

"You have yet to apprehend that within that has already apprehended you," he said. "You have yet to surrender to your own deeper, real knowledge within. . . . You already know that your surface existence doesn't belong to your surface existence. It belongs to your knowing and to your seeing. This that you're knowing isn't an interesting category within yourself that you can bring into your life to add greater meaning. This that you're knowing and seeing and in touch with within is what you come from. It is what you completely belong to. Everything that's yours belongs to the same that you belong to."

He spoke about reaching an agreement within myself, a full-heart's agreement with what I know the truth of. He spoke of "waves of change," and of an incorruptible knowledge within me. "This first knowledge within is incorruptible," he said. "You can cover it but you can't alter it. It resonates clear through anything you put on top of it. This knowing is you. You are waiting for you to agree with you."

He spoke some more and I listened with a rapt and sheeplike expression (I know because I saw the video later). After a long pause, I thanked him, content to end the talk there. There was a longer pause, then he said: "*What are you going to do?*"

It sounded almost like a challenge. I had never heard John ask anyone a direct question like this (not even on all the tapes I'd listened to). "I am going to agree with myself," I said at last.

"And that won't be making meaningful decisions," he said. "It will be meaning, making decisions. Your decisions as meaning will be uncharacteristic to what self you had. You will be that way. Your entire self will change. The very patterning of your self won't remain the same. You'll be meaning that has a being. A meaning with being that has a self. A meaning-being-self in person moving through life, doing from within that that you first are. You won't be governed anymore by emotions and will, feeling. Meaning-you, meaning-knowing will be covering, integrating everything that you haven't integrated yet. *A massive clean, clear growing up of the innermost outwards, manifesting an entire life.* Being that which you are born for. Meaning the full, complete coming into you."

"I see a flower opening," I said.

"It will petal your life instead of want and need doing so. You'll be meeting every threshold in your self that you've been running away from. You'll be healing every line within, every line of knowing that you've crossed. In a living way you'll be healing yourself. You'll be setting your self beautifully right."

I told him I couldn't have done it without him. He gazed at me for a time. I didn't notice it until I saw the video later, but at this point a tear ran down his cheek. "You'll be as awareness," he said, "freeing yourself of bondage of unreason, freeing your self of the habitual misuse of reason. You'll be freeing your self of the addiction to the misuse of reason. You'll be setting your mind right. You'll be thinking as reasonableness. You'll be thinking with the sensitivity that love has. Your mind and your deep heart will be by you made to be congruent. Softness of heart with a sharp mind. Openness of heart with the will brought to one fine point, moved by meaning."

"When you speak of the sharp mind," I said, "I think of a sword, and I think of Christ saying that he brought the sword and not peace. I think of how I've been a warrior for my whole adult life, until recently, when I felt it was time to put down my arms and surrender." I paused. "Am I still a warrior?"

We sat in silence and I realized he wasn't going to answer my last question. I hadn't really expected him to. When I watched the video of the meeting, however, he seemed to be nodding his head very slightly.

The Dying Portal

"You can't fool me! There ain't no sanity clause!"
—Chico Marx, *A Night at the Opera*

On the fourth day, I approached John with his wife outside the university building where the meetings were held. The thought of approaching him filled me with apprehension. It was like meeting a childhood hero—e.g., Clint Eastwood—and it required a concerted act of will and courage to do it. I put my arm around my wife, steering us over to where he was. My wife seemed as nervous as I was. She asked John if it was okay to say hello. He nodded. She introduced herself to Leigh Ann, and we both shook Leigh Ann's hand. Automatically, I extended my hand to de Ruiter. I had met someone who claimed to be enlightened in London in 2007, and they didn't allow physical touch; so as I extended my hand I said to John: "I don't know if you do handshakes," thinking this would spare us some embarrassment if he didn't respond.

He took my hand in a firm but gentle grasp. I gazed into his eyes. He had an eerily placid smile on his face and his eyes were unlike anything I'd ever seen before. There was an indescribable motion to them; it was as if the pupils were swimming around inside the irises. It was a bit like gazing at the night sky. He looked the way people look when they are on LSD or magic mushrooms. He had a baby's eyes. I saw boundless wonder in that gaze; he seemed to be drinking in my being.

I told him that I was an author, and asked if he'd like me to tell his story. He looked at me for several seconds, then softly, almost apologetically, he said, "Someone is already working on it."

I did my best to conceal my disappointment, expressed enthusiasm (genuine), and asked if it was a regular biography or a (ghost written) autobiography. "Regular," he said.

"I do desire a personal connection to you," I said. "I think it's to do with something you said the other day. 'An innocent heart . . . uses intelligence to get closer to what moves it the most.'" I had paused on "innocent heart," doubting my heart's innocence. He nodded again.

I was aware of Leigh Ann pulling on his arm. She said something about having to go and I realized that their taxi had arrived. My wife made a polite comment to ease their exit, and they left without another word.

*

During the Bristol seminar, a volcano erupted in Iceland and all flights were cancelled. Since de Ruiter and crew were unable to leave as planned, they set up more meetings in Amsterdam, and my wife and I followed him there. We were on a grand adventure, on the trail of Christ. I knew I was starting to sound like a brainwashed cult member, and that it was an experience few people would understand. It was hard for me to understand that others *couldn't* understand it. This was more than a part of my life, it *was* my life. Everything I did, "John" was doing it through me. I was an extension of his being.

There had also apparently been a shift in what de Ruiter was doing. He had done an interview on Bristol radio, talking almost like a normal person—an unusual occurrence at that time. He was having someone write his biography. He had just got married, more or less the same time I had. There were so many resonances that convinced me of the deep affinity between us. I was ready to move to Edmonton and sit in front of John for the rest of my life. I knew that was nonsense. If I did move to Edmonton, it would be to serve "Truth" in some way. But surely that wasn't the way it worked? It was an extending consciousness, and I would become an extension not of John but of what John was an extension of, which was what I already was anyway. There was no need to move to where he was. But then again, to be able to actually *report* to a living embodiment of that—the idea of it changed everything.

When my wife and I left Bristol, I had a powerful, visceral sense of being embraced by the energy and awareness of de Ruiter. I felt it around us, like a nest. I sensed a hidden latticework of connections that John was at the center of. It was inevitable, I had always known it would happen; but to have actually made personal contact with not just somebody in that realm but with . . . I didn't *know* John was the One. I didn't *know* he was Christ. I only knew that he was beyond anything I'd encountered before, so far beyond it that I couldn't imagine anything beyond what he was, and I didn't feel any need to. From where I was standing, everything was over. Everything was vibrant and alive and shimmering with beauty and intensity and searing honesty, reality. I was on the line. I had been hooked.

The first Dutch meeting was in a tiny village called Lage Vurrges. The venue was extremely hard to find but we managed to get there at the last moment. Just before the meeting began, I ran into John again. He was in the toilets, waiting for his wife to wash her hands. I came up behind him on his right and he swiveled around like he was on a pivot; our eyes met and I said, "Hey John." "Hi," he said, with a twinkle in his eye. He seemed pleased, and perhaps surprised, that I had come all the way to this obscure Dutch village to sit at his feet again.

At the meeting, my wife and I sat on the floor in front of the little stage, the closest I had ever sat to John. For the first part of the meeting, I experienced extreme physical well-being in which I felt as though I might levitate. John was speaking to a woman about awakening, and I began to get the clear impression that he was tuning into my consciousness, "mining" my experience to add it to his own. I couldn't quite explain this impression, but it was unmistakable and clear. The next day we traveled to Amsterdam for the rest of the meetings (three more days of them), and it was there, on the last day, that I had my third direct encounter with de Ruiter.

I'd brought with me a copy of my book, *The Secret Life of Movies*, published earlier that year, to give to John if the opportunity arose. I knew he was a film fan and that he screened special "truth movies" for his congregation in Edmonton. I didn't know if he read books, however, so I inscribed the book to Oasis as a collective offering and handed it to one of the crew, Dorine, on the last day. Dorine insisted I give it personally to John. I reluctantly agreed, though it was what I'd secretly hoped for. Before the last meeting, in the lobby of the American Hotel, Dorine had me wait in an armchair outside the meeting room. Waiting to meet the man of my dreams was like waiting for the firing squad. Seeing my nervousness, one of the women on the team, Carla, reassured me. "John is a lovely man," she said. "How could he not be?" I replied.

De Ruiter arrived with his wife and I did my best to look casual and at ease. Dorine waved her hand at me in a "No" gesture. John and his wife stopped in front of me, facing the doors of the meeting room. Neither acknowledged my presence. I was invisible, my input was not required. I had no choice but to sit there, book in hand, while the royal couple waited to be announced. I looked at John for several seconds, and finally he looked over (I was on his right) and said "Hi." It was an acknowledgment, but not an invitation.

*

Soon after returning to Canada, I was pleased to notice that my Bristol dialogue with de Ruiter became the first video download at the College of Integrated Philosophy website, and was numbered "001." I took this as a secret sign from the Master, letting me know that I was the One, the beloved disciple, the chosen apostle, the Messiah's right-hand-man. Watching the video was an uncomfortable experience, however. I looked like a frightened rabbit caught in the glare of headlights, a New Age sucker under the spell of his guru. I looked like just the sort of person I would once have despised.

*

"In your life be me instead of you."
—John de Ruiter, 2017

On June 17th, my brother was found dead of a heroin overdose in his apartment in Soho. I flew back to England for his funeral. I spent time with my mother, whose health had deteriorated rapidly since my last visit (more from malnutrition than cancer), and I considered staying in England to be near her. In the end, I decided not to. In late August, less than two months later and a few days after a long telephone conversation with her, my mother went into a coma. I flew back a third time, and after two days at her bed side, she died.

In my dialogue with John in April, he had predicted "waves of change," and a "massive, clean, clear growing up." Now I was coming of age whether I wanted it or not. During this period, I had also begun to develop sciatica pain, and the night before my mother's funeral, it became severe. By the time I returned to Canada a few days later, it had not improved. Soon after, despite repeat visits to a chiropractor, I was walking with a cane. My father began to walk with a cane in his early forties—roughly the same age I was. In the last years of his life, my father was confined to a wheelchair. By the time my wife and I flew to Edmonton to attend the Oasis autumn seminar, in October 2010, my condition was severe enough for me to use a wheelchair at the airport. Although sciatica is not related to my father's condition, the symmetry was too exact to ignore. An ancestral wound had opened up.

I had never seen John in his habitat before, and we arrived a week before the seminar so we could attend several of the ordinary meetings. In the weeks leading up to the trip, I had been getting to know people in the Oasis community ("John-ites") a little by posting at the Google group, "Birds of Being." One of the group, Kesh, had offered us a place to stay in Edmonton. Kesh was a former follower of Osho who had been in Edmonton for ten years. Kesh went to all the meetings so we had easy transportation back and forth—essential in my condition. We had timed it so that we arrived just before a Friday evening meeting, and Kesh took us straight there.

The College of Integrated Philosophy was an impressive building. Built by Oasis in 2003 under the direction of de Ruiter and his common-law wife, Benita von Sass, it held meetings four times a week ($8 a meeting), and seminars throughout the year ($30 a meeting), which sometimes lasted as long as two weeks. The rest of the year the space was rented out for other functions. The front part of the building was the Jewel Café, designed by Benita.

As I entered the café, I noticed an air of excitement and expectancy hanging over the gathered crowd. People looked at me with curiosity, possibly recognition. I suspected they had seen the Bristol download and/or found out about me via my various internet media. Just about everyone I spoke to recognized me from the Bristol download, and they all complimented me on it. I felt myself being absorbed into the Oasis community the moment I walked through the doors.

These weren't the normal quick, furtive glances of strangers. They were warm and open gazes that invited conversation. Behind them was an unspoken assumption: if you were here for John, you were a kindred spirit. Potentially, you were a new member of the Community—a fish fallen into the net.

The meeting hall was impressive. With marble columns and crystal chandeliers hanging from an extremely high ceiling, it was like a cross between a church, a movie theater, and a five-star hotel lobby. Rows of very comfortable, theater-style seats, perhaps five hundred in all, were arranged around a small stage. On stage there was an adjustable leather chair and a table with the ubiquitous vase of flowers and glass of water—John's props. On both sides of the stage was a large screen. Two cameras were mounted on metal poles, one directly in front of the stage, the other off to one side, to capture both side and head-on angles. At the back of the room was a sound-proofed recording booth.

That first meeting, on Friday evening, the 1st of October 2010, John was less talkative than when I'd seen him in Europe. I put it down to his being with his own crowd and not needing to cater to non-initiates. The questions he was asked weren't especially profound, and neither were John's responses. Towards the end of the meeting, however, I had a visceral experience of being connected to everyone in the room. For some reason, I imagined all of us dying at the same time as we entered into "the more of us." I focused on my brother and my mother, now passed over to the other side. I thought about my wife's future death, John's, and my own, all inescapable events in the very near future. It seemed possible, desirable even, that we all go together. We were there to let go of our false identities, and John was the focal point of that surrendering motion. He was the portal through which we would all be passing, at the designated hour.

When In Rome

"You are the only light there is
For yourself, my friend
There'll be no saviors any soon coming down
And anyway illuminations
Never come from the crowned"
—"Illumination," Gogol Bordello

After the first couple of meetings, I felt raw and vulnerable. The "kingpin of sovereignty" was coming loose and I was dying to life, freefalling. I felt an undercurrent of anger without object, mild but persistent. I attributed it to my ego putting up inevitable resistance. My wife experienced some discomfort being at the café because so many people approached her and identified her as "Jason's wife." (My wife is autistic and prefers to pass unnoticed.) She had lived for over three years in Edmonton, so she was also being recognized by people in the community who were surprised to see her back. (The impression I got was that generally, when someone leaves "the fold," they do not return.)

We were told how, since Benita left, or was pushed out (stories varied), and Leigh Ann had replaced her as First Lady, the atmosphere at Oasis had improved drastically. The warmth and openness so apparent to me had not been there before, people said, and this extended to John himself, who now hung out in the café before meetings, interacting freely with his community. (During Benita's "reign," this would never have happened.) We were told that John liked to meet new arrivals and would probably want to chat with us. While I was hoping for just such an opportunity, I was also wary of trying to force it.

In the months leading up to our trip, I had interacted with Oasis several times, via email or telephone, and had become aware of an unpleasant tendency in me, a constant, only partially conscious attempt to get special attention. As often as not, this came out in the form of subtly questioning John's authority. For example, when I found out my talk with John in Bristol was available as a download (for $32), I emailed Oasis and asked for a free copy. I suggested it might be a good policy to give free copies to people who were featured in the videos. I was told they would check with John and get back to me. A day went by and I began to have misgivings. Was I just trying to get daddy's attention by creating a scene? Did I really want to bother John with such trivialities and become known to him as the guy looking for hand-outs? I quickly emailed Oasis and assured them I didn't want special treatment. I received a prompt and grateful reply.

A similar incident occurred when I volunteered to assist with the Victoria, B.C., seminar in September. I had assumed that volunteers would, at the very least, be given free entry to the meetings; but when I asked about it, I was told there were no perks beside the delight of being part of John's team. I made a skeptical sound and was told that the seminars often barely covered their costs, and that a large part of the revenue came from the volunteers. I accepted this explanation at face value, and agreed to help on those terms (I never went to Victoria in the end, as funds did not allow).

Earlier in the year, I had heard from a friend in England, the afore-mentioned Gifford, that de Ruiter traveled first class (at least he had when Gifford worked with him). This idea caused cognitive dissonance for me. John preached a philosophy of surrendering to discomfort as a means to "go finer"—and he liked to fly first class?! After thrashing it out in my head for several days, I eventually decided that, if it was true, it might not have been John's decision but that of one of his wives. Maybe he had simply gone along with it in his supremely surrendered fashion? This put my mind at ease, for a while at least.

When I heard about Oasis not being able to cover the costs of the seminars, the doubt resurfaced. Were volunteers helping to pay for John's first-class air tickets? The bottom line was that I didn't actually *know* ("stay in what you know"). As always, I returned to the fact that this was *John*, and all bets were off when it came to living embodiments of truth. His goodness, honesty and straightness were not in question, and that effectively canceled out all my other doubts. Who was I to judge a man like this, based only on hearsay and rumor and what were, at best, pieces of the puzzle? I didn't trust myself not to make a mountain out of a molehill and turn trivial details into excuses not to surrender. (From what I'd heard, John even smoked cigarettes!) John taught his followers not to trust thoughts and feelings but only "what they knew." What did I *know* here? That I *did* trust John—*he* was trustworthy, and I was not. The rest was idle speculation. Perhaps, by not paying volunteers, John was providing them with an opportunity to surrender, to do what they knew in their hearts was true without receiving any perks for their persons?

I already had a track record of being rebellious and of questioning authority, of either breaking the rules or demanding they be bent to suit me. Did I want to bring this sort of energy to Oasis? Wouldn't it just create unpleasantness for others and be painfully exposing for myself? Wouldn't it be better if, for once in my life, I respected the rules and honored Oasis' way of doing things? The bottom line was that, if I trusted John as my guide, guru, and "*nagual*," couldn't I trust him to run his own business affairs? The real challenge was to surrender my doubts and trust John, all the way, regardless of anything my thoughts or feelings might be telling me about him.

When in Rome ... surrender to Caesar.

The Garden

"I know nothing, except the fact of my ignorance."
—Diogenes

In order to give the reader a better sense of my overall experience during the seminar, here are some thoughts I expressed via an audio journal at the time:

It's very hard to talk about John or describe him without expressing religious awe, without wanting to use terms that are going to be meaningless, if not offensive, to people who haven't encountered that goodness, that subtlety of goodness, which he is. Of course everyone here is in awe of John, and many do worship him, have a worshipful relationship with him, or to him. I don't think he takes any of that anymore. I haven't really interacted with these worshipful ones, though I sense them. It may well be that there are two types of people here: the worshippers, and those who are beginning to embody what John is. Though they also look to John with awe, wonder, love, and adoration, it is without projecting to the same degree their own wants and needs.

I know the Aries [my astrological sign] thing is to do what you're afraid of. I'm afraid of just going up to John, if there is an opportunity, when he's just standing there, and saying Hi. There's nothing forbidding about him. He's the opposite of that. It's in myself. The implications are so huge, of going and talking to this man who is like a cosmic point of awareness, like a node of perception of the Universe: you just don't walk up to that casually. It's like entering into—or getting very close to—a portal to infinity. It could just pull you right through it. And yet, he's also just a man, so one can just go up and say Hi, and be "adorably awkward."

John's wife, Leigh Ann, is a very pretty country girl [actually, a Texan heiress] *with real presence, tall and a very sophisticated dresser with her grey suit, yet not masculine. She came out to the front at the beginning of the second meeting, her face glowing. She said that John and she had been talking about what was happening and that they were both very excited about what they were seeing. The best word they could find, she said, was "burgeoning." There was a blossoming happening in the group, something new was coming into being. Hearing her, I felt glad to be there, to be part of that burgeoning. It felt immense, the implications of it. This was the center of the awakening of the planet, or at least one of the centers, right here. Maybe it really was the center. It certainly felt like it. A very slow nuclear reaction, as John once put it, now speeding up. Shifting gear, right there and then, at that seminar. And our being here was part of it: we were adding our energy to that shift.*

Sometimes when other people talk about John, I want to say, "Oh come on, he's only a man." Sometimes I come from the other way and say, "This is John you are talking about here!" There's definitely a feeling of envy. Why don't they talk about me the way they talk about John? Or, Wait till they see what I can do. It's not strong, they're not thoughts and feelings I give energy to, because they're absurd. And yet John's a father figure, and the desire to defy the father and even usurp the father goes very deep. So it can't be left out either, it has to be owned and integrated; and to some extent maybe it even has to be acted out, to be experienced and recognized.

More than most people here, I think, I see myself as John's equal in potential. I know that I am far from what he is in action, but in terms of my potential, I don't experience a great distance between the two of us. I don't know how much I delude myself there, but there's also a part that wants to believe the opposite, that wants to be a disciple and defer to him. But I know that he doesn't want that (I think I do anyway), that he actually wants equals, people who will step up, give their face and their voice to the subtleties of goodness as he has done, and become "forward benevolence." It's foolish to compare, and this is a big part of what I am letting go of now. The idea that I am better than other people because of having a more profound awareness of reality within, this is a distortion, and also the result of a distortion. The distortion feeds more distortions.

That profound reality is in everyone, so to be aware of it in myself and not aware of it in others is to separate myself, to turn myself into something I am not. That's an illusion, and the main pin for me, or part of the main pin, of sovereignty: that I can measure my self-worth according to my profound sense of reality. So then, if I see others who aren't as aware as I am, then they are worth less than I am. In this case in John's eyes: they are less like him than I am, so then he'll love me more. That's a distortion. It's untrue, and it's the need to believe that that's creating this constant dissatisfaction in me, the need to have that. It makes what I am seeing that is true, untrue. Then I become less than everyone else. And the first gets to be the last.

This distortion is one that I have put a lot of energy into.

On the first evening of the seminar, my wife and I took seats close to the Chair, in John's direct line of sight. A young woman asked him about her mother's passing, clearly upset. John spoke of the generosity of her passing. "The generosity to you ... is the opening, granted ... making dying a kindness. In that way, *what occurs in dying shows you how to live.*"

Since I had mentioned my own mother's passing to John, I believed he was addressing me also, and I was deeply affected by his words. They brought a new acceptance of my mother's death, and it suddenly made sense to me in a new way. What he said was true: my mother's death allowed me to become more rooted in what I knew, in my heart, and to open my heart whenever I needed to simply by thinking of her. Her death was indeed a gift.

On the third day of the seminar, John looked at me after the meeting, just before getting up to leave. I was in my heart rather than my head and I looked back without fear. Whenever John glanced over at me, it was like I had been given something, validated in some way. I kept still and felt an awareness welling up into me, body, mind, heart, tears falling down my face as I was gazing up at him. He stared at me for some time, and I sensed that he was gauging to see what had changed in me.

Besides the café, the occasion on which I came closest to a personal encounter with John occurred in the Oasis garden. The garden is no doubt a source of much pride to the community and, so far as I could determine, it was (like the building) designed by Benita, with (as-ever) unspecified input from de Ruiter. It consists of a large stone patio with a double square design at the center (a Masonic symbol), grassy banks on either side, a few trees, some shrubbery, and a small pond in one corner. At the end of the square there's a raised area with several steps leading up to it, behind which are more shrubbery and trees, as well as some vegetable patches.

On the first Sunday after my wife and I arrived (the 3rd of October), we were informed of a lunch picnic in the garden which John and Leigh Ann would attend. Like everyone else, we brought our picnics. I was hoping, even assuming, this would be the ideal opportunity to interact with John. We sat on the steps with the other community members all around us. John arrived with Leigh Ann and they sat a few feet away from us, on our right, a couple of steps above us. John was not quite within hearing range (especially since he speaks in such a quiet tone of voice). My wife was in the café when John arrived, and when she got back she sat next to me and wondered when John was going to show up. "He's right there," I said, and nodded my head towards him. My wife looked over and laughed, then buried her head into my coat.

The archetypal nature of the encounter only occurred to me later: Adam and Eve in the Garden, with their teacher (the Serpent) on the level above. I was even eating dried fruit at the time. Perhaps it's also significant that I was amusing myself, and I think others, by repeating the more peculiar phrases John had used in the last meeting, some of which verged on incoherent. I found it very funny, and was laughing openly about it. It occurred to me at the time that John might be aware of my making fun of him. I hoped he was.

Into the Fire

"You can be what you know the truth of, within; or, as-awareness, you can lie to knowledge and fool your self. Either way, you will be paying a great price. Cost is constant. The cost will be to your self or it will be to your own core, depending on the way you choose."
—John de Ruiter, 2010

As the reader has seen, my experience of de Ruiter was of being uplifted, filled with a sense of meaning, purpose and truth—all of which I attributed to John himself. He was the source of that meaning, and the catalyst for all the feelings I was having. *He was it.* The proof was that, after the meetings were over, I felt devastated, crushed, destroyed. Being in that space, connecting to John and even "merging" with him (whatever that means), inevitably led to the moment when he was gone and ordinary reality took over. It was similar to being away from one's beloved: life suddenly seemed dull and empty. It was not a comedown so much as a profound contrast. The fullness I felt in his presence brought home the emptiness I felt without it. I told myself that, the longer I spent in his presence, the more transformed I was becoming. Maybe a junky tells himself the same thing about his heroin, and what I didn't consider until later was the possibility that I was becoming more and more dependent on de Ruiter, and on the "Truth-high" he provided.

As the seminar progressed, a lot of people were asking me if I was moving to Edmonton. This was a standard question for new arrivals—at least after they had shown the kind of gushing enthusiasm I had. The assumption was, if you were getting it, you would want to keep on getting it *all the time*. You've tried the drug, you've seen how *good* it is, why *wouldn't* you want to keep using? I told the people who asked me this question what I had learned by then to say: "I can't see any good reason not to." It was true, I couldn't. I was hooked. I wasn't only hooked on John's presence but on the whole community vibe. It answered a deep emotional need in me—the need to belong.

Add to that the excitement of being part of a planetary awakening, and my overall feeling was, "Just try and *stop* me from joining this party!" The feeling answered a sort of apocalyptic longing which I had had since my early twenties: the profound sense that I was destined to play a central role in a global shift in consciousness that would, to paraphrase the song, be *the end of reality as we know it*. As if to cater to that deep predilection in me, there had been an unmistakably cosmic dimension creeping into John's teachings that was generating some excitement in the group. I felt like I had showed up right on time, just as the real show was about to begin. For the first time ever, CDs of the meetings were available before the seminar had ended. John-speak was coming hot off the presses. History was in the making.

"The conversion of your self," John said on the penultimate day, "is the highly accelerated evolution of your self, making up for time, far beyond any scope of your life, bringing you into the more-of-you, accomplishing shared responsibility in where everything—*is going*. By the time that *lands*, something entirely different *has landed on this planet*, appealing only to the innermost of what this planet is. Appealing not to its understood structures; appealing not to its ways; giving invitation for awareness from within its outermost, to surrender to knowledge coming up from within its innermost—*answering everything*."

"*Something entirely different has landed on this planet.*" I didn't know if John was talking about an alien invasion (he was talking a lot about a "black ship"), a day of reckoning, a planetary awakening, the arrival of Christ consciousness, or all of the above. All I knew was that I wanted in.

In the meantime, my sciatica had become so severe that I was facing the possibility I might wind up like my father, crippled for life. I lay on the bed in pain and wondered if I would ever walk, run, dance, or make primal love again. Could I be "warmly okay" with that? In the end, what choice did I have? My relationship to my wife was not providing much comfort or solace, either emotionally or physically. Outside of planet landings, my personal future looked bleak. When I told her of my fears, she asked me to imagine having to choose between the use of my legs or John.

"That's easy," I said.

"Well then," she replied. I realized that she thought I would choose John over my legs! I had put John before my mother, family, friends, my clientele. I drew the line at my legs. When I'd told John I needed help, he had said all I needed was me. Was that a subtle rejection? Or was he setting me up to stand on my own two feet? Was there a difference? I looked to John as to an almost unfathomably wise, all-knowing father, a teacher and a

Master, an embodiment of the divine. At the same time, I saw myself as his equal. What was wrong with this picture? I knew that I was neither wise nor all-knowing. I was constantly floundering in a sea of patterns and unmet wants and needs, hovering between the edges of despair and my best imitation of "tender okayness." I reconciled this paradox by telling myself that it was all part of the process. I was letting the conditioned self come unraveled; I was burning in the fire of the patterns, those patterns which, courtesy of John, I could no longer allow to define me. I was going finer.

The Good King

"And some of us are hoping
To end up with a perfect life
I'll trade you everything I got
For the chance to be someone else"
—David Byrne, "Self-Made Man"

On one of the last nights of the seminar, I dreamt that my father's business was all in chaos. Whoever was running it came to me for help. He wanted me, as the heir, to take over the business. He knew I could turn it around because of the blood I carried in my veins. Part of the dream had to do with the last *Omen* film, *The Final Conflict*, and the Antichrist. John was peripherally present throughout. I gave advertising advice to a representative of the business that confirmed what he had hoped, that I was the man for a job. (I heard John's laughter on the periphery.) I asked about the hours. They were minimal, something like two weeks a year, but the pay was extremely generous. With that in mind, I accepted the job.

On the last day of the seminar, I made a vow to speak to John, if possible and without forcing it. It had been weighing on my mind more than any other single factor: did I have the balls to face the father? I had done it before, and I knew it wasn't really *that* hard. But still I was divided as to whether it was actually necessary. I couldn't sort out my motivations. If I was going to approach him, I wanted to be in character. But who was I exactly? What was my role at Oasis and in John's life? I decided finally to ask John if there was a reason to keep my distance from him, both in terms of approaching him in the café and in the larger context of moving to Edmonton. Maybe the town wasn't big enough for the two of us? Maybe we were like two planets that shouldn't get too close together?

During the first meeting of the last day, I began to silently ask John this question, curious to see if I could get my answer this way. Suddenly, it struck me that my question was a kind of vanity. John wouldn't turn *anyone* away; for me to think I was different was just inverted pride. I then had a little epiphany: My coming to Edmonton was the return of the prodigal son. The prodigal son was Lucifer (it's the same myth roughly, except that the Lucifer myth has no happy ending)—and I had long identified with Lucifer.

I was playing the role of the rebellious son because, deep down, I felt like a *rejected* son. John had reinforced that feeling by turning down the gift of my book. (It's a perhaps significant detail that, one of the only times I can remember my father expressing approval of me was when I published my first book, *The Blood Poets*, also about movies.) It wasn't up to John to placate or satisfy that part of me; it was up to me to integrate it by *not* acting on it. Only then would there be a clear space to connect to John. Knowing John had presented an opportunity for me to let go of all the doings and beliefs which I'd built up around myself when I was still *trying* to be a man, trying to create an identity that didn't *need* a father (in imitation of my brother, who hated our father). So if I wasn't actually the rebel son but the returning son, it was time to let go of those rebel-myths I'd used to construct a sovereign identity. It was time to return to "the heart of a child," to get to an older myth, one sourced more deeply in childhood, a simpler and cleaner myth. In that myth, I was not the One, was neither Lucifer nor Messiah, Christ nor Antichrist. I was only a wayward son, returning home.

All of this was playing through my mind while I gazed at John in his chair. I felt such love and awe for him that I began searching for a word to express what he was to me. My Lord? My Master? Neither seemed to fit. Then I hit on the word I was looking for. The myth of Camelot came to mind and matched the feelings of love and loyalty I was having. Like Arthur, John was the Good King whose law was "right is might." He had spilled over from myth into reality.

In retrospect, though I didn't consider it at the time, the seed of this idea—that of the good king—had been planted by John himself, two days earlier when he spoke to Kesh, my host in Edmonton. Because of our positions, the three of us made up three points of a triangle, and I imagined I could sense the energy flowing between those three points. The feeling was so intense that I experienced a mild stage fright, as if John and I were working together on Kesh. At the start, Kesh was uncomfortable and clearly wasn't speaking from the heart. He seemed to want to approach John as an equal, perhaps because they used to have a personal relationship. (Kesh was John's driver in the early days. This might also have been part of why, until now, Kesh hadn't ever got in the Chair.)

What John said to Kesh: "Your self is in your care, and not as king. If your self is king you will be a bad king." My experience of being one point of an energetic triangle with the two of them was a visceral, bodily experience. I spontaneously remembered that Kesh was a father, and that a bad king was a bad *father*. Kesh had three children, two boys and a girl, fully grown. Thinking of his desire to be a good father, I felt deep empathy for him. Like Kesh, John was the father of two boys and a girl (also fully grown), and this was the same configuration in my family: I was the youngest, with an older brother and sister. So there were three triangles, of one girl and two boys, which itself mirrored *the original triangle* of the mother, father, and son. My talks with Kesh revolved largely around his father, and I had mentioned my father to John on the last two occasions we spoke. The wave of empathy I felt for Kesh, as a father and a "bad king," was especially poignant because John had brought up the ancestors in the previous meeting. Now he was speaking of Kings.

Two days later, when I had the epiphany of John as the Good King, it seemed to have emerged fresh from my own consciousness. And the more I thought about it in those moments, the more right and true it seemed. Everybody wanted to be the special one and to receive special attention from John. He was the supreme father figure, which is what a king *is*: an impersonal father to his people. That's also what a guru is, and an avatar—a "guru of gurus" as John was sometimes called—was a father figure for the entire world.

As a child, though I hadn't been especially taken by the Arthur myth, there was another, even older myth-story that *had* caught my attention for a time. When I was around ten years old, I had been taken to see *Jesus Christ Superstar* by my mother and stepfather. My brother and sister were there, as well as some other family members (possibly my stepfather's children; I was definitely the youngest there). There had been a mix-up and we had ended up short of a ticket. It seemed like an insoluble problem: if one of us couldn't go in, none of us could. Then my stepfather suggested a solution. On his suggestion, they all bunched around me until I was concealed at the center of the group, and we moved forward as a mass while I shuffled along inside a cocoon of warm bodies, excited and comforted at the same time. At the door, the ticket collector took the tickets, counted heads, and let us pass. I sat on my mother's knee throughout, and adored the show. The character that impressed me the most was Judas, and my favorite number was "The Judas Song."

As I gazed at my King, some thirty five years later, I pictured myself as a Good Knight, kneeling at John's throne and offering eternal allegiance. I imagined myself as Parsifal, the fool, and as Lancelot, the most loyal of knights. I didn't think about Judas. Then I remembered that Lancelot betrayed Arthur by sleeping with Guinevere, and this sparked uncomfortably Oedipal associations in my mind. I pushed them away. I would never betray my King, whose goodness and power was not in question. His mightiness was his righteousness, his authority the supreme authority—that of Truth.

There was no doubt or question in my mind as to my undying loyalty to John. I didn't experience any misgivings about subjugating myself to another man. It felt deeply right to place myself utterly in his service. At the same time, it felt strangely empowering.

I had "entered"—all the way in.

Part One: Snake in the Garden

The author, on returning from Edmonton

Part Two
Intervention

"For so many men, the spiritual path is a road for those who don't know how to be their own fathers, who crave to relive the crisis of clashing with authority, to retest themselves, perversely enthralled by the strange virtues of the bully. There's an erotic self-hatred in it: it feels good to rub yourself raw and then to rub yourself away against an absolute. It feels like justice, like what you deserve."
—Matthew Remski

"I bought a million lottery tickets. I won a dollar."
—Steven Wright

The Black Glove

"With knowledge doubt increases."
—Goethe

The single most discordant note for me during my time in Edmonton was a seemingly trivial one. While I was driving home after a meeting with Kesh, he pointed out the movie theater that John had rented to screen *Avatar* for his congregation. Kesh referred to the movie as "Blue People" and it took a moment for the penny to drop. I had tried to watch *Avatar* some months before and found it moronic. Hearing that John—the living embodiment of truth—endorsed it caused a brief moment of cognitive dissonance in me. "Taste," wrote Pauline Kael, "is the great divider." Was this the great divide?

I had taken a guru. I had pledged my allegiance to the King. But was I in full agreement with myself? John had said to me in Bristol: "What you give your heart to isn't the same as the deepest that you know the truth of in your heart." If there was a division in my heart, it was inevitable I would eventually start to act from that split. Even as I was exalting John, was I secretly plotting to bring him down to my level? I wasn't cut out for complete subjugation to another; sooner or later I was bound to begin questioning the guru's goodness and infallibility. I had already done so in small ways: his on-going smoking habit (still unconfirmed); his preference for first-class air travel. When Kesh had mentioned that John didn't dance, I had argued that an enlightened being who couldn't dance was not an enlightened being. But it wasn't until I was confronted with John's taste in movies that something in me—that old "trouble maker" persona—was fired into action.

I initiated a debate at the Birds of Being forum which went on for several days, until one of the long-time John-ies, a man named Baba, made fun of the discussion, and specifically of me, suggesting that I was an egomaniac interested only in showing off how smart I was. "Smart: good," he wrote. "Too smart: not good." I replied curtly, and Baba received a flurry of support from the women in the group, who "lined up" to kiss him on the forehead for his wonderfully childlike sense of humor (of which I was the butt). I was chastised for wasting people's time with trivialities that did not "support realness." I meekly apologized for being a smart-ass. Since I knew I was regressing to a former personality, I was willing to admit it and come clean about my mixed intentions. That effectively ended the discussion.

After the seminar, I had been ninety percent convinced I would be moving to Edmonton. This despite the fact my wife and I had a very comfortable set-up, and besides John and the enticing prospect of being part of a community, Edmonton had very little to offer us. My wife had lived there for almost four years and felt like "a prisoner" because of the landscape (around Edmonton it is a visual wasteland). While she wasn't eager to move back there, she wasn't completely opposed to it. I was planning for both of us to return for the winter seminar, and take part in the Oasis New Year's celebrations.

For the previous year and a half, I had been running an online group for "existential detective work," pattern recognition and identity deconstruction. Some members of the group were intimidated by my association with de Ruiter, others were turned off. The oldest member was suspicious of my gushing descriptions of John and Oasis, was convinced our group was rapidly turning into a cult, and did all he could to convince the others. A private female client (who was not part of the group) underwent a similar crisis: John gave her "the creeps" and was obviously a conman. Both of them ceased dealings with me soon after.

My work with them and elsewhere had become increasingly informed by John's voice and teaching. I considered myself a kind of "energetic extension" of de Ruiter. I had even considered asking him about it at some point, to make sure he approved. Now I began to have doubts about whether I was in any position to guide others when it was becoming increasingly apparent how lost I was. As the doubts mounted, I began to consider ending my business and taking stock of everything I had done until then. An eerie symmetry was revealing itself. I recorded a final podcast in which I admitted having abused my power and authority as a quasi-guru. I expressed the disturbing possibility that I might have unintentionally turned my clients into prisoners as a means to secure a steady flow of income, and for the ego-gratification of being "a somebody." I had fallen into the guru trap, I said, and it was time to climb out before it was too late. Two nights after I aired that final podcast, I had a dream.

I win a six-month stay on an island, as the only inhabitant, in a large house. The island is British, very flat and green. After I install myself in the house, John shows up. He is to live there too. He lies beside me in a double bed, close but not touching. He tells me something about energy grooves that I can't even begin to describe. He energetically places his body around mine. It is like a hand inside a glove, his body being the glove and mine the hand. I arrive at a school where John is constantly instructing different groups. I seem to be moving about a lot, on the edge of activities more than part of them. I have the sense that somehow John is only there when I am not, and vice versa. I get repeated glimpses of him, but no direct contact. A group is sitting at long tables chanting. I sit opposite an Indian guy and join in chanting, but the session ends. John arrives and comes over to my left side. He puts his hand on my shoulder to signal that the class is over: I arrived too late. There's a black glove in front of me, it's supposed to be mine but he gives it to the Indian because I have no use for it. He leaves the room.

Word from God

The day after the dream, I received an email from a young guy I'd met in Edmonton who called himself "God." A friend of Kesh, God had joined us for lunch in downtown Edmonton during our October visit, while I was visiting a back specialist for help with my sciatica. God was an outsider to Oasis and was considered a trouble maker at Birds of Being. According to Kesh, God (formerly Paul) considered himself not only to be enlightened but *the most enlightened being on the planet*, superior even to John. Because of his cheekiness and unpredictability, his posts were monitored at Birds of Being (Kesh was the moderator), and he had recently been "silenced" at the Oasis meetings, according to God by none other than Leigh Ann herself. (Apparently God had a habit of "laughing inappropriately.")

The email I received from God was sent to undisclosed recipients and included an attachment of documents from a court case, currently in process, between Benita von Sass and John de Ruiter. Benita claimed her employment at Oasis had been terminated without due cause or notice, that this was a breach of contract, and that she was suing for damages. Though the case began in February of 2010, this was the first I'd heard about it. God claimed not to have read the affidavit but pointed out that, in his testimony, John denied having had intimate relations with Benita, meaning that he lied to strengthen his defense. I read the document with interest but I didn't find any solid evidence of John's lying, and told God as much. I then read Benita's testimony.

It took me several days to realize the full impact of this affidavit. At first I didn't feel as though anything much had changed. Having read it, I felt more on a level with John. I no longer regarded him as a father figure so much as a "brother" and a friend. I also thought he was in trouble. I wrote a letter to him to offer my hand of friendship and support. In the letter (the draft I sent), I said that I wanted to get to know him better, and mentioned that Oasis, as well as the world, might be headed for difficult times.

At first, like my wife (though not to the same extent), I took Benita's testimony, damning as it was, with a pinch of salt. I told myself that the word of a woman spurned was not reliable. But the more I thought about it, the more I realized that, even if only half of what Benita said was true—if only a tenth was—then John was not what he appeared to be. If I'd had a less lofty idea of him, hearing about his strange behavior would have been easier to take. But how much margin for error does a living embodiment of truth have? The actions Benita was describing not only contradicted John's teachings; they were completely at odds with his public persona. The picture she painted was not of a soft, gentle, surrendered paragon of love, kindness, and "core-splitting honesty," but of a Machiavellian manipulator with a runaway Messiah complex. It depicted de Ruiter as less a man of knowledge than a spiritual psychopath.

Besides the affidavit from God, there was another intervention that helped me in coming to my senses. Although this person prefers not to be included in this account, in the interests of transparency I feel obliged to mention his role in this story since it was such a key one. I'll refer to this person as "Charlie." Like John de Ruiter (though they could hardly be more different), Charlie is a spiritual teacher, one I met (in the flesh) the year before I met de Ruiter. We stayed in touch on and off over the next couple of years and exchanged words here and there about de Ruiter. (Charlie had crossed paths with John on several occasions.) I didn't try too hard to hide my belief that Charlie was not in the same league as de Ruiter, though I put it in more diplomatic terms by stating that Charlie had had a relatively small impact on me compared to John. Charlie said something about how I had come to John via my wife, and that this had primed me for the experience. That made sense to me, but I was still convinced that, whatever level of awareness Charlie had attained, it was kid's stuff compared to de Ruiter.

Immediately after my mother's passing, Charlie and I spoke via Skype about de Ruiter. Until then, I'd suspected that Charlie was in competition with John, even that he felt threatened by him. During our conversation, however, I realized that Charlie was more than merely skeptical: he was actually suspicious of de Ruiter. He asked me questions about my experiences, and told me anecdotal stories which he'd heard from some of his own students and other people he knew. Questioning de Ruiter's goodness was unthinkable for me at the time, but I was too curious not to want to talk to Charlie, and I did my best to cooperate.

After the funeral I flew back to Canada; a few weeks later, on the verge of physical, emotional, and mental collapse, I emailed Charlie a one-word message: "Help!" I didn't really expect a response, and I didn't get one at first. Then, while I was in Edmonton for the seminar, we resumed our dialogue. Charlie was curious to hear anything I had to report about my experiences and provided short, pithy comments by way of feedback. (When he heard that I was not feeling ballsy enough to approach John, he said simply, "Grow some.") He was particularly interested in hearing my impressions of the Oasis community, and I kept him informed within the limited time I had between meetings. Perhaps a week before the affidavit landed in my inbox, Charlie contacted me again and we embarked on a series of dialogues about de Ruiter. Again, I felt threatened and defensive, and again, Charlie seemed disappointed by my lack of openness. I was still in crisis mode concerning my back, my marriage, and other matters, so I consulted Charlie in a more professional capacity. John had dismissed my cry for help by telling me that all I needed was myself. Charlie had responded to it by providing me with the one thing de Ruiter couldn't or wouldn't give: a personal connection. It is no coincidence, then, that the ostensible reason for this personal connection was to lead me gently but unerringly to question my belief in de Ruiter's "goodness." And Charlie's character was the polar opposite of de Ruiter: he was fast-talking, meandering, irreverent, and refreshingly ordinary. His guidance was also much more down to earth and practical than de Ruiter's vague and abstract statements.

The first clue I had that something wasn't right was in my responses to Charlie's questions and anecdotes. When Charlie brought up evidence that de Ruiter might be less than "straight" or "clean," it seemed absurd to me, because my mind was already rigidly convinced otherwise. John's goodness was beyond question, and that was the extent of my "argument" with Charlie. I was threatened by the mere suggestion that de Ruiter was less than perfect, and my response was essentially: "Why are you questioning John when I already know what John *is*?" It wasn't that de Ruiter's behavior was irrelevant to me; I wasn't that far gone. It was that I rejected the context in which Charlie was scrutinizing it: his skepticism and doubt. To me it was all right to question de Ruiter's behavior, but only in the context that he was the living embodiment of truth, because *that* belief was beyond challenging. Based on my conviction, whatever he did, there *had* to be an explanation for it. In the past, I had always fallen back on the belief that de Ruiter was a surrendered being, and if he *seemed* to do anything dodgy, it was because he went passively along with what *other people* wanted. Why? Because *he had no preference*. He was literally "beyond good and evil." By this logic, any suspicious behavior became further evidence of his surrendered nature.

Charlie was suggesting a different point of view. He was suggesting that de Ruiter might have a hidden side that was fully in control of his actions and decisions. Charlie wasn't saying de Ruiter was up to anything dodgy; he was merely asking if that *could* be the case. He was asking me to look at the evidence before making my mind up. The trouble was I had already made my mind up. Since I couldn't allow the idea that de Ruiter was untrustworthy or deceptive to enter into my mind, none of the evidence mattered. The case was already closed, and I blocked Charlie every step of the way. Ironically, it was this very act of blocking that allowed me to see that something wasn't right, and after a couple of conversations, things began to shift in my mind. I realized I was *preventing* myself from seeing something that was right in front of me.

It was at that precise moment that the affidavit arrived.

An Empire of Self-Interest: The Document that Overturned the Rock

"The shame for Benita . . . is that she never saw it coming that one day she would be old hat just like everyone else. So she stitched herself up. She set up a whole organization with him at the top of the tree in such a way he was pretty untouchable. Although you have seen the affidavits where she reveals a fair bit one can be fairly sure there is a TON more dirt on John . . . It is an empire of self-interest. It's obvious. All the usual suspects: power, control, self-interest, money, glamour, sex; the blondes of being they used to be called."

—ex-Oasis member

What follows are the pertinent parts of the affidavit which landed in my inbox that decisive day in November of 2010. I have italicized the parts which I consider especially relevant, and to which I may refer later on.

I, JOHN DE RUITER, of the City of Edmonton, in the Province of Alberta,

MAKE OATH AND SAY AS FOLLOWS:

1. THAT I am the Defendant in the within action and as such have personal knowledge of the matters hereinafter deposed to, except where stated to be based on information or belief.

2. THAT I was trained as a shoemaker. I was drawn by profound spiritual feelings to the study of theology, later serving as assistant to the Pastor of a Lutheran Church in Edmonton. Continued study led to my separation from the Church, eventually becoming a philosopher and teacher. I earn my living by speaking at meetings of people who are interested in my ideas and insights in Canada and throughout the world.

3. THAT my teaching gradually became more popular during the 1990s and by 1999 I was employing several people and had about 60 volunteers. I began to hold weekend retreats at a rural venue (a lodge) near Edmonton at the invitation of its owner, Peter von Sass, who, I understood, was a financier, and had previous experiences with other similar speakers and philosophers.

4. THAT I met the Plaintiff in 1996 at a meeting in Edmonton at Mr. von Sass's lodge. She was a student in Calgary where she lived with her 2 boys. At the time I was married to my wife, Joyce. The Plaintiff began to volunteer at various meeting that I held in Edmonton and Calgary over the course of several years.

5. THAT the Plaintiff applied and was admitted to the Faculty of Law of the University of Alberta, Edmonton, in the fall of 1998, on the basis of a BA 1997 from the University of Calgary.

6. THAT my marriage to Joyce broke down at the end of 1999. We have 3 children, and generally, at that time, very little assets. The Divorce proceedings took 3 years.

7. THAT I began to have an intimate relationship with the Plaintiff in 1998. I commenced an intimate relationship with her sister, Katrina, within the year. I told the Plaintiff about that relationship, and she was not concerned about it.

...

17. THAT the Plaintiff had told me during our entire relationship that she had not gotten over her experience of deep love for her youngest son Felix's father, and she often spoke of wishing to have back what she had with him. She traveled to Tokyo in October 2008 and visited with him there, I believe, in hopes of rekindling their relationship. *The Plaintiff virtually refused all intimacy in our relationship from 2002 to 2007.*

18. THAT the Plaintiff did not object to my relationship with Katrina. She supported my relationship. When Katrina was having some difficulties, I stayed with Katrina for 3 months at one time. *I also stayed longer at Katrina's when I could not face going back to the Plaintiff's house.*

19. THAT I never promised to marry the Plaintiff. We never had a domestic contract. We did not own anything jointly.

...

22. THAT during the last several years of our relationship, the Plaintiff would confront me with issues that she perceived were important. She continually denigrated staff, her sister, her children, and her parents. I found this very upsetting, and could not respond to her remarks.

STATEMENT OF DEFENSE

9. On or about August 8, 2009, Oasis terminated the employment relationship with Von Sass for cause. The particulars of the cause included:

a) Misappropriation of funds;
b) Misappropriation of business records and equipment;
c) Insubordination;
d) Insolence;
e) Breach of trust;
f) Harassment of staff;
g) Mismanagement and Incompetence;
h) Misrepresentation of her position within Oasis to other employees of Oasis.

SUPPLEMENTARY AFFIDAVIT

I, BENITA VERA VON SASS, of the City of Edmonton, in the province of Alberta, MAKE OATH AND SAY THAT:

...

3. In response to paragraphs 2 and 3 of the Defendant's Affidavit, the Defendant speaks of the interest that people have demonstrated in his ideas and insights. This is an understatement. Many people have moved to Edmonton from other countries to be near the Defendant further to his suggestions that a close proximity to him is desirable because of the benefits that his "energy" will have upon them. Accordingly, the Defendant's popularity grows with followers believing it is desirable to become a volunteer or staff member to increase their spiritual growth. *The Defendant's insights, whether positive or negative, are taken to be directives that come directly from truth and God, and become those of his followers.*

...

7. It was extremely painful when the Defendant announced shortly after moving in with me as my husband in early 2000, that he now also knew from God that my sister would also be his wife. I struggled emotionally and mentally coming to terms with this arrangement. I cried many hundreds of times over the years following, learning to cope with the daily psychological pain, and enduring what the Defendant insisted came directly from God. I obeyed the Defendant's instructions to "let the pain be what it is" while believing that a greater good was being served in my submission to him. The Defendant's claim that I was not concerned upon hearing about his new relationship, is completely untrue.

...

9. In response to paragraph 9 of the Defendant's Affidavit, the Defendant stated that God had directed him to buy a million dollar house in Westridge. The Defendant stated that "it stirred from God" to purchase this home with a large indoor pool. He told my family that for educational purposes, to teach Katrina about power and responsibility, the house would need to be entirely in his name. The entire intended down payment of $410,000.00 came from Katrina's life savings alone. She obeyed.

...

14. The Defendant assured me that giving up my law degree and developing/managing his company was the best use of my skills and time, stating conflict of interest would prevent me from ever being able to defend him if I became a lawyer anyway, and stating that what I had already learned in law school would still be of great use in the coming years. I obeyed, and began to receive a salary in April of 2000 far below my actual worth, working 12—18 hours days on average, 7 days per week.

...

21. In response to paragraph 17 of the Defendant's Affidavit, I was surprised to read for the first time, the

Defendant's relationship fears regarding my prior invitation with my son to visit with his estranged father in Japan at his place of work. I went to Tokyo because my son's father, who was married at that time, wished to reconnect with my son. I did not want for this to happen without my being there. At the completion of this trip, my son returned to Canada, but I traveled directly from Japan to Germany to accompany the Defendant to a regularly scheduled Seminar.

22. *The suggestion that I stopped marital relations with the Defendant at any point beyond what would be considered entirely normal within the day to day course of a marriage is completely untrue.*

23. In response to paragraph 18 of the Defendant's Affidavit, in the midst of extreme personal psychological and emotional pain, I did my best to accept the Defendant's relationship with Katrina inasmuch as I believed it was, as the Defendant told me, ordained by God and therefore true.

24. In response to paragraph 19 of the Defendant's Affidavit, in 2000, the Defendant informed me that we were married and that this was so as per God and the Defendant *in his authority as the Christ.* On March 16, 2008, the Defendant led a ceremony at the Oasis Conference Centre renewing our vows as husband and wife. He told me that he could not legalize our marriage as this would hurt Katrina too badly. The ceremony took place on the Conference Centre stage, then celebrated at the Hotel McDonald directly after the ceremony in a special suite.

...

29. The Defendant's allegations in paragraph 22 are a distortion of the facts and completely untrue.

30. Strange difficulties and disputes with family and staff members developed during the last two years of my relationship with the Defendant. *I came to understand these originated from*

inappropriate conversations and deleterious comments that the Defendant made about me behind the scenes, and his encouragement that others do the same. Upon finally reconnecting with family members he had, in this way, alienated me from for years, including my parents and my sister, we came to discover that the Defendant had spoken disparagingly behind the backs of all involved, thereby creating deep divisions within the family alone. The Defendant was not pleased with our regained relationships. *The Defendant had been successful in isolating me from almost all supports.* This, coupled with much of my work being conducted in my home office where the Defendant further did not allow guests, left me in a particularly painful and isolated place.

31. When I attempted to address the strange difficulties and then later the disparaging remarks I came to understand the Defendant had made, the Defendant's response was for the most part *a treatment of silence.* Later, when accounting concerns and irregularities created by the Defendant were brought to his attention by myself and my father (the Defendant's business advisor) we both received a treatment of silence. Shortly thereafter we were both terminated.

32. *During the last 2 years of my common-law marriage with the Defendant, I could no longer reconcile his increasingly bizarre and self-oriented personal behavior with his claims of having no personal interest in power or personal identity. The Defendant's focus on personal time with his followers and corporate staff, his late night encounters with followers with no explanation, his avoidance of direct explanation with a reliance on others to speak on his behalf, his utter avoidance of home responsibility or caretaking, his elevated personal expenses, his questionable treatment of accounting, and his use of semantics to alter his story when convenient, were in direct contravention*

even of his own teachings. My concerns and questions to the Defendant became extensive.

...

35. In response to paragraph 26 of the Defendant's Affidavit, in early 2000, as I have already stated, the Defendant informed me with one witness present, that he "knew from God I was now his wife". He said this was true in all senses of the word, physical, emotional, and spiritual, and that we would now live together in my condominium with my children as husband and wife. He moved in with me and my sons, whom he encouraged to call him dad for many years.

...

37. The Defendant told me I was the "sweetness he abided in," eventually telling me we were "two sides of the same heart" and that I alone was "his soul".... He told me that I alone completed him and that I was the key to his complete understanding of himself on both surface and profound levels. The Defendant maintained that this was ordained by God and that on that level we were profoundly compatible. I trusted the Defendant. For years the Defendant and I walked into and out of seminars and meetings with his right arm around me as a public demonstration of our union, which was recorded on select video tapes of the Defendant's meetings.

38. To read the Defendant's allegation that there was no marriage and no shared vision, is incomprehensible. My entire life's work and common-law relationship with the Defendant demonstrate the shared vision we had and my commitment.

I, BENITA VERA VON SASS, of the city of Edmonton, in the Province of Alberta, MAKE OATH AND SAY THAT:

...

9. Since then, the Defendant's weekly Edmonton meeting audience has grown to over 300 regular attendees, many of

whom have arrived from all over the world, with a further extended audience attending his many international seminars. He has held seminars in such places as England, India, U.S.A. (until he was denied entry and work in approximately 2002), Israel, Germany, Holland, Austria, Australia and New Zealand. The Defendant claimed then, as he does today, that he is a spiritual teacher with *a supernatural calling from God*. He has been holding informal local and international spiritual development seminars for over 10 years. The Defendant offers these in a question and answer format. In this fashion he has come to receive millions of dollars in contributions and seminar fees from his followers. Obviously, the Defendant provides a message and experience that is initially compelling. The Defendant, however, *fosters a spiritual obsession and submission to his teachings*. Having been drawn in by the Defendant and initially convinced he was an entirely honest man with deep and great integrity and knowledge, I have come to learn that the Defendant is fraudulent. *It has taken me years to come to understand this.*

10. *The Defendant told me he knew from God to single me out and teach me about truth, and that this necessarily involved sexual intimacy. The Defendant convinced me to sexually submit to him, reminding me that this was "God's will." The Defendant stated he was the "Christ on earth" and that defying him was to defy truth, goodness and God.* Accordingly, I obeyed and submitted.

11. *The Defendant later told me God had willed deviant sexual and other behaviors as well as relationships between himself and four married female followers. He was at that time still having regular sex with two of them in addition to his wife and to me. One of the husbands had been aware of the activity, the others not.* The Defendant currently and at that time, publicly preached a message of marital fidelity and honesty. The

Defendant explained to me that *part of his "burden from God" was to act against his own message and to violate his own marriage so as to prepare him inwardly for his upcoming battle with Satan. He spoke in soft convincing tones, claiming to be a kind of willing victim suffering God's will.* He claimed this preparation was further "profound evidence" of the truth of his "calling" from God to be the "embodiment of truth," and that what "may appear or may be suffered on the outside" is not "in reality what is happening on deeper and profound, unseen levels."

...

17. The Defendant preached a strict type of fundamentalism concerning honesty and allegiance to truth during seminars, and most notably at home. *He often spoke of "dark forces" and "principalities of evil" that were ever lurking, and that he would one day be responsible for facing and annihilating as part of his role as the embodiment of Truth. He asked me to consider as a mental exercise the possibility of killing my own children to reveal my true "allegiance to truth".* I told him I would be unable to commit such an act, even if it came from God.

...

20. I sold my condominium and in approximately 2001, purchased a house in my name. The Defendant modified my home to suit his requirements, including increasing the size of the garage door opening to accommodate his monster truck, installing an expanded shower, *installing security cameras, purchasing a large Rottweiler guard dog and installing a security fence.* I continued to pay all household bills from my salary and completed and arranged almost all domestic indoor and outdoor work and upkeep. Oasis Edmonton Inc. ("Oasis") paid all associated costs, including food, grooming, training, fence construction and surveillance fees. The dog was hit by a car and killed in October of 2008. I purchased another large security

dog, a Great Dane cross, in February of 2009 and Oasis continued to pay all associated costs. The Defendant continued to live with me with my two boys through 2009 until my eldest son, now twenty four years of age, moved out. The Defendant's son came to live in our home for a period during this time as well.

21. My office was in my home. The Defendant did not allow the public to know our private home address. Our phone number and address were not listed in the phone book. Social contact, even with my sisters, brother and parents, was strongly discouraged by the Defendant, and we did not have guests. Over a 10 year period, we may have had 5 visits to the house. The Defendant's former wife and three children moved to Holland with her new husband and had little contact with the Defendant before their departure, followed by strained contact with the children after their departure. *I wrote possibly hundreds of letters for the Defendant in his name to his three estranged children, to help him further his relationships with them for many years. The Defendant was not able to type well or formulate his thoughts in the form of personal or business letters.*

...

30. ...I personally oversaw the receipt of *millions of dollars of contributions* from philanthropists attending the Defendant's meetings and interested in supporting the Defendant's public message of honesty, accountability and higher values of altruism.

31. I was the mind and management behind all corporate policy, strategy and operations, including the creation of all corporate forms, reporting and filing systems. I created the entire pricing scheme for public rental of the facilities and advertising vision. I created the entire corporate structure for the new Conference Centre, defining and delegating jobs and hiring approximately 15 key employees, including *Leigh Ann Angermann whom I met in Germany during one of the*

Defendant's seminars and for whom I prepared work and immigration documents to allow her to work in Edmonton as a Conference Host. [Angermann became de Ruiter's wife in 2009.]

...

38.

...(n) repeated comments over the years by the Defendant assuring me: "this is not my company, it is ours," "your job security is iron-clad", "nothing should ever make you feel like your job security is in question", even if you were to be unable to work you would be taken care of completely", "I can hardly believe you would even question your job security", and so on. The Defendant told me his dream would be for the company to be able to run itself and he and I would have the time to ourselves with my no longer needing to work. The Defendant said he did "not relate to the companies or the building belonging to [him]", saying they were created for a reason beyond personal ownership". Knowing that staff looked up to the Defendant as their spiritual teacher and therefore held any comments from him in high esteem, the Defendant told staff to treat my comments and directives to them in the corporation as equally authoritative. He told staff to see us as "the same" and to treat my words and directives as though they were coming from him directly.

...

39. As the Defendant's behavior became less and less consistent with his message of profound honesty and goodness, and as the Defendant began to privately exhibit increasing intolerance to my questions about his behavior and integrity, especially concerning his use of power and persuasion, he continued to publicly preach a message of "dearness, honesty and transparency". *The Defendant adopted a virtual silent treatment of anyone not in direct support of him and his*

teachings. Publicly and privately the Defendant's motives and behavior were in direct opposition to each other. The Defendant portrayed himself as a "victim" of anyone not in support of him, enlisting sympathy and support from his followers and creating fear in his followers that anyone opposing his teachings is a direct threat to his organization and is "dangerous".

...

42. The Defendant was aware that I had no savings, as he had directed all available monies to go directly to the businesses. Over the years the Defendant expressly discouraged my suggestions to find supplementary work for myself to supplement any income, saying it would "split my focus" and detract from the purity of my commitment. The Defendant had for years recommended charging to the company any household or personal expenses (such as dental, home repair or improvement and so on beyond the regular monthly expenses) as part of my salary. I paid taxes yearly on the combined total sum. Many home improvements and other purchases had also been made on my personal visa or line of credit to keep money in the company where possible, resulting in significant visa and line of credit debts. Accordingly, with bills mounting and no reply from the Defendant, after my sudden termination, I continued to pay my usual monthly fees by credit card and cheque, including Voxcom (Reliance Protection) security, dog costs, pool costs and janitorial. In addition, I paid a Westworld computer repair cost for the laptop computer I had been working with, kenneling cost for the Defendant's dog while he was on holidays, 20 Oasis cell phone use reimbursement (for use from Jan 08—July 09) and concrete pouring cost (as explicitly approved by the Defendant months earlier in the back yard of my home).

43. My home security was cancelled unilaterally by the Defendant July 23, 2009 without my knowledge. Two cheques

written by me for my usual janitorial services were bounced by Oasis, dated July 28 and August 4, 2009, as well as cheques I had written for our usual pool service, and bills for my security system and cement pouring. I did not receive the usual tithe salary cheques for July nor August 2009 amounting to approximately $2,250 monthly, nor receive reimbursements for any of the expenses outlined in my emails to the Defendant. I believe this was all part of a deliberate tactic by the Defendant to compel me to continue to use my corporate visa and chequing to cover my bills, resulting in "continued spending of company monies on personal items" which was identified by the Defendant in his letter of termination sent August 8, 2009. I have been strong-armed into returning all Oasis materials in my possession by threat that I will not receive a monthly salary cheque beginning September 1st without compliance. As I have been advised by counsel to retain all corporate materials in my possession as the only evidence of my extensive career in the development and management of these companies, I did not return the materials to the Defendant (the content of which he already has through e-mails and hard copy originals over the years, and which remain in the corporation's possession on the Oasis premises). I had already delivered all personal effects (clothing and sundries) to the Defendant, July 17, 2009.

...

47. Within a three week period beginning mid July of 2009, the Defendant has demoted me, unilaterally removed me as a corporate officer, removed my salary, terminated my employment, ended our marital relationship without speaking a word to me, consummated a secret relationship with one of our staff (for whom I had prepared immigration documents), legally married the staff member, damaged my reputation with employees and College attendees as well as with my bank and some of my associates, and left me with no savings and mounting debts.

A Living Paradox

"We are so acutely aware of our deficiencies, and he has so well programmed us not to trust ourselves, not to trust what we think, not to trust what we feel, that the hardest battle we ever have is having courage to say, 'I may not have everything together, but I know something is wrong with you.' That is the hardest thing for us to do, because we've been trained and taught and indoctrinated not to trust ourselves and not to be arrogant in our opinions. So who are *we* to look at John and say, 'Something's wrong, John'? That's a terrifying thing to us. This is why the battle to leave John is so hard."
—Joyce de Ruiter-Kremers, 2010

Once the elements of the affidavit began to crystallize in my mind, the cognitive dissonance I experienced was enormous. What made it even more difficult was that my wife took this new information casually, almost with indifference. Her perception of de Ruiter was seemingly unchallenged by hearsay or anecdotal evidence.

Just a week earlier, I had been thinking of moving to Edmonton to be near him. Now the accounts I'd heard (not just the affidavit but others) combined with and gave substance to a growing intuition (though de Ruiter admonished his followers not to trust intuition) that *something wasn't right*. De Ruiter was immensely powerful, that was more than just a seeming. But now I had to ask myself an unsettling question: if he was as powerful as he appeared to be, was he powerful enough to deceive people?

The impression I got at Birds of Being was that, although many of the group had read the affidavit, either they didn't believe it or they didn't care. (I later found out that they were being discouraged from reading it.) Benita had already been demonized by the group—she was unpopular even before the split—so, like Joyce before her, anything she had to say against John was not to be taken seriously. But at the very least, surely the affidavit was evidence that de Ruiter was severely challenged when it came to containing his women? Even if Benita were making up wild stories to get back at him, the fact remained that this was the woman (one of them) he had chosen as his wife and trusted to run his business. (In fact, as we'll see, the von Sasses were a major financial force behind the creation of the Oasis center.) The best you could say about de Ruiter at this stage was that his judgment was poor. If he had responded to a "movement of being" by jumping in the sack with Benita and Katrina against his wife's wishes and behind her back, it was a movement that had set him up for some major headaches. However you sliced it, the affidavit proved that de Ruiter was a human being with all the flaws that go along with it—and possibly some more serious ones too.

The consensus view of de Ruiter in the Oasis group—a view I had recently shared—was that John was beyond such weaknesses. Allowing that he had flaws at all opened the doors to a massive overhaul of belief about him. If I'd been wrong about that, what else had I been wrong about? How much was my perception of him based less on a reality than a mixture of de Ruiter's performance skills—his sorcery—and my own projections? Between us, had we created a magical illusion of a Christ embodiment, a good king and perfect father? And as the illusion was coming unraveled, was I getting to see that the father was only a man after all—or would I find a bad king? Countless theories began to weave their way through my brain. Of *course*

John had a dark side, and naturally it was a side he was careful not to let his followers see. He had to maintain an image of perfect truth and complete goodness, so effective a persona that even my wife—usually the inverse of a gullible or trusting person—had bought it hook, line, and sinker. And I had followed suit, from that first dream on, until I was down on bended knees with my head bowed, waiting for the chop.

If I wanted to know what de Ruiter's dark side was like, what the real man behind the curtain looked like, the obvious place to enquire was with his (ex) wives. The affidavit was like the fruit in the Garden that opened my eyes. The initial result of this massive internal shift for me was positive. I might be losing my religion, but I was gaining a new sense of my own truth.

It's possible that what follows is just my very limited mind's attempt to make sense of an unbearable paradox, a paradox as old and archetypal as that of the Son of God who is also God-the-Son (or the Serpent who is also the Savior). De Ruiter's words reached me at as profound a level as I had ever been reached by words; they formed the basis of a whole new way of seeing and being. I spent dozens of hours listening to his tapes. I fully believed he was the Way, the Truth, and the Light. He was my ticket home. I gave myself to him, internally and without conditions. I offered complete loyalty and devotion. There was no doubt in my mind, none at all. Now there was nothing *but* doubt. Whatever I had come to suspect recently, even if true, it didn't really detract from my perception of de Ruiter's enormous power. All my experiences of that power and *seeming* benevolence were still intact. But now the new evidence contradicted it all. If he was that powerful and *not* benevolent, only one conclusion was possible.

I made a few inquiries at Birds of Being about how to meet with John privately but I received little by way of encouragement: write him a letter, contact Leigh Ann, ask to sit with him in the café, get in the Chair. If I could have set up a private meeting with him, I would have flown to Edmonton in a shot. The funny thing was, since I had started to believe de Ruiter might be corrupt, I was less afraid of facing him than when I thought he was pure goodness. Now I *wanted* to face him, to ask him all the questions that no one dared ask or that he blocked with his stony silence. I wouldn't take silence for an answer. I would confront that figure of darkness and of light. The more I mulled it over, the more I believed de Ruiter had an *unconscious*, shadow side, and that his identification with being—and being seen as—an all-good Messianic truth-embodiment had caused him to completely disown that shadow, and so be possessed by it. He would then be justifying morally questionable behavior under the delusion that he was battling external "forces of darkness"—when in fact it was his own shadow he was wrestling with. "Battle not with monsters, lest ye become a monster."

On the other hand, maybe he really *was* Christ, and in the interests of a full planetary integration, he was embodying the satanic energies too? This was what (Benita's testimony claimed) de Ruiter believed, and I was prepared to give him the benefit of the doubt, at least for now. But if this was the case, *when exactly was he planning to let his followers know*? I remembered the sign de Ruiter placed outside his shop in the early days: "Christianity is Satan's masterpiece." He also used to claim Jesus had been his own private teacher. So what did that say about John-ianity? Was Oasis the *anti-John's* masterpiece?

From what I could tell, a lot of people in the Oasis community, maybe most of them, believed de Ruiter was synonymous with goodness. From such a perspective, any hint of a dark side would be met by a fierce wall of denial. The situation might be similar to a child who finds out his father is doing some really messed up things, but who gets a clear signal from the rest of the family *not to talk about it.* Unable to corroborate the new reality with anyone, after a while the child learns to pretend it's not happening. The child has to "forget" what it knows in order not to disturb the smooth surface of the household. This process of suppressing knowledge to maintain a cover story is crazy-making. Perhaps something similar was at work in the Oasis community?

I *knew* my experiences of de Ruiter had been real. It hadn't *all* been projection. His power was beyond question: I had seen it with my own eyes; my whole life had been (superficially) transformed through his influence. The picture I had of him was too extreme to allow for some watered down in-between. If he wasn't a living embodiment of truth, then he was a master of deception. There was no way for me to reconcile de Ruiter's depth and power with the idea of a simple huckster chasing after money, sex, and worldly power. If he was in any way corrupt, that corruption would have to be manifest on the same level on which he appeared to operate, that of "the Deep." If he was corrupt, he was *deeply* corrupt.

On the other hand, if, as a result of his over-identification with Christly goodness, de Ruiter were embodying "antichrist" energies, would that make him any less valuable a teacher? Possibly not, provided one knew it at least. But it would mean he wasn't someone to blindly follow (or follow at all), and that his wisdom-teachings might be laced with something else besides wisdom.

While I was beginning the investigatory work that eventually led to this book, I went to de Ruiter's website to check a detail in his bio. To my surprise, the whole site had been overhauled. Within days of beginning my investigation, the site had abandoned its austere, simple design for a much more dramatic New-Agey look, dreamy and bright with Neptunian blues.* Had Oasis begun the damage control already? If de Ruiter was expecting serious court costs and damages to his public image, was he going for the hard sell? A placidly smiling John was standing in front of the ocean, promising, "The easiest, most effortless and perfect answer can be known by all."

Curious, I went to the online store to see if the video download of my Bristol talk with John was still available. It took me a while to find it because the numbering system had been altered. Now, instead of being number 001 at the top of the page, I was halfway down the page, numbered 037.

It was official: I was no longer John's number one.

Enter Joyce

"Behind every great man is a woman rolling her eyes."
—Jim Carrey

One day, I found Joyce's account on Facebook via a Google search. Since I didn't use Facebook, I asked a friend to contact her and tell her about me. Once I had her email address, I emailed her. Joyce responded quickly with the following:

> I have always expected that eventually somebody would turn their experience with JdR into a book. Many should. I truly believe in unveiling, as you so aptly put it. In fact, this is one of the first things I too did 10 years ago, when my crisis hit. At the time, many told me that I should "write a book." I am not a writer, but nevertheless, I did begin. I wrote 200

---

* Astrologically, Neptune is the planet of surrender, of redemption, and of Christ, but also of addiction and escapism.

> pages of my 18 years with JdR. I still have it, and may one day work on it and publish. I have reasons for which I don't. One is my children, and two is that I have a semi "gag order" on me. Part of our divorce settlement was that I "would never do anything that would potentially harm [his] earning potential for as long as I am getting child support." Since my two sons are now living with John, I am attempting to terminate child support; thus this constraint will perhaps soon be lifted. Despite that, I am not sure I am ready to publish. I am glad you are—extremely glad, especially because I see you are a talented writer. I have always hoped that the first book that comes out about JdR is tasteful and well written. . . . Naturally, this "gag order" does not necessarily mean I cannot speak about my past life, but I know John, and I am quite certain he would take action at this point. My child support has not been terminated yet, so this is still a fragile time to begin to speak.

In a second email, she wrote:

> When I left John 10 years ago, I truly had no idea what I had left. In fact, while I was with him, I had no idea who I was with. . . . I recall believing and saying to him that I was quite sure that if he saw the grave error he was making, I truly trusted that he would "repent" of it. In other words, when I left, I believed he was merely deluded. I called it an innocent illusion. Over the last 10 years I have become more uncertain. Over the past 10 years I have seen what seems much more like malice, cruelty and corruption. I understand that malice, cruelty and corruption could still fit in with his own deluded perception of his own purity and innocence. . . . I understand how that works. The one thing I always claim to not fully

know, is whether he truly believes his own lie or not (i.e., is he deluded or mad?).

Since I left I have read hundreds of books of other spiritual teachers, gurus, cult leaders, mind control, etc etc etc. I have spoken to endless people. I feel very clear on the issue. I would say Andrew Cohen, Barry Long, Isaac Shapiro, Neelam or even Osho are clear examples of who John is. I doubt he will ever get as "big" as Andrew Cohen or Osho, because he simply does not say enough or does not say intelligent enough things. His silence and paradoxical statements are limited, in my opinion. About his capability to seek revenge, I have no doubt. I have been in litigation with him for almost 10 years. Recently, I realize he attributes much of that revengeful or unkind behavior on Benita. I don't know. I knew Benita, but I am sure John authorized her actions.

When I left the group, my body left. It took years for my mind to leave. It seems a part of my spirit will always be there. John was my husband and spiritual teacher. The wounds go very very deep.

I imagine you are well aware of the newspaper articles that have been published years ago. John was and still is very angry at me for this, by the way. I hear you about his secret desire to be "found out." I don't know. I have only seen him fight hard to protect his image. He has threatened to sue, he has tried to ban publications, and he has paid good money to keep certain things from being made public (or for the fear of this occurring). But, I agree that transparency and openness is essential. I understand that the group is being discouraged from reading the affidavits. This is a shame. This shunning of information shows so well the depth of close-mindedness. Why not be a critical thinker? Why not strive for transparency?

Part Three
The Evolution of a Guru

"He really is the living embodiment of truth. He is established in being on this earth, just as Christ Jesus was; basically he is the very foundation that the truth is able then to build itself upon and have brought in this world. Not just this world, the whole universe, every dimension. The truth is now able to move in a way that is able to do what the truth can do, and apart from John being here, then there's no way in which the truth will move in that, it won't fully manifest itself."
—Bob Emmerzael, 1998

"You will notice though that the kind of people who turn to Jesus tend to be the sort of people who haven't done that well with everybody else."
—Dylan Moran, 2006

Early Years & "Awakening"

"Give me a child until he is seven and I will give you the man."
—Jesuit saying

Even with Joyce to help me, I couldn't discover much about de Ruiter's early childhood. Of those who were present at the time, and of the very few who ever got close to de Ruiter, I spoke to only a couple. What I was able to glean came mostly from Joyce and the official bio at de Ruiter's website.

The child of Dutch Catholic immigrants, de Ruiter was the first-born son. He had an older sister, Rietta, and was followed by Frank and Cecilia. The youngest child, Cecilia, adored John and is numbered among his followers to this day. According to Joyce, John bullied Rietta and Frank (Frank is still with John today; Rietta has never been part of his group). At least partly because of his aggressive behavior and his love of "pranks," family life generally centered on John. As Joyce recalled, "His father always used to say he was the life of the party; things were always exciting when John was around. He needed the most attention; he was a troublemaker but colorful and gregarious." John's official bio (attributed to one "Atticus Cutter," a pseudonym) makes no mention of either his pranks or his bullying, however; instead it focuses on his "golden hands" and generosity. It does however quote his mother describing him as "restless" and "always on the go."

> John was not an easy child to bring up: in trouble frequently, not because he was bad or deliberately mischievous, but because his unceasing curiosity dissolved boundaries: open doors beckoned the stand-alone child out to wonder-worlds under a wider sky, toddling with unspecific purpose down

the lane, time and again. Truly a trial-child of his mother's vigilance and care. But at home and right through school, his father said and his teachers too—there was the fire alarm incident—that "John was always truthful, owned up, no question."[1]

Open doors beckoning, trial-children, wonder-worlds and wider skies—did de Ruiter hire the ghost of Walt Whitman to write his bio? Such awkward use of language cries out "spin." But what is being spun? Having stated that John was not an easy child, the bio reassures us that he was not "bad," or even "deliberately mischievous." Omitting to mention pranks or bullying, we're told that his "unceasing curiosity dissolved boundaries." Later on, in a different context, the bio refers to de Ruiter's "propensity to push boundaries." A phrase like "truly a trial-child of his mother's vigilance and care" suggests a pain in the ass who demanded ceaseless attention; so why not say it that way? Perhaps because de Ruiter wants his impeccable aura of truth to extend backwards through time and transform his past? So does the language of the spin—as well as the webs being spun—provide clues as to what is being concealed?

As de Ruiter entered adulthood, the bio refers in passing to the fact that his "intelligence had not responded tellingly to his classroom studies."

> In his early years the practical skills that attracted John were the first clear manifestation of a propensity to push boundaries. This pertinacity became a characteristic of focus on all levels of his interests—spiritual, psychological, academic and physical, as instanced in his progress from shoe repair to the making of shoes, refining this still further when, under the employ of Salamander Shoes (1981), he became accomplished in the craft of orthopaedic

shoe-making, described by John as "the learning of a beautiful trade"; a skill that would support his young family and himself for many years ahead in Edmonton, Alberta.

"Pertinacity" implies persistence—presumably intentionally—but also suggests stubbornness and obstinacy (perhaps less intentionally). According to Joyce, her husband hardly worked at all in those early years, making the bio's comment about de Ruiter supporting his family at best a generous exaggeration. As Joyce recalled, "I think there was probably only the very first year we both worked: he was making shoes. I think that was the only year he worked full-time. Then there were one or two years when he worked sixteen or eighteen hour shifts, two very long days. He basically never had normal work hours." Did John's "pertinacity" amount to diligence at earning a living—or an obstinate refusal to get a job? Aversion to working for a living would hardly be remarkable in a young man, even one who had been put to work at a young age by his (Christian) father.

The official bio states that John was taught shoe repair by his father as a boy, and that de Ruiter senior was "one of a long line of fine shoemakers from De Bildt in the Netherlands." (The Van de Bildts is a royal bloodline if ever there was one.) John worked on repairing shoes after school, mainly on Saturday mornings, from the age of twelve. We're told that "His work was good and his father paid him fairly, earning the boy more than usual pocket money for a child of his age." Apparently John's father, Cornelius, was determined to turn his son into a tradesman and put him to work at the earliest opportunity. John's cobbling skills would later provide him with his first and last real job; before that, he applied his "golden hands" to carpentry work—a suitable occupation for a Messiah-to-be. Cutter continues:

> In the school workshop, twelfth grade, John had been encouraged by his teacher, Ignace Miazga, renowned in Stettler as a superb craftsman in wood and stone, to take on an exacting carpentry project by making a full suite of bedroom furniture worked in walnut. . . . Seeing John's sedulous [another obscure term which has the meaning of persistent, diligent] concentration in the shaping of this work, his parents and teachers grasped at the opportunity to settle such an aptitude in an apprenticeship, *calculating that perhaps by this means a direction might be secured for an otherwise quite restive boy, about to leave school, whose intelligence had not responded tellingly to his classroom studies.*" [My italics.]

What that last, convoluted, paragraph-long sentence translates to, as far as I can disentangle it, is: de Ruiter's parents were worried John was not too bright and lazy to boot ("restive"); concerned he might wind up as a vagrant or a drug addict, they "nudged" him into a carpentry career. It's safe to assume that much of the pressure for young Johannes to make something of himself came from his father.

At seventeen, de Ruiter had his first "awakening" experience. In the bio, he describes it as follows:

> When I was seventeen I just stumbled on to being awakened to something that was profoundly amazing, wonderfully life-giving, without understanding the source of it. I wasn't looking for it, I never related to anything like that being in existence, then all of a sudden there was a flowering inside, that made everything in this existence pale in comparison. That

flowering, that awakening inside, opened up my awareness to everything in existence to be something more beautiful than I had ever seen before.

According to Joyce (who met John when he was twenty-one), de Ruiter said nothing about this experience during the years she knew him and she only heard about it when he began to describe it to his followers. After that, it became part of the official history.

> I have obviously read this many times, and I think, "My God John, you've changed history!" The story he always told me is, he was a bully, he was a horrible kid, nobody liked him, he was a brat, a vandal, etc. At age seventeen, he wanted to work for a horse person, someone who did something to do with horses, someone named Sergio.* John wanted to get a job and the person said, "Well, I will have to pray about this, to seek God's guidance." That just amazed John, he had never heard of someone having such a relationship with God. He was raised probably nominally Catholic. He was fascinated by this, got the job, and through that guy he became a Christian. He started going to a pretty alive Baptist church, and that's all I know. The first time I started hearing this stuff about an awakening was maybe fifteen years later. Nothing of that was ever communicated to me, although he was very open to me about those years. It was expressed in radically different terms. I can imagine that he would have experienced some kind of high, because he was really a jerk before he became a

---

* When de Ruiter described this experience in a 2011 interview for *Conscious TV*, the employer in question was a cabinet maker.

> Christian. The family does tell me that he really changed after that, that he became a much nicer person. All I can think of is that he probably was walking around on some kind of high, it was easy to be nice to his family, he was experiencing some kind of joy, gratification, from that. The experience he talks about now and as it is in his bio is nothing like what he communicated to me over those years. He was just a radical Christian. All this awakened stuff, never. He didn't use any of that language back then. He was a very typical Christian, except [he was] extreme.

If it seems unlikely de Ruiter could have had such an experience and not have told his wife about it, even less likely is that she wouldn't have been aware that, as the official bio and John's own repeated testimony has it, he became *re-*awakened a couple of years later, roughly two years before he met her. (I read older accounts that estimated the second awakening happened around ten years later, a curious inconsistency, and not the only one.) Joyce's version was that John became a devout Christian at seventeen and *adopted a whole new personality*. Until that time, she told me, de Ruiter was disliked by just about everyone. Not only his siblings, whom he bullied, but his classmates and others found him a mean, insufferable presence.

Besides Joyce, the only person from those early years that I have managed to persuade to speak to me was Jason Gerdes, who roomed with de Ruiter for several years in the late '70s and early '80s. Gerdes did remember de Ruiter describing some sort of awakening while he was working in the shoe store. Gerdes said he was never sure if it was the cobbler's glue that gave de Ruiter his revelation—that "sweet thing," John called it—but he remembered how "he always wanted to get that back; that was why he was always reading these books and going to all the churches or groups or organizations. He was in this endless search, he didn't know if he should go to official training." According to the official bio, de Ruiter kept that first awakening for about a year and then lost it as mysteriously as he had found it. The bio quotes de Ruiter:

> "And that lasted about a year, then all of a sudden, it was gone. . . . In the same way as I couldn't comprehend how it started, I also couldn't comprehend how it ended, or why. Once awakened, it seemed to me inconceivable that it should ever go away. Once it left, I was profoundly disturbed because I knew I had been connected to something that made the whole universe live, and that without being connected to that, I knew nothing was worth living for. . . . I then committed myself to spending my existence in looking for that reality, not knowing what to look for, although I knew the flavor of it, knew what it was like when alive." Holding course through years of anguish, no back-down considered, de Ruiter drew upon all his inner resources, to bring to light what had so inexplicably appeared and gone, accepting spells of despondency, brushed by hazards of lostness, and overwhelming darkness and pain, yet throughout those experiences he recalls—"though I had got myself in so deep, moved so far away from the familiar, there was no thought that I might be unable to get out of this, not be able to repair myself and sort of live normal again."

Whatever really happened, it's doubtless significant that John's taste, and subsequent loss, of paradise, occurred when he was on the verge of manhood. De Ruiter entered into a state of completeness and fulfillment—he came of age—but, for whatever reason, he was unable to sustain it. What happened? The bio isn't saying, and de Ruiter described it in terms that require no external cause, either for the awakening or for the fall from grace. It's possible there wasn't one; it's also possible—and maybe more likely—that something happened which de Ruiter isn't talking about. Something to do with sex, maybe—a subject he has a recurring history of *not talking about?*

Unconditional Surrender or Blind Submission?

"Essentially, I suppose, according to John, I undermined his status as an evolved person. I also often used Christian terms (albeit less and less as time went on) which he was trying to eradicate from his repertoire. I think I was just a reminder to him of who he once was."
—Joyce, 2010

According to de Ruiter, in his online bio:

> "After about two years, when there was nothing more that I could turn inside out, there was nothing else to peel and make raw, nothing left but a state of what seemed to me to be never-ending pain; . . . what I did, without fatalism, without any edge of hardness or bitterness or resentment or any seeming wastage or regret, was to surrender in a very sweet way to be in that deep, in that darkness, in that pain, with an absolute letting-go of ever needing to find that reality I had so wonderfully tasted and lost. . . . Then, to my total surprise, I was astonished when that same reality that I had once tasted, flowered again in the midst of the rawness and the pain, in the darkness where I had unconditionally made my home. . . . I surrendered to it unconditionally, understanding that it does not need to bless me, that I'll give my life to it and it

doesn't have to give anything back. I would exist for that reality."*

Joyce claimed to have heard nothing about this second awakening either, even though it would have occurred *only two years before they met*. What de Ruiter *did* share with her about that period of his life (according to the official timeline, this would have been between the ages of eighteen and twenty) involved his participation in a "mini-cult" run by a Native American called Len, and some extremist Christian practices with a young man called Ross. De Ruiter told Joyce that Len and his wife took derelict types, young teenagers, into their home and "trained" them, in what Joyce called a "mini-cult." She didn't remember if the group had a specific teaching or a philosophy, but she believed "it was more about behavior. John called it very, very abusive." He recounted being on a restricted diet of one meal a day (a McDonald's meal), and how, if they expressed hunger at any time, they were heavily chastised. Punishments included doing a thousand pushups, which would take John two or three days. "He would have to walk through the streets and stay awake and do these pushups. They would have boxing matches . . . punching until there was blood."

Joyce voiced her suspicions to me that there had been a "distorted, perverted aspect to it," citing how "Len would drive them around a certain area in Edmonton, near Jasper Avenue, checking out all the prostitutes." She didn't specify what kind of perversion, nor did she have an opinion as to why de Ruiter would submit to such abuse. When I suggested that he might

---

* Yet in a 2012 interview with a Dutch show, *NonDualiteit*, when Patrick Kicken asked de Ruiter if he had gone through a period of suffering prior to his awakening, De Ruiter denied it.

have been doing penance for his own bullying, she was noncommittal.

> John talked about it as a heavily, heavily intense time of being disciplined. He always said that he recognized some of the craziness of it, but for him it was just a matter of learning to surrender and be submissive to this person. He used it often to tell me about being submissive, because he strongly believed in my being a submissive wife. He used pushups on me as a form of training me to be submissive, when I would swear, in my early years of marriage. If I would say "fuck," I would get twenty pushups. It was something he apparently learned from that time. John spoke about [Len] as an opportunity to learn surrender and obedience, blind submission.

If Len was de Ruiter's first teacher, it raises the question how much his influence continues to inform de Ruiter's own teachings, the fundamental requirement of which is "absolute surrender." Making your newlywed do pushups for using the word "fuck" is unusual behavior even for a radical Christian; and since these methods of "discipling" came from Len, it suggests he was still under Len's influence even after leaving him. The possibility de Ruiter had been terrorized—and victimized—by Len was supported by Joyce's impressions on meeting Len: "I was shocked because John always talked about him as this big, burly, American Indian [but] he just seemed mild to me. . . ." Apparently de Ruiter's perception of Len was influenced by being under his psychological control. Jason Gerdes had the same impression.

"He was really under this guy's personal power," Gerdes told me. "I don't think it was a physical power, it was a personality power that he felt enslaved by."

Gerdes and John were roommates for a time, and Gerdes recalled a time when de Ruiter heard that Len was back in town and trying to contact him, causing de Ruiter to become extremely anxious. "That was the first time I'd seen him as a weak person. He became less than who he was when this Len guy came into the picture."

*

Although the chronology is unclear, by Joyce's account it was after his involvement with Len that de Ruiter met Ross, at around nineteen or twenty. Joyce remembered that Ross was "more of a peer to John. He was a sort of cohort in their extremism, taking Christianity to an extreme." She recalled how they were "devouring books" by an author called Charles Finney, on "a very intellectual pursuit of how to be genuine. His family talked about that time when John would come home, very drained, lifeless." During this period, she said, de Ruiter was "harsh, he was cold, he was judgmental, very self-righteous. He was pursuing this true path and intent on labeling everything that was false." She remembered hearing how he and Ross took food out of the bins behind the grocery stores, how John talked about getting up at four in the morning and sleeping in churchyards. It was "a very extreme time of thinking, 'If this is what is expected of me, then I will do it, 100%.'" For de Ruiter, following the will of God entailed becoming a vagrant and eating out of garbage bins, as well as being especially harsh towards his family—suggesting that his Christian extremism was a form of rebellion.

Joyce described it as "a time of 'Pharisee-ism,' following the letter of the law, but not a very joyful time. There was no mercy, no softness, it was very hard." After, de Ruiter became involved with the People's Church, "which was filled with young, born-again Christians, radical Christians, and he started reading some books." He was interested in Calvinism and he "absolutely fell in love with the gospel of grace, which completely turned him away from Pharisee-ism." He started reading books by Andrew Murray, and it was at that point that he met Joyce. This was a time "when he was overwhelmed by the theology of grace." Joyce found it strange, she said, that de Ruiter wanted to deny the Christian component to that period, "because he was flying high in euphoria of grace, grace, grace. That's what I knew John was dealing with. [There was] nothing about awakening."

Comparing de Ruiter's version with what Joyce remembers, it seems like the time of "darkness" which he described (the loss of his awakening) coincides with being taken in by Len and taught the value of "blind submission" under an extreme, probably abusive, disciplinary regime. This period overlapped with his self-righteous Christian period, before he discovered "grace"; the latter would then roughly coincide with his second "awakening." Since the official bio excludes any mention of external factors, of cobbler's glue or mini-cults, it creates the impression that de Ruiter's awakenings were *internal* affairs wholly independent of outside influences. That's consistent with de Ruiter's later teachings about "going finer," while at the same time it subtly reinforces the idea that he was mysteriously touched by grace. But is it accurate, or is it, as Joyce believes, a case of de Ruiter rewriting history and creating a myth for his followers to believe in?

Early Christian Influences: Finney and Murray

"Just as a servant knows that he must first obey his master in all things, so the surrender to an implicit and unquestionable obedience must become the essential characteristic of our lives."
—Andrew Murray

Charles Grandison Finney (August 29, 1792 — August 16, 1875) was a Presbyterian and Congregationalist figure in what was known in US Christian history as "the Second Great Awakening." His influence during this period was such that he had been called "The Father of Modern Revivalism." A cursory investigation into Finney reveals several striking parallels with de Ruiter: Finney's many innovations in preaching and religious meetings included having public meetings of mixed gender and the development of the "anxious seat," a place where people who were considering becoming Christians came to receive prayer. At de Ruiter's *satsangs*, anyone who wants to have dialogue with him must take a seat in what is known simply as "the Chair."

According to "The Sinner's Prayer," Finney made many enemies because of his innovation. The Anxious Seat practice was believed by some to be "a psychological technique that manipulated people to make a premature profession of faith." Accusations were made of "an emotional conversion" influenced by the preacher's "animal magnetism." Finney's method might be seen as "a precursor to the techniques used by many twentieth century televangelists."[2]

Finney was also known for his use of extemporaneous preaching, which included preaching with no written preparation. Once again there was a parallel with de Ruiter's history, specifically a turning point during his early days of preaching:

> "In that service I just died inside. I knew I could have used a sermon of mine from the Three Hills Institute; all my notes were there with great clarity. I could have just walked through, preached a sermon, no-one would have known. I knew. I just had to be faithful to that one voice." [The bio continues:] And still moving forward, certain of his way, he determined not to preach "anything that doesn't happen fully to me first, because if it doesn't happen, I can't preach it. It can't flow through me, because it's not in me. I'd always try to figure out, how am I able to preach with revelation and not be breaking down all the time."

Further parallels between de Ruiter and Finney: Finney never attended college, but his *six-foot three-inch stature, piercing eyes*, musical skill and *leadership abilities* gained him recognition in his community. Finney was married three times in his life. Counting his spiritual/common law marriage to Benita von Sass, the same is true of de Ruiter (to date at least). All three of his wives assisted Finney in his evangelistic efforts, and accompanied him on his revival tours. Snap. Finney was described by one who knew him as "a man of the wilderness, not damaged by religious or traditional thought patterns, but trained and raised of God and filled with the Holy Spirit."[3] Once again, the description fits de Ruiter (at least from a sympathetic perspective) to a "T." The two men's demeanor might have been similar also. Finney's advice with regard to manners befitting a minister of God was to always avoid levity and "all winking and roguishness," to be "grave but not morose, dignified but not sanctimonious." Like de Ruiter, Finney also had an awakening experience and a personal relationship with Jesus. The following is from Finney's "Memoirs," chapter two, "Conversion to Christ":

> As I went in and shut the door after me, it seemed as if I met the Lord Jesus Christ face to face. It did not occur to me then, nor did it for some time afterward, that it was wholly a mental state. On the contrary it seemed to me that I saw Him as I would see any other man. But as I turned and was about to take a seat by the fire, I received a mighty baptism of the Holy Ghost. ... the Holy Spirit descended upon me in a manner that seemed to go through me, body and soul. I could feel the impression, like a wave of electricity, going through and through me... My sense of guilt was gone; my sins were gone; and I do not think I felt any more sense of guilt than if I never had sinned.... Nor could I recover the least sense of guilt for my past sins. Of this experience I said nothing that I recollect, at the time, to anybody; that is, of this experience of justification.

Such outpourings notwithstanding, Finney was not without his enemies, one of whom charged that, "No single man is more responsible for the distortion of Christian truth in our age than Charles Grandison Finney."[4] Another claimed that, "Finney's ministry was founded on duplicity from the beginning."[5]

The parallels with Andrew Murray, de Ruiter's second major Christian influence, were less obvious. There was one striking similarity, however, and that was Murray's aspiration to be an imitation of Christ. Murray wrote over two hundred books, including such titles as *Abide in Christ, Absolute Surrender, Be Perfect, God's Will: Our Dwelling Place* and *Like Christ*. In "Andrew Murray—Christlike AntiChrist,"[6] by Christian exponent Victor Hafichuk, I found a less than impartial account of Murray that was nonetheless interesting in relation to de Ruiter:

> Murray put on a great show of imitating Jesus Christ as he perceived Him. It was all religiosity, a product of flesh born of the Tree of Knowledge of Good and Evil. Murray pleased and impressed men by imitating Christ. . . . This copycat mentality and attitude, in essence, is Andrew Murray's great sin. . . . All Murray's writings are self-exaltation. In *Absolute Surrender*, one must take his word that he is absolutely surrendered; *we assume he wouldn't talk about it if he wasn't*. . . . As I scanned his sermon—The Power of Persevering Prayer—I could find no substance, nothing practical; it was all theory and condescension. [My italics.]

I have no idea how accurate Hafichuk's charges are in regard to Murray, but there's no denying they could also be leveled at de Ruiter. De Ruiter's claim that he only ever preached from experience, quoted above, would only reinforce the assumption that *anything de Ruiter describes he must also be embodying*. That assumption creates an inevitable blurring in the mind of the listener between the message and the person who delivers it. Implicit in that blurring is the idea that, if they want to surrender to truth, they can do so *by surrendering to the person embodying it.*

The idea of blind submission to a human being is entirely foreign to Christianity. Pastors were not Kings, because there was only one King (only one god-embodiment) for Christians, and that was Christ. But there is a clear antecedent to such worship in the East: *the guru.*

A Seasoned Warrior

"I know the majesty that John has, that he actually wears a majesty because of who he is. There's power in that majesty, there's glory in that majesty. It's a full representation of truth, and along with that is a warrior, a seasoned warrior."
—Bob Emmerzael, 1998

Before he found his calling as a guru (a.k.a. integrated philosopher), de Ruiter tried the more conventional route of a Christian pastor. As the bio has it:

> John de Ruiter preached first in 1979, aged nineteen, in the Shiloh Baptist Church, Edmonton. This prevenient occurrence made known a rhetorical gift which de Ruiter developed, hearkening to the voice of Early Church origins, finally elevating the delivery of his sermons with full commitment to revelation in the latter half of 1986, while at the Bethlehem Lutheran Church in Edmonton. . . . There he placed himself under the tutelage of an understanding man, the resident Pastor, who provided him with an office and an informal dispensation to preach: but despite his intense application to study, and his dedication and devotion in preaching, it was here that his final break with established Christianity happened in 1987.
>
> There were divisions in the Lutheran Church hierarchy over acceptance of de Ruiter's return to the mystic practice of the Apostles, of preaching only with revelation, by aspiring to deliver his sermons in a continuous stream of spiritual insight. These divisions were exacerbated when de Ruiter questioned the protocols for election of church Elders. Directing their attention to an apostolic

precedence in this regard, where elders were appointed, not elected, a return to appointments made in recognition of a transcendency [sic] of spirituality, allowing due place for inner gifts, natural talents and abilities, but irrespective of age, popularity, or academic qualifications. On these issues and their implications a schism among Lutheran Church Elders was averted by the intense opposition of one faction, leaving de Ruiter no choice but unacceptable compromise, and so finally bringing to a close his involvement with the Bethlehem Lutheran Church, and formal Christianity as a whole.

According to the official story, then (for those who make it through the tortured prose), in his early days as an intern at the Bethlehem Lutheran Church in Edmonton, de Ruiter was given his own office by the resident pastor, Don Rousu, as well as "an informal dispensation to preach." Even in the rather vague and convoluted account above, it's clear de Ruiter had aspirations of becoming a pastor. The suggestion is that the only way he could gain a position within the church was via "a return to appointments made in recognition of a transcendency of spirituality" (in other words, I presume, being a "spiritual person" would count for more than all other considerations). De Ruiter's plans were terminated by the "divisions in the Lutheran Church hierarchy," and when de Ruiter couldn't persuade the elders to recognize his legitimacy, he refused to compromise and left. While the bio attributes the disagreement to de Ruiter's "mystic" preaching style and his questioning the election protocols, I was getting a different story from people present during the period.

Even as it is increasingly clear that this was a turning point in de Ruiter's life, and the beginning of his "ministry," there is a great deal that remains unclear about what actually *happened.* Of the players involved, I was able to speak to Hal Dallmann, assistant pastor under don Rousu, his wife Candice, also present, and Barrie Reeder, the chairman of the elders at the time. I had only a brief email exchange with Don Rousu, who would not go on record and gave me very little. De Ruiter himself, unsurprisingly, did not respond to any of my attempts to speak to him.

Over the course of several telephone conversations, Barrie Reeder described de Ruiter to me as a "whistleblower" who approached him at a certain point with information about illicit activities involving two of the pastors; as a result of de Ruiter's disclosures, the two pastors, Hal Dallmann and Don Rousu, were asked to leave the church. Shortly after, de Ruiter was also asked to leave by Reeder. Joyce's memory of events mostly supported Reeder's version, while she also suggested some kind of adulterous desire on the part of one of the pastors. There was one key difference, however: up until the time I made my own inquiries, Joyce believed that her husband *had left of his own choice*.*

Hal Dallmann, who arrived at the Bethlehem church in 1977, told me in 2010: "It was real good till John got there." According to Dallmann, Rousu, the head pastor and Dallmann's

---

* "Then [John] got involved in a scandal as well. There were two pastors there, the first one was Hal Dallmann. Some of the facts are fuzzy, but I know there was a thing when John confronted one of the pastors for ... lusting after the pastor's wife. There were two pastors, both were married and had kids. There was an accusation or a holding accountable on John's part. John assumed this position to confront these pastors, both very established. There was a lot of that going on. [John's] bio says he confronted them for not using the apostolic form of choosing elders. I don't remember that. *He initiated a lot of scandal.* He also spent an enormous amount of time with the pastor's wife. I don't have any suspicions about that. Things just got messy. Eventually John left. I wasn't always privy to this information. I sort of heard trickles of it. It was [over] a few months." [My italics.]

immediate superior, wanted to start training interns as pastors and chose de Ruiter as his "first experiment." Dallmann agreed that de Ruiter had promise. On the other hand, and somewhat contradicting himself, Dallmann told me that he went to John once for counseling and was not impressed. About de Ruiter's preaching, Dallmann said that

> John was way too focused on demonic stuff and not enough focused on God. . . . The way he went about it was "I'm the great healer," not God. Those were things that set off red flags in my head. The elders invited John to present what his vision of the church would be. As I recall, John talked for almost three hours and gave his vision, and he never mentioned Jesus Christ as part of his vision for the church. All he talked about was all the evil demons that were crawling on the walls, and in the community, and that we had to do warfare against them. But never in the power of Jesus Christ; he never mentioned Jesus' name. He finished and my impression was, the elders were . . . shocked at what he had shared.

According to Dallmann, Rousu then told the elders that he agreed "one hundred percent" with everything de Ruiter had said, and offered his resignation. Dallmann's memory wasn't clear on the sequence of events, but he claimed he had instigated a complaint against de Ruiter because of something de Ruiter had said to Dallmann's wife, Candy. Dallmann believes "John wanted to stay as far away from the elders as he could, until he saw there was no way around it," i.e., once Dallmann lodged a complaint against him. De Ruiter then counter-attacked by claiming that Dallmann's preaching was "coming from the demonic side of things."* Regarding the nature of his complaint, Dallmann told me that his wife had been going through a spiritual crisis and he had suggested she speak with de Ruiter. What de Ruiter said to Dallmann's wife was so disturbing that Dallmann complained to the elders, setting in motion the events that led to de Ruiter's departure. After that, Dallmann was "totally opposed to [de Ruiter's] involvement in any kind of leadership role in the church, counseling, preaching, or anything else." Because of this, Dallmann claimed, the division between himself and Rousu became "more distinct."†

In my conversations with him, Barrie Reeder had very little good to say about de Ruiter. He called him "an interloper" who "was always looking for an edge, always looking for an opening. . . . When he realized that he couldn't wrestle the church out of our hands and that he had no ability, he had to leave or admit that his vision was wrong." While avoiding such implications, de Ruiter's official bio confirmed that the events brought "to a close [John's] involvement with the Bethlehem Lutheran Church, and formal Christianity as a whole." It was a turning point in de Ruiter's life, and the beginning of what Joyce termed "the evolution of a guru." According to Joyce, de Ruiter only began earning a living when he assumed the role of spiritual teacher to a small group of Christian fellows and started receiving *tithes* (ten percent of the congregation's earnings). At the same time,

---

* This echoed something Barrie Reeder said to me on more than one occasion, that people at Bethlehem were accusing each other of being possessed by demons. Reeder became so fed up with it that he temporarily stepped down as chairman.

† More bizarrely, Dallmann told me that "Don Rousu preached a sermon out of the Apocrypha books, about the light-haired woman minstrel who would lead him astray—obviously a blatant reference to my wife, who was a worship leader who played a guitar, blonde. Don told me that he didn't think he could counsel me anymore because he was in love with my wife."

she recalled how her husband "rapidly dropped everything to do with Christianity . . . we stopped reading the Bible, we stopped praying, we stopped singing, but we did tithe. . . . That's Old Testament! That always seemed so weird."

Jason Gerdes also remembered that same turning point, a moment when de Ruiter came to him in a state of excitement and said, "'I never thought of this before but you can get people to pay for your rent and your mortgage and your food! You don't work anymore!'" According to Gerdes, de Ruiter "thought that was like the most amazing thing. . . . It just seemed to dawn on him that he could do it, become a religious organization to officially get paid to preach." If this was the moment de Ruiter found his calling, and shifted gears from an aspiring Lutheran pastor to a Christ-ian guru, the bio sums this evolution up in two (large) sentences:

> On leaving the Church, with prospects of moving forward in that outward life ended, John de Ruiter, and a following of eighteen people mainly from a group within the church, began holding regular Sunday meetings in his home, with further gatherings arranged on other days in the houses of friends. On through the 1990's many more people attended, until in 1996 the first public, non-residential venue was opened at the Akashik book store in Edmonton, replacing and ending the years of Sunday morning meetings in de Ruiter's home.

Over a period of fifteen years or so, de Ruiter's leadership of a small group of Lutheran apostates would grow into a multi-million dollar non-Christian "church," of which he was sole, sovereign minister.

Silence is Golden: JDR the Game Player?

"I never really saw John as a materialistic person. When I met him he certainly wasn't. At the same time, he was the child of Dutch immigrants who came here to make some kind of life in the new country, and although his parents were not materialistic either, I know that they cared about making a living, moving up in the ladder."
—Joyce, 2010

One of the primary questions I had was whether de Ruiter's rise to power was the result of conscious manipulation or, as his supporters believed, simply a "movement of truth." If, for example, like most human beings (especially the visionary type), John had been reluctant to get a job, that reluctance may have partially accounted for his decision to become an independent preacher and accept tithes. As extraordinary a young man as he was, he may well have been at a loss, in those early years, about what exactly he *could* do. Joyce described him as lacking a basic sense of self-worth. She saw him as "extremely talented and somebody who would always make a living doing whatever." At the same time, she remembered how

> He did frequently say, "You know Joyce, I actually don't have anything. I have no tickets." He knew I saw him as a capable person, but he probably didn't see himself that way. . . . In retrospect, I have often wondered if John felt that he couldn't make it on what he had. He was just a shoemaker. I often have thought, did John realize that he was never going to make it financially?

Timothy Gallagher became a follower of de Ruiter in 1998 and was a friend of my wife during that same period. I met him in Bristol in 2010 (he was attending the seminar) and then, when the story about Anina's death broke in 2015, I spoke to him over Skype. I will get to Tim's unique take on John in Part Four, but regarding de Ruiter's career path, he had this to say:

> I know that he really believes his own stuff. . . . I actually think he didn't fully factor in the guru effect on himself. I don't think most gurus take that into the equation. "What will people sitting at my feet do to me?" You don't get to know what that's like before your awakening. . . . I think he hit a comfort zone with it somewhere. He said once, very early, he said, "If the structure around what's happening here ever takes over, I will just walk away. Now he definitely didn't and it definitely did. He's still sat on the throne. So I would say he's rather comfortable and he doesn't want to have to find a job as a shoemaker. He'd be pretty unemployable right now.

While Jason Gerdes "never saw [John] grasping after money or things . . . never saw him as a guy who was avaricious," on the other hand, de Ruiter's peculiar technique for haggling suggested he *was* highly conscious of his poverty and on the lookout for ways to overcome it. On one occasion which Gerdes shared with me, de Ruiter wanted to buy a circular saw and went to a private house to look at it. The woman wanted at least $25 for the saw and insisted she couldn't go any lower. De Ruiter offered $15 and the woman repeated that she couldn't possibly accept less than $25. Gerdes' impression was that the woman was waiting for them to leave, but de Ruiter simply sat there, revving the buzz saw and staring silently at the woman until she agreed to take the $15. Gerdes believed de Ruiter "had no clue of the consequences of his actions" and didn't do it maliciously. "He just zones into, 'This is what I want, I don't know how to leave so unless they drag me out I'll just stay here.'" According to Gerdes, de Ruiter "got tons of sales that way!"

Gerdes remembers de Ruiter as someone who was determined to get his own way and incapable of adjusting to circumstances when he couldn't. Besides being possibly autistic behavior (Gerdes' opinion today), de Ruiter's actions are similar to a child's sulking when it can't get its way. Today, de Ruiter claims—and many of his followers believe—that he is living in service to truth and that his actions are devoid of self-interest or "personal agenda." One of the principle mysteries I found myself confronting while looking into John's past was how much of de Ruiter's life and circumstances were the result of conscious intentions. This was a mystery even his ex-wife couldn't answer. Gerdes' anecdote was a useful example of this uncertainty principle. Was de Ruiter trying to get the buzz saw cheap, or was he simply tongue-tied and miraculously obtained the desired result through silence? Gerdes' opinion was a bit of both:

> It's like Pavlov's dogs. Somehow he's been conditioned throughout his life that this strategy works for him; it's a survivor's strategy to be successful in the world. "If I talk to somebody I'll probably lose, but if I'm quiet I'll probably win." Wherever that started in his life, he just kept doing it, it became part of his being. So I don't really think it's a spiritual aspect, it's just who he is, and he'll apply it either to making a joke, a sale, or a religious thing.

Gerdes' interpretation allows for two possibilities to co-exist. De Ruiter could be acting unconsciously, in a "childlike" or even autistic fashion, while *at the same time* another part of him, the opposite of guileless, adapted to what it learned and discovered "a survivor's strategy to be successful in the world."

Pure and impure motives co-exist, until none can say where the one left off and the other began.

The one thing that seems clear is that, perhaps even before he found his calling, de Ruiter had found his "ticket." Silence.

*

"It's like a chess game. He thinks fourteen moves ahead, so he has to prepare. His whole life was this game-play. He loved telling a story, and for you to buy into it."
—Jason Gerdes, 2010

As I continued to dig for dirt on my former guru, I found another, peculiar characteristic of de Ruiter's that hinted at darker undercurrents: his penchant for pranks. Gerdes talked at length about John's proclivity "to see if you were naïve, to see if you were gullible." He remembered how de Ruiter would talk about "sky hooks," "muffler bearings" and "hydraulic floor mats" to see if a person would get "hooked into these things." When people believed him, de Ruiter was "like a child with a toy—he just loved it when people bought into his fake statements." While Gerdes never interfered with de Ruiter's pranks (by letting the "mark" know they were being conned), he insisted he never fell for them either. "That's maybe why he liked me, because [I was] not a sucker.'" While Gerdes was smart enough to see through de Ruiter's trickery (most of the time), he was also "game" enough not to spoil the fun. "His pranking was just like a child having fun," Gerdes told me, "like a ten-year-old who could tell a whopper and everyone bought into it. He felt he had power. 'I got adults believing that I did such a thing. Wow!'"

When de Ruiter felt insecure, Gerdes told me, "he would lean towards his silence; or if he was talking, he would play these other games, because what else is there to talk about or to be? So there was insecurity there, is how I viewed it. Bullying comes from insecurity as well."

In another anecdote, Gerdes described a day-trip he took with de Ruiter, from the same period (late '70s or early '80s, when both men were in their early twenties). De Ruiter suggested they go to Ram Falls, in Provincial Park. He wanted to hike in and camp over the weekend. Initially, he told Gerdes he was afraid of bears, and told Gerdes to procure a license to carry a gun. Gerdes got a gun permit and they brought two shotguns and a rifle with them. They took a very difficult, pathless trail through brambles, "a long walk through hell," as Gerdes remembers it. Once they'd arrived and set up camp, de Ruiter began calling for bears. When Gerdes asked what he was doing, de Ruiter replied that he *wanted* the bears to come.

The next day, as they were leaving, de Ruiter let Gerdes know that there was a regular path out, the path he had used the first time he came, with Joyce. It was an easy twenty-minute walk back. Gerdes realized that John, wanting to see if they could make it through the wilderness, had tricked Gerdes into thinking it was the only way. Gerdes didn't see it as malicious behavior, however. "He was just living in his world, doing what he wanted to do, and figured, if he could do it, I could do it. . . . I think that's why he played those games." De Ruiter's *modus operandi*, Gerdes believed, was only to reveal his full intentions once it was too late to back out.

> He would only tell you certain parts of the story, it was always his plan, his desire, his goal. [Then you realize:] "Oh, *that's* the real thing, that was the full plan!" I would always learn that there was more to it; that's why I called him a chess player: he'd plan this whole thing. He really knew what he was doing the whole time, but he only let you know certain parts

> that you needed to know to get you to go along, so that you wouldn't argue. I think John takes advantage of the simple and those who don't think ahead. I think the people who have left [the Oasis group] are the smarter, more intelligent people. The people who have stayed behind are probably the less intelligent.

In Gerdes' view, John "put people in [boxes:] 'How I can interact with them.' And those he didn't, he was more silent with those people. When he doesn't know what kind of a person they are, he tends to fall into silence." For de Ruiter, silence was a way to take the pressure off himself and get other people to reveal things about themselves. This then gave him a better idea how to interact with them. Apparently the silent treatment, as in the haggling incidents, sometimes had the unexpected effect of causing others to bend to his will and give him what he wanted. His pranks seemed to be a somewhat more aggressive way to determine what people were made of, and to what degree he could manipulate them by persuading them to believe things that were untrue.

The Key to Satan's Masterpiece

"It's all so different from how you normally see this. It's in a very underhanded way. Half the time I think, 'Are you just stupid John, or are you brilliant?' Somehow there has to be a bit of both. He's not educated. But clearly we can't think of John as stupid, he's a mastermind. It was my battle, all of our marriage. Is he that? Who is he? Who is John?"
—Joyce, 2010

At some point in those early years, de Ruiter erected a sign outside the shoe store (where he worked on and off for several years) that read: *"Jesus Christ says Christianity is Satan's masterpiece."* Perhaps John was quoting the Lord directly, since this was also the period he claimed to have had a personal encounter with Jesus while driving his truck. After that, Jesus became his teacher and showed John everything he knew. It's not clear whether de Ruiter held this unorthodox belief while he was embarking upon a career as a Christian minister (albeit a radical one), or only *after* his plans were thwarted by the elders. This is a significant detail, obviously, but John's personal history is currently lost in the myth.

According to Joyce, her husband got into trouble with authority during the first Christian seminary, after which they went to a different Bible school. Joyce assumed they would continue but de Ruiter decided to drop formal education and become an intern apprenticing under a pastor in the Lutheran church, hoping to learn more this way. It was through internship that he got closer to the Lutheran leadership, when Don Rousu and others recognized him as a unique individual with a "special connection to God." De Ruiter and Rousu apparently had a shared vision of de Ruiter being "the key" to the Church; as a result of that vision, de Ruiter gained access to deeper levels of the church infrastructure. It was then that he decided there was no point going back to Bible school or pursuing formal education. "At that point," Joyce remembered, "I think he started meeting every morning with either one or both the pastor and his wife. This is when it started to become a little secretive."

De Ruiter decided to abandon any plans for a formal education—and presumably whatever career he had in mind—once he realized he could gain special status within the Lutheran church. It was unclear if he became an intern before his unique qualities were recognized or only after, but in either case, it was an unusual development. Christians are usually extremely wary of false prophets and all-too ready to cry "heresy" at the first sign of unorthodoxy. In de Ruiter's case, the miraculous seems to have occurred. How did he impress his Lutheran fellows and gain access to the higher echelons of the elders? Was it simply by being himself, or had he consciously set out to woo them? Again, from what I could determine, it was a little of both.

As Joyce recalled, her husband didn't preach much and only stood in the pulpit maybe three times.

> John's a procrastinator; he's lazy at heart, extremely lazy academically. Not physically, he can stay up all hours of the night and work on his truck; but academically he's lazy. He was due to preach a sermon one Sunday and he was up all night, wasn't preparing anything, going through trauma, turning it into some huge spiritual experience. It may have been valid, I also just thought, "Whatever, John, just get on with it, do what you're supposed to do, don't make this into some woo-woo spiritual thing." What I remember is, five or six in the morning, him calling Pastor Don Rousu, who was his mentor, and saying, "I don't have anything, I don't have anything." . . . I think that was the day when he came to the pulpit,

had not slept, had not prepared anything, and started weeping behind the pulpit, and repeating, over and over in a sort of weeping tone, "God wants to set you free, God wants to set you free, God wants to set you free." It was a huge, controversial thing, it was so abnormal, so beyond the norm. "What is this? Is John being a fool or is it just really spiritual?" [That] really characterized my entire life with him, not knowing, being able to see both perspectives.

Maybe de Ruiter was finding out that silence was good for more than just a good deal on a buzz saw? One of the original apostates that followed de Ruiter out of Bethlehem, "Paul" (not his real name), described de Ruiter's peculiar manner as being quite similar to autistic behavior:

> [H]is stare and willingness to wait for conversation was unnerving. There was so much awkward time. Everything he did seemed different. Taste in vehicles. Obsessions with dog training. I can't remember all the things but by themselves they were okay, but the total package was strange. . . . The best thing we could come up with to describe John was he was socially awkward. I really tried to not let that interfere with my perception of his spiritual gifting, but looking back I think I gave him too much credit. Some of those things that made him look really deep were just part of his weirdness.

Autism is often characterized by an inability to verbalize. "Intense world syndrome" (a less known theory of autism) posits that an inability to verbalize is the result of autists being *unusually attuned to their environments* and receiving an overwhelming amount of sensory data that makes it extremely difficult for them to function or express themselves. If de Ruiter experienced something like "premature enlightenment" at age seventeen, might the symptoms of such an awakening have been similar?

In 1998, de Ruiter, described his awakened state in terms that match those of intense world syndrome:

> [E]verything you touch, everything you do as consciousness, every contact that you are in, every circumstance, every relationship with everything around you, people, things, you are constantly as a sphere of consciousness, everything is touching you. And everything that touches you, you become. So, as you are present in this life, as vast expansion of consciousness that is happening, which creates an amazing flow. And in all of that expansion, there is no identification with anything. . . . The universe is what it really is when you as unconfined consciousness is simply being with it. Then everything outside of you, you experience as yourself, because there is an instant merge with everything that you touch as consciousness. For you to integrate the universe-as-consciousness, you turn into it.

Gerdes had a similar impression of de Ruiter to Joyce's:

> He did this silent thing way back then, just as a regular person, unnerving everybody. . . . Maybe it takes a long time for things to boil up out of his brain and into his mouth. So it makes everyone nervous and they start rambling and it fills the space up, and he can just sit there in his silence and it doesn't reveal that he's nervous too. I [saw] this behavior years before he use[d] it as a religious thing.

In the face of such behavior, it's easy to imagine how the members of the Bethlehem Church could have been divided about de Ruiter. Was he insane, deluded, or (worst of all) a flaming heretic; or was he touched by God, a holy fool? And from what I got from Barrie Reeder (one of the elders at the time), de Ruiter's unworldly/otherworldly presence literally divided the Church—making him less the key than the sword. Reeder was even divided in himself when he spoke to me. On one occasion, he suggested that, by creating an upheaval within the church, de Ruiter was "hoping to pick up the pieces" and "end up with the spoils."* On another occasion, Reeder stated that de Ruiter "wasn't capable of that kind of strategic thinking," and referred to de Ruiter as having "a dysfunctional mind."

Regarding de Ruiter's mind, Joyce had this to say about her third year of marriage with John, a time after their first year of seminary, when they were living with John's younger sister Cecilia: "That summer John talked to me about how he believed he was becoming schizophrenic. He would spend hours and hours lying on his back. It felt like he was having some kind of a breakdown." He also suffered from narcolepsy. "John took Ritalin for narcolepsy for a few years. He fell asleep all the time and he was diagnosed as narcoleptic in the early years of our marriage. I think he took Ritalin when he needed to stay awake, rather than on a daily basis." When I brought up the idea that her ex-husband was autistic, however, Joyce rejected it. After eighteen years living with him, she saw him as all-too-aware of what he was doing. She saw his actions at the Bethlehem church in a similar light:

---

* In an email to me, Reeder wrote: "It was like divide and conquer tactics. When John realized this strategy wouldn't work he seemed perplexed and wasn't able to come up with any other avenue to become the spiritual leader of the church. In Lutheran Churches Pastors are called and must be ordained and John was neither."

> It was a bit like he was this young person coming in to take over the church, to say it simply. He was assuming a lot of power... After John and I were divorced, I decided to go back and talk to Don Rousu and his wife. A statement that Don made at that time fascinated me. I asked him, "What was it about John? What did you see?" He had been pastoring fifteen years at that point, so why would he have given John so much power? John wasn't educated, he had no experience in ministering, but [Don] really was handing over the reins almost: "Here, have my church." I asked why and he said, "I think it was John's certitude, more than anything." He had until then never encountered somebody with so much certitude.

On the one hand, I was hearing stories about a fumbling, bumbling, possibly autistic "idiot" who was barely able open his mouth in company. On the other hand, there was an equal number of tales about a cunning, willful, unbending manipulator. But by all the accounts, however it happened, de Ruiter's brief stint at the Bethlehem church was the moment when de Ruiter's guileless fumbling and/or wily pranking gave way to a new authority and confidence. Whatever conviction he possessed about his divine calling could only have been strengthened by Rousu's faith in him and by the buzz that grew around him, like a forest fire. This was the turning point that would eventually lead to the creation of a spiritual empire.

The Demon-Carrier

"Bob was carrying our demons; that was one of the strong suggestions."
—Joyce, 2010

The turning point in de Ruiter's career, at least on the surface, appears to have been the famous "nine-hour testimony" which he gave before the gathered congregation at Bethlehem, an incident which he described in 1998:

> What I was doing during that nine hours, I would go into, it's like my own space developed over all those years, from about seventeen years on. I would go into that space and I would just be on the inside now and just describe how things developed, and I would go from one time to the next to the next, and each time I would be inside of that space, I just talked about it. What that did to people who were listening is it took them inside of that space. Because it wasn't the words that I was using, it was the space that I was in.

Joyce was not present for the marathon testimony but she heard a recording of it afterwards. She summed it up for me as "extreme narcissism; those are like the early signs." No doubt others in the church would have agreed, but there was at least one person who experienced something else. That was Bob Emmerzael, and besides John, Emmerzael is the most enigmatic and evasive character in de Ruiter's history. In 1998, at a public meeting in Edmonton, Emmerzael described his conversion to the group (the transcript is from a tape recording):

> The biggest change for myself was when John gave his testimony, which was I think a nine-hour ordeal;

> it was from early evening till late in the morning. For me, that was the key. It was for me like the picture of truth just dropping into place and fulfilling itself. From that point on, it was knowing truth and actually being inside of truth instead of trying to make it work, that I actually knew the truth and the picture was clear and it was there, it was complete. Right from that moment on, things took off for myself.

In those early days, Emmerzael became Tonto to de Ruiter's Lone Ranger, Robin to his Batman, John to his Jesus. Today, Emmerzael is no longer among de Ruiter's followers, however, having gradually ceased attending the meetings in the early 2000s. Despite being diagnosed with cancer over fifteen years ago, I knew from Joyce that he still lived in Edmonton and that he had never spoken about his reasons for leaving the group (reputedly not even to his wife). Yet Emmerzael was perhaps the most central player in de Ruiter's rise to prominence.

As Joyce recalled it, Bob was an elder of the church who became de Ruiter's confidant after that nine-hour testimony. From that day on, the two men went out together on average four nights a week, from eight at night sometimes until six or seven in the morning. They spent that time talking in restaurants and in de Ruiter's van, and Joyce would often get up in the morning to find them both sleeping in the front seat of the van. "I didn't think they were fooling around with women," she told me. "It was an area of conflict. I didn't like that he would sleep in all morning and stay out all night. I always thought, apparently [he managed] without much sleep, but I realized later, OK, you probably are sleeping with Bob in the van."

Years later, once de Ruiter was fully established as a (non-Christian) spiritual teacher, Bob, the beloved disciple, sometimes held meetings in Edmonton when de Ruiter was touring. So far as I know, none of these recordings are available, but there is a recording of the meeting (in 1998, the tape is called "Bob's Story") where Bob gave his own testimony, a testimony which concentrates exclusively on the impact de Ruiter had on his life.

> I was caught up in this thing that was way bigger than me. It was phenomenal, the description of fireworks going off was constant, truth opening up. It was even apparent then that what was happening was happening with John, and I was really along for the ride. I was benefiting just by being with John, and the more I've been with him, the more that that's actually been the case, that that became established more and more, [that] what was actually taking place was a cornerstone of truth being established here in this place, in this world, so that everything is built on that, and everything that took place then is to have that cornerstone shaped, formed, and completely usable, and then just doing what the truth would do. And for me, it was me being a part of it, in a way that was like a useful tool.

Throughout his testimony, Bob states his belief—his "knowing"—that de Ruiter is "the living embodiment of truth." While apparently Emmerzael was the first person to believe this, by the time of his testimony, others believed it too and de Ruiter was making the claim publicly (it was even printed on the early tapes). But in the period Bob is describing, Bob may have been the *only* person to believe this about de Ruiter—except possibly for de Ruiter himself. Describing the relationship from his side, at the same meeting, de Ruiter said:

> Once it was clear that I moved in truth and [Bob] was taken into it, like I took him inside of my space. Once

that happened, he dropped his space, he just didn't bother with it anymore, he didn't listen to it. . . . He didn't hesitate. He didn't want to use up his energy trying to fit things in when he could just drink. I would open up truth and he would just bathe and bathe and bathe in it. . . . for him it was like, everything's over. For myself, *he was just like putty*. I would open up truth and it's like I'd be working this putty while I'd be opening up truth. *I could mold him.* [My italics.]

What was de Ruiter "molding" Bob into? Presumably, both men believed de Ruiter was molding Bob into "truth," otherwise Emmerzael would never have consented to the process for as long as he did. But besides taking their word for it, it's impossible to say what kind of internal "molding" de Ruiter performed on Emmerzael, or just how beneficial it was, to either of them. What we do know is that Bob, an elder, became de Ruiter's confidant and his first official "follower," and that it had a ripple-effect on others in the group, who followed Bob's lead and joined de Ruiter's party. At the 1998 meeting, de Ruiter said:

> When people that were close to [Bob] before and really respected him before, they were amazed. They could see that a lot of people would follow me and be deceived, so to speak. They were most amazed when Bob followed me because that didn't make any sense, because he was stable, he was even, he was smart, he knew where he was. He wasn't moveable like most other people would be, and yet he would just totally follow. They couldn't understand that, that didn't make sense; of all people, that didn't fit at all.

In Bob's own words:

> This little straggling group that remained with John, in spite of the fact that the rest of that Christian community was chattering with fear as to how deep the deception was. It was basically only a week and a half, I think, that everything blew up. Then after that, the response that the rest of this group had towards us was that we were just powerfully deceived. In many ways it would be fair to say that it was like being, well it isn't fair to say but the equation can kind of be given of being like guinea pigs. Like everything was new, everything was . . . this stuff had never been written and taught. The only one who lived this way was Jesus Christ. That stuff being written down had been misinterpreted for centuries and mis-lived for centuries. That which was opening up was entering into total newness because there was nothing that was able to give the picture of who Jesus was, of what the truth was. There's nobody to explain that to John. I tried. John was not seen as this huge threat and powerfully deceived individual until after I joined him.

When de Ruiter left Bethlehem—whether by his own choice or because he was ejected from it, as Reeder claimed—Bob Emmerzael spear-headed the exodus. The exodus formed the core "cell" of de Ruiter's private Christian group.* That cell group (many of whom are still following de Ruiter today) eventually multiplied into a three or four hundred strong congregation, the Oasis community.

---

* According to Reeder, Emmerzael did not voluntarily resign as an elder from Bethlehem either.

"I Am That": A Man After God's Own Heart

"John shared with me about encountering 'the Beast' in Revelations, and doing battle with the Beast. Extremely early on, probably four years after we got married, he and Bob came home and needed to tell my sister, Bob's wife, and myself [their] revelation . . . that Bob and John were in fact the two witnesses in Revelation. We were never supposed to share that with anybody. It was hidden knowledge. Shortly after that, maybe within the year, John shared that he was the fulfillment of a different scripture, from Isaiah 53, a classic scripture about the coming of the Messiah, Jesus Christ. . . . We were never, ever, ever to share that."

—Joyce, 2010

One thing that became clear as I proceeded with my investigation was that de Ruiter's teachings, for all their mutations, remain essentially Christian (and ascetic) at their core, even while the outward form (and, as I would discover, de Ruiter's own private behavior) veered further and further from his Christian roots (see Appendix Three). So what sort of a Christian leader had de Ruiter been? Joyce assured me he wasn't much of a preacher, more of a teacher. Those first meetings were long, she said, starting at ten or eleven in the morning and continuing until two in the afternoon. This created the sense that "something big was happening, because it took up our whole day. It was different, it was big and exciting." That first stage was followed by one or two years of silence, sitting on the couch, doing and saying nothing. "We'd get together in the morning, everybody would sit down, nothing would happen, a little bit of small talk, and we'd all sit there, and sit there, and sit there, and sit there. People would fall asleep, and eventually it would be two or so in the afternoon and it would be over, John would say that was it."

Bethlehem apostate Paul described the group as "disaffected Christians" who created "a new kind of Church based on the Bible." They weren't tied to any denomination, he said, but craved spiritual experiences and relationships with others who were equally committed. "For most of the time," he told me, "I think even John was trying to figure out what his authority was. I just thought he was well-read and was working out some neat explanations for things." They started with Bible studies once a week, focusing on Revelations. Since open prayer and worship wasn't considered appropriate, there was "a lot of sitting and waiting for someone to share thoughts." As time went by, de Ruiter did more and more of the talking. Sometimes, Paul recalled, there were strange manifestations: "physical or vocal expressions that would have to be considered very abnormal." Participation from the group became less and less and the silences became longer. De Ruiter's "vocabulary changed over a period of time and the use of the Bible quickly became less." He became more outspoken about his ability to interpret spiritual things, and dreams and visions were shared and explored. As Paul remembered, the women became less and less involved with the regular meetings. "There were a lot of questions from the wives who were less enthusiastic, but John would encourage us by calling us 'pillars of this church.' We often mocked the traditional church for how it worked in the Flesh (made things happen by strength of Man versus trusting God)."

The increased periods of silence were explained as a form of "weaning" from the need for anything concrete, including a teaching. Joyce was skeptical.

> We were told that it was good for us. I just thought, "This is bullshit, nothing's happening here, people are falling asleep, this is a joke." But I did my best. It was in my home, so I tried. It wasn't just [John] being

lazy and a lack of initiative to prepare something. It was partly that, but that was also conveniently covered up by [his saying] "There is nothing, I have nothing for you." We were being shed of all of our preconceived notions and constructs, rapidly dropping all of the traditions that we had once held onto. Which is why it's so ironic, because somehow we kept this one tradition where we had to tithe towards our pastor, of all things. It was under the pretense or understanding that we were shedding our religiosity and so on; but it was just a vacuum.

De Ruiter's conviction—his own standard of integrity—was never to preach what he didn't know from direct experience. So the moment he became unsure of himself, he would fall into silence. Ironically, that silence became the nature and meaning of the "sermon," and even the *reason* for the meetings. By redefining what had value, de Ruiter turned a *lack* of anything tangible to offer into his offering, and transformed an apparent failing into an ostensible virtue. Once again, silence saved the day.

*

Based on Joyce's accounts, de Ruiter decided that he was the living Messiah—not merely "the key" but "the One"— shortly after leaving the Bethlehem church (where aptly enough, this "savior" was born), and while brain-storming with Bob Emmerzael. It was a *folie a deux* that the two men were unable or unwilling to keep to themselves. Joyce remembered it as a pivotal point—who wouldn't remember the moment her husband came home claiming to be the Messiah? At the time, she asked him, "Are you the Second Coming, or are you the one coming before?" but he wouldn't answer. She was confused. Historically, Jesus had already been and gone, so what was

John's purpose exactly? The way she understood the Second Coming, it would be a big deal, and people would know about it everywhere. None of what was happening met her expectations of the Second Coming. Yet John's claim wasn't exactly to be the Second Coming, she said, it was more that he *was* the Messiah. "It didn't make sense for John to claim to be the fulfillment of Isaiah, because that was about a savior who bore our sins, if you will. So who was John in that picture?"

The news that John was the Messiah, in whatever form, was to be kept strictly under wraps. It was only for the elect to know. But of course word got around, and even if open claims of his being the fulfillment of the prophecy were not encouraged, de Ruiter sometimes compared himself to Christ and talked openly about having Jesus as his personal teacher. Bob testified publicly to John's divinity while de Ruiter sat in the room, his silence endorsing all of Emmerzael's claims. At the same meeting, de Ruiter also talked about his "apprenticeship" under Jesus:

> In my relationship with Jesus . . . he would be with me in a way that I knew was true and I had no comprehension. . . . I was put in that situation because there was actually a purity of heart. It's like Jesus taking a clean heart and a pure heart and putting it in a space that it can't comprehend and nothing will ever take place if you don't integrate that space, and that can only be done to a heart like that. *There was already like a perfect heart, a pure heart*, to do that with a heart where there's anything less than a purity or cleanness, it'll just hurt itself. For him to transfer what he was to me, then it's like that had to take place, basically the hard way, and with a heart that was clean and that was pure. Anything less than that would just automatically disqualify it on every level. I just started surrendering, and once that caught, it was

> like a wild fire and I never did anything to ever slow it
> or stop it. Once it started I never drew back. I never
> hesitated.

While De Ruiter speaks in a gentle, diffident, almost tentative tone of voice on the tape, using searching, naïve, often childlike terms, at the same time, in the most disarming of ways, he is alerting others to his own supreme specialness, his "perfect heart." He is telling the group how he was chosen by Jesus Christ to be His disciple and earthly representative, His successor. While de Ruiter may have only referred to himself as "an Apostle," his descriptions imply that he considered himself far more than that. Towards the end of the meeting, he said:

> If you had to do it the way that I did it, you would
> never do it. I know that you would never do it.
> Because the way that I did it, you don't get another
> chance. It's like if you blow it, you're disqualified. . . .
> My guess is that a lot of people who were in my place
> would have started and just got disqualified. That
> that would have happened a lot. And with myself . . . I
> was just clean. I never drew back, or I would have
> been disqualified.

Although there were many contenders for truth-embodiment, evidently there was only one winner. The self-professed status of living embodiment of truth does not invite peers, collaborators, or even disciples. It requires followers. "There is no such thing as a 'knowing' that John does not agree with," Paul said of that time.

*

"I distinctly remember John saying to me that he had no friends. I distinctly remember those exact words and I thought it was very strange. It may have been regretful, but since he didn't actually show emotions, I don't know. It was more of a neutral statement and I thought it was odd. But I have thought about it a hundred times, that he probably didn't have friends [because] he couldn't confide his deepest feelings. Bob Emmerzael became a friend."
—Joyce, 2010

According to Joyce, de Ruiter carried more authority than any ordinary pastor would. "There was something in the air, that he was different, that he was a radical, that he had 'a pure heart,' that would have been the term. There was always this sort of hush that John had this amazingly pure heart. In that way, he was different. He wasn't seen as just one of our equals who played that role." Whether it was by conscious design or not, from the start de Ruiter was placed above his fellows. Even his wife was under the spell:

> I believed it, somewhat, and his [younger] sister projected that on him. Bob would have somewhat projected that on him, from that elders' meeting on. Probably in some subtle way John asked for it. Because he teaches this stuff, there is the presumption that he lives it. Because he talks about this, in that kind of a mesmerizing, mystical, hypnotizing way, you cannot help but think, "You wouldn't talk that way unless you knew this." It was more the air he had as he spoke, as if he *knew* this.

Joyce mentioned how, in the Old Testament, David was described as "a man after God's own heart." "Somehow," she said, "that little phrase got slapped on John." That was her primary contribution to the evolution of a guru, she said. She believed in the perfection of her husband's heart and that such a thing was possible; she wanted "that kind of person in my life." When she'd met de Ruiter, she had fallen in love and believed his heart was pure. "From that point on, he kept trying to convince me of that and reaffirm that and confirm that." Whenever things didn't add up, she *had* to believe that he had a pure heart; that was what he *told* her to believe, and that, since his heart was pure, whatever impurity she was seeing wasn't true, because he had a pure heart. "I never ever gave myself permission to see otherwise, because [I believed] 'John's not like that.' That's the fatal error we all make."

The belief that de Ruiter had a pure heart would eventually come to be held dear by hundreds, perhaps thousands, of people. "Why do we let that be our premise?" Joyce asked me. "For some people [it's] because of the way he looks, his stare, maybe the aura we see around him. It's very complicated, a lot of it is because a few hundred people believe that, have been believing it for a dozen years, so it must be true. I think that's how all these personality cults work." As perhaps the first person to believe it about her husband (though John's younger sister may have beat her to it), Joyce made "the fatal error" that "started the ball rolling."

My own suspicion is that, if anyone (besides de Ruiter) got the ball rolling, it was Bob Emmerzael. During his testimony in 1998, Emmerzael describes his experience within the Christian church, when he met a lot of "top-level Christian leaders." He worked overseas with a Christian group and met big-name authors and missionaries, leading pastors and "TV people." (By giving this personal history, he is laying out his credentials for the group.) Even while he was involved with all this, Emmerzael said, he had to justify the Christian leaders' behavior by saying that "these were just human beings so that's why there can be such a difference between what is true, or what is true of Christianity or whatever, and what their lives are." While there were certain areas in which these men lived "cleanly," he noticed "huge chinks." He claimed never to have seen such chinks in de Ruiter. "I became aware of that fairly quickly, that the more I knew him, the more that is on the surface very amazing, because it still never has happened. I'll let you know if it does." (Laughter from the group.)

Emmerzael's point in his testimony is that, while the Christian leaders who so disappointed him were "just human beings," de Ruiter was something *other* than merely human. "By just valuing John," he says, "valuing the truth, I gain what is true. It becomes what I live in. It had nothing to do with me having any initiative in it. It wasn't my initiative to establish myself in truth." In other words, it was truth that took charge of his life in the form of de Ruiter. For Bob, they were the same thing. Emmerzael talks about de Ruiter like a man in love—maybe because that was what he was at the time. He was in love with truth, and since he believed de Ruiter was the embodiment of truth, he was in love with John.

> In twelve years, there's never been any confusion. I've never had any confusion. In being established in what is true, it never, ever was a picture of myself wrestling with whether truth or what I knew of truth was true. What was true was absolutely true. I don't see that as just because I had all this time with John, although that didn't hurt. It was like what was true was absolutely true and that was settled. Whatever's happened since, if there was anything of what would appear to be confusion on the surface, it would be like, that's just something that appears to be confusing; it has nothing to do with what I know.

It's hard to tell from Bob's babbling who he is trying to convince. He is speaking of doubts and lack of trust in such a way that he appears to dismiss the subject, yet it is still what he chooses to speak about. In fact all he is really saying, throughout his entire testimony, is that he loves John. His awareness of "who John was" allowed the truth to establish itself more and more in him, which in turn allowed John to be established more and more in him: "knowing him, and in me knowing him as the embodiment of truth." The trust Emmerzael had in John allowed him to know John's heart fully, and to know that his heart "never, ever, ever missed. It never once deviated from what I knew of truth and what was always there before us. It's been about twelve years now and that's an incredible picture even on the surface, to know that somebody's heart never once, never even once slightly deviated from what was true."

It certainly is an incredible picture. By painting it, Emmerzael elevates not just de Ruiter but his own discernment into the realms of the absolute. De Ruiter's wife had a very different story to tell, but of course, she wasn't asked to testify; Emmerzael, meanwhile, was never married to de Ruiter. He remained in perpetual courtship with him, and so the illusion of his beloved's perfection remained intact (for a while at least).

> [T]o actually be inside it and be who I am, I don't see that happening to anybody anywhere, apart from what actually is established in John, what John is is actually allowing the truth now to be brought about in this world. That wouldn't have taken place, I don't know, the only way that that can take place is through what is happening with John.

Though Emmerzael doesn't come right out and say it, the implication is clear: *anyone who doesn't believe in John is doomed.* To be saved—"established in truth"—they have to go through him. By taking his Christian beliefs and transposing them onto de Ruiter, Bob gave de Ruiter the power (and the glory) of *embodying* those beliefs, thereby bringing meaning to his own life.

Emmerzael was the first of de Ruiter's children to testify, and he set the pattern. "His heart was perfect," he told the congregation in 1998. "I would have never imagined a heart like that. I couldn't even imagine. The only thing I could have ever equated it to was Jesus Christ, because he was God." John was Christ, therefore John was God. Throughout the meeting, de Ruiter was in the audience, making occasional comments or corrections; since he didn't correct Bob at this point, he was tacitly giving the nod to Emmerzael's wild claim. "Yes," his silence says. "*I am that.*"

If it was enough that John was here and belief in him was not required, why was it necessary to testify to all of this? What possible effect could it have upon the listeners except to increase their awe—and worshipful love—of de Ruiter? Besides that, there appears to be no purpose to Emmerzael's testimony.[*]

---

[*] For more on Emmerzael, see Appendix One, "The Things Bob Had to Swallow."

Who Am I This Time—Myshkin or Machiavelli?

"[T]he teacher (himself, particularly) was 'empty'—code for 'lacking inherent qualities'—or 'the blank slate' upon which the student was shining his own needs, and, more starkly, the qualities of his own mind. Which then meant that the teacher's own day-by-day nuts-and-bolts behavior was forever indefinable, baffling, and blameless. This would be true whether the teacher "seemed" outright manipulative or just plain stupid."
—Matthew Remski

As I pressed on with my investigations—receiving rejections or non-responses from almost everyone I approached—I began to despair of ever reaching an understanding of de Ruiter. If his own wife of eighteen years still didn't know who he was, what chance did I have? Was there any way to determine how much of his life was the result of calculated action and how much of it "just happened"? His loyal followers believed de Ruiter was a spotless vessel of "pure goodness." His ex-wives (if I included the von Sasses in that category) told a different story. Who was likely to know de Ruiter better?

I knew the arguments against trusting the testimonies of ex-wives, yet my many conversations with Joyce convinced me that what she felt towards her ex-husband was less ill will than a fervent desire to understand him. She told me she never knew who her husband was. He had a normal side, she said, and she loved that normal side. But there was also a lot of confusion around him, including "just whacked stuff." Joyce was entirely convinced that John was an ordinary man, in terms of having no superhuman powers at least. "John is human, he's a very, very mixed up human being. There's nothing otherworldly about him. There's just a lot of confusion going on. That is something I am convinced of. But I can't explain that confusion. I don't know what it's all about."

> I think John is shy, which is why in social situations he becomes a kind of a blubbering fool. He's not that good socially. He makes up for it, but he never was. When he started conducting weddings at his own meetings, it blew me away because suddenly he looked like a fool. He didn't know what to do with his hands, he would kind of sway, he hardly knew what to say. It was like a radical, black and white difference.

Apparently even Emmerzael, despite all his supposed "knowing," experienced the same confusion. He described himself as de Ruiter's "guinea pig," and as clay for the master's molding. Naturally he would have had a vested interest in believing his soul-sculptor was trustworthy. But based on his testimonies at the time, a significant part of his trust was because he wasn't sure *what* was going on. "There would be pictures, like visions or things," he said in 1998, "but we weren't practically aware of how all of that stuff was going to take place." Presumably such "stuff" included the building of the Oasis Empire—so was de Ruiter as "practically unaware" of this process as Bob was? Did he simply become "a living embodiment of truth" one day and follow what he "knew to be true" all the way to a multimillion-dollar corporation with hundreds of followers? Or was it all worked out behind the scenes, "embodying truth" being the best shot he had at making an honest living without going to college or kowtowing to Christian orthodoxy? Was becoming a living embodiment of truth something de Ruiter had to *work* at, like any other career path?

One piece of evidence I found for the latter perspective was Joyce's account of de Ruiter's interest in body language. During the early years of their marriage, she said, her husband was reading up on the subject.* Though Joyce apparently didn't consider her ex-husband especially intelligent, she came to believe that he developed "some sort of a skill to read people, to read their insecurities, to read their needs: were they needing a father, a lover, a friend, a teacher? Reading that from things they said and from their body language, and becoming that for them." Only later did it occur to her that he had kept a lot of those particular books around the house and that he was fascinated by the subject of body language. "Definitely it was something he was engaged in and took up as a study," she said.

Was de Ruiter's interest in body language a continuation of his desire to get a "read" on people and determine how best to approach them? If de Ruiter is neurodiverse, to whatever degree, it might be that he didn't quite "get" neurotypical human beings.† In the early days, maybe he had trouble understanding social behavior and lacked the basic tools to respond appropriately? Neurodivergents (I am one) can fail to pick up the simplest of cues. Vocal inflections or physical gestures that are quite obvious to other people can totally pass an Aspergerian by, and autistic types can also be literal-minded to the point of apparent idiocy (they often don't get innuendos).

---

* According to Joyce—and despite collecting thousands of books during the early years of their marriage—de Ruiter was not a great reader. She said that, besides some of those formative Christian works, he mostly read Western novels, such as those by Louis L'Amour.

† The terms neurodiverse and neurotypical are alternatives favored within autistic communities for "normal" and "autistic," and pertain to neurological hardwiring and its effects on perception and social behaviors.

At the same time, neurodiversity often entails being finely attuned to other people's unconscious agendas, and that can be a primary source of confusion. If a person is saying one thing while thinking another, autistic types often don't know which signals to read and are unable to respond. Gerdes said something similar about de Ruiter, "You ask him questions and he's like, 'Why are you asking this question, are you seeing through me?' So that's why I think maybe he's autistic, because he doesn't think I'm truly asking what I'm asking, he thinks there's a double meaning to it. Conversations with him were really surreal."

As children, we learn behavior through imitation; so if neurodivergent children are picking up signals that are hidden to the naked eye and ear, they would have difficulty knowing what to imitate. They would be like beings from another planet: the harder they tried, the weirder they would seem. Perhaps the same is true of de Ruiter? His desire to correctly imitate human behavior might also account for his predilection—bordering on obsession—with movies. De Ruiter was a movie lover even in the early days of his marriage to Joyce; later he developed the concept of "truth movies," and told Joyce that taking his followers to the theater was part of his work. To date (as far as I know), he still has screenings at the Oasis center. If de Ruiter's fascination for movies stems from a desire to figure out what makes people tick, perhaps such vicarious experience is exactly what he is looking for? According to Joyce, "John always identified with the hero in a movie like *Braveheart* or *Matrix*, all these kinds of movie. He became that person and took on that identity. I think it had to do with being different and being misunderstood. I think John did a lot of that, identifying with these characters and building himself some kind of persona thereby."

In those early years, de Ruiter set about building himself a Messianic persona, and apparently he used real-life personalities to gather raw material. Joyce cited several people over the previous fifteen years who were extremely significant in de Ruiter's development. Each one of them, she said, gave something particular to him. There was Chris and Mariel Helmers, two "very intelligent, very analytical, intellectuals" who ran a new-age bookstore which de Ruiter frequented during a long period in the early nineties, as much as five days a week. "They would discuss everything . . . very intensely. John would go to the store every day and just hang out at the store and people would meet him, sort of like a doctor. I think sometimes they set up appointments and sometimes they didn't."

Then there was "Boots" Beaudry, who owned a massage clinic which de Ruiter frequented over a two-year period, five days a week, "partly to get massage and partly to talk about stuff. John learned a lot from Boots, and that's clearly when all the lingo changed. He started talking about Kundalini, *chakras*, third eye." Boots got her nickname from her many years spent in the army. Joyce recalls it being a high position, and also that Boots had a very rough childhood (my wife remembers Boots talking about being sexually abused as a child). According to Joyce, Boots (like John?) "had a nasty side, and a sweet side; she had a childlike side and a very domineering side."

> She poured into John all her "new age" knowledge about chakras, third eye, bilocation, astral travel, energy, brain waves, etc. She also massaged him as she was primarily a body worker. John, of course, was discipling her. She often said that all her knowledge was worthless in light of what John was giving her—teaching her how to "be." It was a real exchange. It was also clear that she loved her special position around John. I have often said that it was obvious that all the people with whom John spent a lot of time had something unique to offer John—

whether that was money, position, knowledge or otherwise.... It was during that time that John spoke extensively about his astral travel and bi-location.

Joyce remembers finding John "lying on the floor in one of Boots' therapy rooms with a brainwave machine hooked up to his head. Measuring beta waves, etc. I guess that was the learning element." She also remembers this as the time de Ruiter started the "connecting, the intense eye-gazing, where people started to experience his face shifting," techniques de Ruiter also learned from Boots: "He would come home and actually practice; he practiced it with me sitting across the table, asked me to stare in his eyes: 'Joyce what do you see?' He tried it with the kids, he tried intensely all the time... 'What do you see? What did you experience?'" Joyce says she herself never had a connecting experience with her husband, much as she wanted to. De Ruiter told her it was because she "knew too much. They were sort of attributed like the miracles of Jesus, the confirmation that he had special powers. I knew too much to need that."

Joyce described a major transition point when her husband met Boots, and then Baba Singh, a *Sikh* from India. A Sikh is a follower of Sikhism, defined as "any human being who faithfully believes in One Immortal Being; ten Gurus, from Guru Nanak to Guru Gobind Singh; Guru Granth Sahib; the teachings of the ten Gurus and the baptism bequeathed by the tenth Guru."[7]

"Up to that point," Joyce said, "he was a teacher ... people treated him as somebody with some more wisdom, some more knowledge, perhaps a purer heart than they had; but people didn't worship him." The people from the South side of Edmonton, whom Joyce called "the Baba crowd," were familiar with the ways of the east and the whole guru culture. It was through their influence that everything changed: "people actually began to bow to him, treat him like a God. I would look at him and think, 'Say something!' And he didn't; he conveyed that sweet, innocent, expressionless look, that blank look; but he allowed it." Joyce believed those were critical times, perhaps even the critical year, during which her husband "allowed it to happen. I don't know if he wanted it to happen or if it was complacency and he allowed it to happen." Joyce saw in John what often looked like "apathy, selfishness, self-indulgence," but at the same time she saw "a lack of self, a lack of ego." She didn't know what to believe, she was losing her ability to trust in her perceptions, because her husband told her how to interpret them every step of the way. "He just carried so much authority. I think a lot of John's development was trial and error—this worked. This way, you have power over people; and so you continue to do that, not necessarily so consciously and deliberately. But unconsciously, you learn how to overpower people."

*

"Machiavelli says that if as a ruler you accept that your every action must pass moral scrutiny, you will without fail be defeated by an opponent who submits to no such moral test. To hold on to power, you have not only to master the crafts of deception and treachery but to be prepared to use them where necessary."
—J.M. Coetze, *Diary of a Bad Year*

The more I hear about de Ruiter, the more convinced I am that he has two distinct sides, sides that seem as dissimilar as Jekyll and Hyde but which apparently co-exist in his psyche and seem to work quite well together. There is the Prince Myshkin, Dostoyevsky's holy epileptic; then there is Niccolo Machiavelli, the author of the famous political text *The Prince*. Prince Myshkin is an innocent who blunders his way through the social ranks of 19th century Russia, causing whirlwinds of activity wherever he goes, never quite comprehending the impact he is having. Except for the time frame, this certainly sounds a lot like de Ruiter. On the other hand, Machiavelli's text, considered the inception of real-politick, is a treatise on the most efficient forms of tyranny and how best to attain power, social influence, and political control. This, I believe, is de Ruiter's hidden face.

In simple terms, Myshkin represents childlike innocence and a lack of cynical agendas, while Machiavelli (in honor of whom the term "Old Nick" was invented) represents the most naked and ruthless form of self-interest. If we assume that, like all human beings, de Ruiter possesses both sides—then which is in control? Does his passivity and acceptance extend as far as passively going along with his own corruption? Does he equate truth with the line of least resistance? If his inherent innocence (his Myshkin nature) prevents him from suspecting the existence of an inner Machiavelli, would that make it easier for the Machiavellian part of him to put such "innocence" *to use*?

If we are to believe his own accounts, even in the early days of his teachings, de Ruiter no longer acted out of self-interest *at all*, only out of a love for what he "knew to be true." But if the results of being true to what he knows are indistinguishable from the results of a ruthless bid for power and control, *what does this say about de Ruiter?*

Unveiling de Ruiter/Weaning Joyce

"I don't think I ever saw anything beyond normal about John, other than his words. Of course his presence, his charisma, sitting in a room silently, but only because people projected that on him. He was not impressive to me on his own. He was a talented person, I admired his courage. I'm not saying that I wasn't impressed with him as a person, but not like that. That's not how John was at home. He was a very average person except that he had qualities. He's good with his hands; he likes adventure so he's quite courageous. He's a great water skier. I admire him for these things. That's it."
—Joyce, 2010

A father feels a duty to set a positive example to his children; a guru or spiritual teacher—even one who doesn't claim to be the living truth—has (or believes he has) a responsibility to "keep up appearances" in order not to let his followers down. Maintaining such an appearance might not be as difficult as it sounds, if the belief and adoration of the followers is enough to sustain a guru's belief *in himself.*

I have seen how de Ruiter's followers have a tendency to dismiss the testimonies of his wives (Joyce, and later Benita von Sass), as prejudiced and tainted by bitterness and disillusionment. Skeptics, on the other hand, tend to take the accounts as conclusive proof of de Ruiter's dishonesty. At the very least, they provide some useful context to the picture of de Ruiter that has been created and maintained by the Oasis PR team for the past fifteen years or more. There is plenty of room for speculation as to why de Ruiter has chosen to keep that aspect of his life carefully concealed. What there can be no real argument about is the fact that he *does* keep it hidden, to the best of his abilities. Yet de Ruiter's teachings are all about "unveiling reality," so when is the veil to be drawn aside so we can gaze upon the reality of de Ruiter?

It's a curious fact that de Ruiter was apparently secretive even with his first wife, perhaps anticipating this very day?*

> I can't know how much John was sharing with me. I think John saw me as a skeptic. We started out as soul mates, deeply in love. I would think I knew everything, but now I realize I guess I didn't. I think at some point he realized he could only share so much with me, because I was skeptical and you're not going to tell someone who doesn't believe; you're going to tell the people who will lap it up. If John had consistently displayed the loving, kind, giving, humble fruit, I would have probably been more inclined to believe his crap. But at some level, he was a jerk. . . . He was incredibly self-absorbed. It was always about him, about what he was going through, his own experience of what he needed, and the path he was on. It was always about the path he was on. How are you going to argue with that?

The official bio describes how John and Joyce first met in the Christian bookstore where Joyce worked, in 1981, when they were both devout Christians. According to the bio, both of them had a strong sense they were to be married from early on, but they only shared this feeling several months later, on their

---

* At the time I first contacted Joyce, she told me that she had a "gag order" regarding talking publically about her ex-husband in any way that might "harm his earning potential." That was part of the court agreement, and would remain in place as long as he provided child support for their three children, who until recently lived with Joyce. (The two boys have since moved to Edmonton and joined de Ruiter's organization.)

first date. They were married in June 1982, and four years later their first child was born. Joyce told me her husband-to-be believed in sexual abstinence before marriage. "When we would fool around and go too far, he went on huge guilt trips and would talk about experiencing grace afterwards, feeling forgiven." Evidently this was a powerful issue for de Ruiter: he would pursue Joyce sexually (she believed they would have gone further if she'd allowed it), but at the same time, "there was a lot of guilt related to it." What's significant about this detail, besides showing de Ruiter's traditional Christian morality (fairly unusual for a young man in the late '70s), is the way his "guilt trips" were followed by an experience of "grace." The picture Joyce gave me was of someone wrestling with sexual desires, giving into them and experiencing the corresponding shame, and then, miraculously, being "saved" (from his sinful nature) by the intervention of grace. There is something familiar about this sequence: it is a pattern de Ruiter repeated, in an almost theatrical manner, when his eighteen-year marriage to Joyce came to a messy end in 1999, also a major turning point in his trajectory as a spiritual teacher.

The first five years of the marriage with Joyce coincided with the period during which de Ruiter was struggling to find his way—his "ticket"—in the world, culminating in his *coup d'état* cum exodus at/from the Bethlehem Lutheran church, in 1986. Their first child, Naomi, was born in 1986, the second, Nicolas, in 1988, the third and last, Nathaniel, in 1990. As de Ruiter's bio has it, "in 1996 the first public, non-residential venue was opened at the Akashik book store in Edmonton, replacing and ending the years of Sunday morning meetings in de Ruiter's home." Shortly after that, de Ruiter met the von Sass family.

Before embarking on the saga of the von Sass sisters, it may be useful to cover an aspect of de Ruiter's teachings which were directly involved in everything that happened, either in terms of how de Ruiter rationalized his treatment of Joyce (both to her and his followers), or as a genuine "spiritual" explanation of them. This is de Ruiter's concept of "weaning." In very simple terms, weaning involves letting go of emotional, psychological and sexual wants and needs, usually in the context of a relationship, in order to become reliant solely upon one's inner resources. Self-weaning would be a conscious inhibition of compulsive desires in order to get free of them, as when a person quits a drug or any other compulsive habit. *Being weaned* by another person is rather less common, and generally only occurs in parent-child relationships (though to a degree also in the military). It depends upon an obvious inequality between the parties involved, as the more "adult"—less dependent—person denies the other certain basic wants and needs in order to help them reach a new degree of emotional maturity and independence. That's the theory of it, at least, and it's something de Ruiter has spoken about in his meetings, though usually in abstract, philosophical terms rather than practical ones. It's also, not surprisingly, something he has allegedly practiced in his own relationships, most dramatically (or at least most publicly) with Joyce.

Joyce told me how their marriage started out as a normal marriage with normal marital quarrels and arguments, and how sometimes her husband would give in and sometimes he wouldn't. If they had a quarrel in the evening, he would leave and go to a movie, sometimes staying out to see a second movie. They wouldn't ever resolve the issues, she said, but eventually he would come to bed and "it would be sweet." Towards the end, however, it was far from a normal marriage. She remembers when her husband told her, over a coffee at Tim Horton's, how "he was now going to cut the marriage down to the roots so that it could grow again." She had no idea what he was talking about, but she was terrified what it might mean. Things were rapidly changing. Joyce pointed out to me, however, that John's explanation of how the marriage ended at the meetings was "after the fact." Her experience was simply that he was cutting her out of the marriage and came up with a handy, "spiritual" explanation for it.

"John spun webs around me and talked in circles," she said, "so I never knew quite what was going on during the last five years of our marriage. I was extremely skeptical, extremely doubtful, for years; but I always said there is not one thing that I can put my finger on." Whenever she hit stumbling blocks, he would pull her over them, "masterfully and artfully." Joyce *wanted* to get past her doubts because she didn't want to lose her trust in her husband. And as much as she wanted to get over the stumbling block of doubt, it was convenient for de Ruiter to help her. But, slowly but surely, her trust was corroding.

She knew he was involved with Benita and Katrina: she had seen the relationship develop for three years. It had all the signs of an emotional affair, but she didn't want to believe it was sexual. When he finally told her that they would in fact be his wives, and that this would mean everything—physical, spiritual, emotional, sexual—something snapped in her. "I knew then, 'you've crossed a line John, you're not pulling me across this line.' I dabbled a bit with, 'Could this be, could this make sense?' If indeed this is true, I will have to accept this as well. But that was just too big of a line for me to cross." After this, she said that nothing made sense: her eighteen years with de Ruiter, all the goodness, depth, innocence that others saw in him no longer seemed real to her. Her husband was asking her to do something that she knew even *he* didn't believe was right. She was convinced he was betraying himself.

Once, when they were in Hawaii, when he was already an established guru, de Ruiter had told Joyce that "he couldn't be

[her] husband until he was [her] master." He had made a clear statement: unless she was willing to be his disciple, she couldn't be his wife. Joyce complied as well as she could, but she struggled with it immensely. She let her husband "be like God" to her. And although she never had visions of shapeshifting or auras and colors, when she connected to him at the meetings, it was a powerful experience. "Looking up at him, usually weeping, amidst the harsh treatment he was giving me, I would say to him inside, 'Though you slay me, I will trust you,' which is what Job said to God." As a Christian, "a very confused Christian," she let him "merge with God for me. And he was brutal to me, absolutely brutal as a husband; but I allowed it, thinking, 'I'm being tested, I will trust you, I will love you.'" This relationship defined the last four years of their marriage. She had trusted him for so long that she didn't know anything else: she didn't dare not to trust him, couldn't even conceive of not trusting him. "The alternative was too scary, because if I actually believed the alternative, he was a madman, he was deceived, he was deluded, he was horrible. That alternative, that scenario, was too big for me. I couldn't handle that."

While Joyce told herself it was all a test, to give this up, to surrender her love, de Ruiter talked to her repeatedly about how much she had surrendered but how there was "still one thing; he wouldn't be explicit about it, but I knew that there was this *bit* that I wasn't willing to let go, and he was always focusing on that bit." Joyce assured me that there was nothing wrong with their sexual relationship, but that, by the time he was sleeping with the sisters, he was no longer comfortable sleeping with her. Joyce believed this was the real reason he had to "wean" her" of sexual desire, and that, as he was weaning her of the need have him as her husband, as she was surrendering all her wants and needs as a wife, he was commencing his affair with the sisters. "Towards the end, the last year or so, finally, he was slowing down [sexually] too; but eventually the explanation was that I had to be weaned of that as well. Don't ask me how it works with a guy when he's had sex with someone else and he comes home to his wife. Things are different then."

Under the guise of being weaned, Joyce was being excluded more and more, not kindly and sweetly but harshly. "What always amazed me was, 'John if you knew to do this to your wife, who you loved dearly,' I would think [I] would feel some of that. If, as he said, he had to do this because he knew to, but he cherished me, I think I would feel that. . . . It was very harsh. It's that twisted thing: I felt like I was the most amazing disciple because all I wanted to do was learn how to endure this. It was kind of [like] being tortured: the whole Stockholm syndrome thing."

Though Joyce was raised to be skeptical, she tried hard to believe. On two separate occasions, she took the Chair and poured her heart out, repented, admitted that he was more than just her husband and apologized for wanting him for herself.

> The group would be in tears because the wife has finally surrendered. That was after India, after Poona, and shortly before I found out about Benita. When I was that surrendered, John could tell me. I am convinced that he believed, finally, I was at such a surrendered place [that he could tell me]. Maybe he didn't believe, but hoped, that I would be okay with it. It was very strategic.

In 1997, de Ruiter told Joyce about a couple he'd met, Peter and Ilona von Sass, who owned a retreat center near Edmonton. According to Brian Hutchinson's 2001 article "The Gospel According to John" (which de Ruiter reputedly tried to prevent from being published), the von Sasses had "a history of attaching themselves to spiritual teachers." Joyce remembers how her husband "just let this family right in. He gave himself to them." Between 1988 and 1996, the von Sasses had followed a Hungarian guru, Imre Vallyon, who ran the Foundation for Higher Learning from River Lodge, a retreat center near Stony Plain, Alberta which the von Sasses had helped secure. Ilona was devoted to Vallyon but when her husband fell out with him Vallyon asked them to leave. Peter von Sass took control of River Lodge and about a year later they heard about de Ruiter. They attended a meeting and Ilona von Sass promptly asked de Ruiter if he would lead a retreat at River Lodge. De Ruiter agreed, after which Ilona invited him to Calgary for some meetings and told all her acquaintances about him. (Apparently her husband was less enthusiastic and only came to meetings out of loyalty to his wife.)

Soon after, de Ruiter began spending time with the von Sasses' eldest daughter, Benita. On his first trips to Calgary, he stayed with Peter and Ilona, but later he began staying with Benita. After Benita moved to Edmonton, he spent many late nights at her home. A few months after that, Katrina arrived from Europe, where she'd been playing professional volleyball (apparently Ilona had sent her a picture of de Ruiter which grabbed her attention). Since she needed a place to stay, she moved into the de Ruiters' basement; now when he was not visiting Benita, de Ruiter hung out with Katrina, watching movies and talking late into the night. Joyce would plead with him to come to bed, but he always refused. He assured her that Benita and Katrina were his "disciples" and that their relationship wasn't personal.

Then, in late November of 1999, de Ruiter and Joyce were sitting in the kitchen, smoking cigarettes, and he was talking about Joyce's "death." He acknowledged that she had "gone through a lot of dying, which was a good thing." She had let go of "ninety-five percent of the life that [she] had to let go of," he said, adding that her "ultimate death would be if he took on two more wives." Joyce thought he was joking at first. She phoned Ilona von Sass and asked her if she knew about it. Ilona said she did but that she didn't know what "wives" meant. After many sleepless nights pondering it, Ilona had decided that if this was "truth," they had to accept it. A few days later, Joyce woke her husband from a pre-meeting nap and asked when he was going to tell her what "wives" meant.

"'Wives are just like you, Joyce,' he said. 'A complete physical, emotional, and sexual relationship, just like you.' That, Joyce says, 'was when reality hit.'"[8]

A Ruse by Any Other Name

"You moved out of the subsequent self because of the pressure. But you moved out of your First-self because of the pain. Going for pain-relief instead of remaining in Knowledge. Going for pain-relief will have you building a subsequent self, one to give you what you're wanting and within that self you will then go for pressure-relief . . . to cover that you have gone for pain-relief. That will have you again building a further self where you won't be going for pressure relief. You will simply put pressure on someone else to cover that you have gone for pressure relief. Within that self, if you don't refer to Knowledge-within then you are well on your way to being lost."
—John de Ruiter, 2011

Joyce told me she simply knew her husband too well to ever really believe in him as a living embodiment of truth. No matter how good a water skier he was, to her he would always be a man. De Ruiter's insistence that she see him as her master rather than her husband betrays a desire to remain distant and aloof even from his wife. Ostensibly, it was for her advancement; but maybe aloofness was also de Ruiter's preference (a preference he preached as well as practiced). Perhaps his dallying with the von Sass sisters—who regarded de Ruiter as a holy man to be revered and obeyed—was an inevitable response to the frustration he was experiencing in the face of Joyce's refusal to "surrender" and recognize him as God? That would be in keeping with his "explanation" that he was taking on two new wives as a means to facilitate Joyce' final and complete surrender to Truth (a.k.a. John). What de Ruiter left out of his explanation was the possibility (literally unthinkable to his more loyal followers) that the polyamorous new arrangement was also meeting his own, ever-increasing appetites, as well as a response to his preference for more "impersonal" (one-sided) sexual relationships.

So far, not only had I heard no persuasive evidence that de Ruiter discouraged his followers from perceiving him as superhuman, I had seen plenty of evidence to the contrary. Everything about his stage persona seemed to encourage the idea of superhuman benevolence. That was how it had impacted me, and everyone I spoke to among de Ruiter's admirers described him in roughly the same terms. It followed that, the more de Ruiter's followers projected their ideas of—and aspirations towards—absolute goodness onto him, the greater their belief in his superhuman status and divinity would become.

Logically speaking, the more a follower sustains the idea of his or her guru's perfect goodness and divinity, the more acutely aware of their own *lack* of those same qualities will become. Based on my own experience (and what I'd seen of Oasians), a follower isn't necessarily aware of this happening, because the blissful high of being around the "master" gives one a sense of specialness—*though only insofar as they are submitting to his "truth."* A follower's sense of self-worth centers on their capacity to recognize the guru's greater worth, and their own corresponding lack of value. They get to be "wonderfully worth nothing," because only truth has value. And if de Ruiter is the living embodiment of truth, then he is the measure of all things. As the group members empty themselves of their prior set of values—including or especially their sense of *self*-value—they become fully receptive to an inception of value(s) by de Ruiter himself.

Ironically enough, all this could simply be the result of de Ruiter being *uncomfortable interacting at a personal level*. His Christ-like persona would then be a sophisticated but *unconscious* defense against any sort of personal interaction, a way to minimize the risk of vulnerability or exposure. If this were the case, it's likely that any obvious movements *away* from a more personal engagement by de Ruiter with his group would correspond with some sort of external "trigger" in his personal life. As it happens, de Ruiter's teaching style *did* mutate—from a more casual, conversational delivery to the slow, halting style for which he later became known—over a relatively short period between late 1999 and 2001, *immediately after he admitted to his adulterous affair with the von Sasses.*

*

"When he presented this thing about Benita and Katrina, I knew very well, 'If I go along with this, I will be the queen forever.' I was very aware of this. In a sense I gave up everything when I said 'This is bullshit John,' because that would have been my crowning jewel, if I could have accepted that. I couldn't, because I didn't trust him. Partly it was the way he told me—he told me in stages. And when he left he didn't have a clue what he was doing."

—Joyce, 2010

On the tape "Stillness in a Hurricane" (recorded on the 5th, 6th, and 12th of December, 1999, Edmonton), de Ruiter compared facing the group immediately after the affair came to light to receiving a death sentence:

> Coming up here, and sitting through the meeting, was like walking to the gallows. It was one of the sweetest nights of my life. I was bathing in every moment. Everything being completely still, and silent. And yet at the same time, sailing through this awesome blue sky. I wouldn't have missed it for anything. So endearing this morning. It is seeing so many hearts being so cracked open, and so fragile, so delicate. And seeing such a deep thirstiness, seeing a depth of a love of truth, hurting-hearts looking only for truth. I love what I see.

Besides taking delight in his follower's broken hearts, de Ruiter's claim is that, by conducting a secret affair with two women (though Benita's testimony says there were other women also), he was only "doing what he knew to be true." So why did he feel like he was walking to the gallows? Was he so afraid of the judgment of his followers, or was it something else?

Joyce told me that John's parents refused to have anything to do with the von Sass sisters once the truth came out; as simple Christian folk, they may have judged their son harshly for his behavior. Did de Ruiter suffer internal conflict about it? His decision amounted to a monumental change in both his private and public life. By taking two new wives, not only was he going against his Christian upbringing, he was contradicting his own teachings about the sanctity of the marriage bond and the need for monogamy.

De Ruiter's explanation was the only explanation he ever gave for anything, whether buying a house with a swimming pool or conducting a clandestine love affair: he was doing what he knew to be true. The implication of these words is that *he had no choice*. So what's the difference between that and compulsive behavior? Outside of his philosophy of truth, and coming from anyone else, de Ruiter's account sounds like the reasoning of someone who acted *against* what he knew and then rationalized it. If de Ruiter felt like a condemned man facing his executioners, does this suggest there was some doubt in his mind, even a sense of guilt? But outside of that one poetic phrase, he never expressed anything of the kind. On the contrary, he insisted on having *no doubts at all* about what he'd done.

Although a handful of followers left, de Ruiter's explanation was accepted by the majority, who chose to side with his version of events rather than Joyce's. They only really had two alternatives: either they continued to believe their guru was embodying truth, no matter how it looked; or they acknowledged that he'd been lying, not only to Joyce but to them. Questioning de Ruiter's version of truth would risk being ostracized from the fold; perhaps worse, it would mean losing the shining image of their guru's goodness and being left with a crippling sense of shame and regret. From my own experiences of shame and regret around de Ruiter, it doesn't seem surprising if hundreds of people chose to ignore what they knew and protect what they needed to believe. People do it every day.

I had known about the affair with the von Sasses and about de Ruiter's lying to Joyce during the two years I was devoted to John, and I had ignored it too. The reason I'd ignored it was that I believed de Ruiter operated on a level beyond my understanding, so, whatever it *looked* like, it obviously wasn't *that*. That was de Ruiter's own reasoning, and it was tactically brilliant in its unassailability. The moment I allowed for the possibility that de Ruiter was an ordinary human being, the scales fell from my eyes and what I saw was a liar and a cheat with an unusual repertoire of magic tricks to cover his ass.

There was one other factor at play in keeping my denial in place, and that was that I was a long-time believer in polygamy, and in the notion that "spiritually advanced" individuals—shamans and sorcerers—were not bound by ordinary social or moral conventions, and certainly not by romantic ones. When I first heard about it, the fact de Ruiter took a shot at having three wives if anything only *increased* my admiration for him. Maybe it was similar for many of the men in the group. Maybe the notion of having two or three wives was appealing enough for them to overlook the possibility that de Ruiter might come sniffing around their own nests? For the women, naturally the possibility of joining de Ruiter's harem would have enormous allure. Considering all these factors, it's easy to see why the consensus in the group was one of acceptance/denial.

It's impossible for me—or for anyone—to know what sort of "knowing" de Ruiter had that led to his clandestine involvement with the von Sass sisters. Outside of his descriptions, we can only speculate what a "knowing" for de Ruiter even *is*. We also have no way of deciphering by what faculties de Ruiter determines something to be a true "knowing" and acts accordingly; the presupposition is always that his own depth of understanding is greater than anyone else's—including, or especially, Joyce's. So if de Ruiter says he had a knowing, that's the end of it. The alternative is to question his authority and his "knowing," which means to open a can of worms that few of his devout followers would want to gaze into. If de Ruiter could deceive himself about something of such magnitude, what else might he be deceiving himself about? At that point, for many people, all rational thought ceases.

De Ruiter's spotlessly impersonal version of events really comes down do: "I did what I did and I'm not sorry, so let's move on." Compare this with Joyce's messy and tangled, wholly personal account, and which one makes more sense?

> When he first told me [about the affair], he said, "I either am or I will be sleeping with them. What difference does it make?" And I acknowledged that.* He went away on a trip to Toronto, came back, we were having coffee somewhere, and I finally said, "Are you sleeping with them?" And he looked at me, and that slow, slow, slow nod. So I'm pierced—he is in fact sleeping with them—but I'm also relieved. Okay, so I finally know. But then he says, "But now I know that I won't be anymore." . . . . Some days later, I find out that he had gotten up very early from Katrina's house, after spending the night with Katrina. "I don't understand John, you said you wouldn't be sleeping with them anymore." He said, "I told you that I wouldn't be intimate with them. I didn't say that I wouldn't sleep with them or be affectionate with them." He sounded like a troubled teenager who couldn't figure out what his lines were. He was going back and forth. [I thought,] "If you're trying to tell me this is something you know, why does it fluctuate every few days?" It really was more like a scandal than like a scene of truth. There was nothing clean and final about it. It was more like somebody in a relationship struggling with their lines, how far they should go and where they should draw them.

In de Ruiter's defense, the whole situation *was* new to him, so maybe he was trying desperately to do the right thing, knowing he couldn't possibly please everyone and tying himself

---

* Personally, I thought it would make quite a difference. And why the refusal to give a straight answer?

into knots in the attempt. But if so, why give an account of *never once* having any doubts about what he was doing, never *for a moment* being torn between personal desire and truth? As far as I know, de Ruiter *never* speaks of internal conflict; he certainly never admits to doing anything wrong or lying to Joyce, even though that's precisely what he did.

When he went on public record about the incident, he said two things which stood out. The first was: "I don't live with lust. I don't struggle with that. It's not a weakness."[9] Yet by most accounts, de Ruiter was and is a highly-sexed person. Apparently, he experienced a great deal of guilt over his sexuality when he was a young man, at least partially due to Christian ideals. Joyce described how his "struggles with lust" would lead to a period of shame followed by the arrival of "grace." In the von Sass affair, while there was nothing (besides that "gallows" remark) that indicated de Ruiter felt shame for his lustful behavior, he definitely managed to turn it into a manifestation of grace; many of his followers even perceived him as holier than ever for his "sacrifice." Under the circumstances, de Ruiter stating that he didn't "live with lust," and that it was "not a weakness," sounds a bit like the Wizard telling Dorothy to ignore the man behind the curtain. De Ruiter was not only denying all charges, he was telling us to dismiss all the evidence *based solely on his word*.* Such total assurance in a case like this is indistinguishable from bald-faced lying. It is also more characteristic of a sociopath than a saint.

The second comment de Ruiter made around that same time was, "I have never once flirted in the last twenty years.

---

* Something similar seems to have occurred around the death of Anina: de Ruiter spoke before his congregation about the "truth" that he never had sex with her as if it was a proven fact, rather than simply his word against a dead woman's.

Never once. I've had endless offers, and they just don't mean anything."[10] Here de Ruiter appears to be offering as proof of his innocence the fact that he never *tried* to commit adultery (at least not via the normal social ritual of "flirting"). And if de Ruiter never flirted with women, presumably he never *had* to because of all the "endless offers"?! De Ruiter's defense consists of: "I didn't ask for this to happen, so don't blame *me*." Like a child, he absolves himself of all responsibility, not only for anything that happened to him, but *for his own actions*. He is claiming innocence *a priori*.

On one occasion, Joyce asked her husband if he was ever sexually aroused by other women. He looked at her and very slowly said "No." It was a relief, she said, to know that, if her husband was surrounded by adoring women, he wasn't sexually aroused by them. She shared this exchange with some friends, and when the truth came out about Benita and Katrina, one of them challenged de Ruiter about his lying to Joyce. Joyce remembered that, "John's answer was, 'I was answering from another place, not from a personal space but from another space.' That was how John dealt with everything. I cannot know if it's complete deception and lies, or if he believes that."

So what "space" was de Ruiter answering from? Apparently a space where a spade is no longer a spade, lust is not lust, and adultery is really a movement of being. So why enter that particular space in order to answer a question put to him by someone clearly *not in that space*, if not to provide the answer that best suited his purposes? If de Ruiter's excuse was that he was enlightened, was he asking his followers to believe that he practiced an *enlightened* kind of lying? The moment his followers agreed to accept his non-denial denial, they effectively agreed to go along with *anything* he said.

"He is extremely evasive," Joyce told me, "which is why he's silent: he just avoids answering. In the years that I have been asking him about these women, he does not have an answer except: 'It's what I know.' And he will always say, 'I can't explain it to you because you wouldn't understand.' I have always been amazed that John never attempts to explain [anything]. He just says, 'It's what I know and you wouldn't understand.'"

De Ruiter's version of enlightenment is every male chauvinist's dream. It means never having to say you're sorry.

Edging Towards the Dark Side

Over a period of two or three years, Joyce watched as her husband's relationship with Benita developed. Although she saw "sexual sparks," she refused to believe her husband would ever cross that line. When she questioned him about it, she was shut out. It was her challenge, learning to be "okay" with Benita. "There was so much denial going on, on his part, that it could happen; but it happened, so somehow he had to, not scramble, because he would never acknowledge scrambling, but somewhere metaphorically he scrambled to justify it and call it 'truth.' It was a huge set-up."

Whenever Joyce asked him about Benita, he would refuse to answer. "He had many evasive lines. His lines were, 'You think I'm that stupid to fall for a pretty face?' 'They're not women, they're people.' 'I'm doing what I know is true.'" When his stock replies ran out, de Ruiter became angry and gave her the silent treatment; either that or he simply left. "If we were in bed and I asked, he would say on occasion, 'If you keep asking I'm gonna leave.' And he has gotten up out of bed at three in the morning and driven away because I asked."

In the midst of the messy breakdown of her marriage, Joyce continued to attend the meetings. She took the Chair to confront her husband. He responded mostly with silence, as was increasingly his wont. Shortly after that, someone else questioned him (recorded on the tape, "Stillness in a Hurricane"); de Ruiter gave the following reply:

> I am not guilty until proven innocent. And neither am I innocent until proven guilty. I am what I am. Nothing to gain, nothing to lose. Just living truth to enjoy and to be as. That is all there is. . . . I am not polygamous. And neither do I endorse it. All there is, is truth, being and expressing itself. And anything outside of that is just the manifestation of illusion that we discover in the presence of want or need. . . . It is not want or need expressing itself through the personality, chasing something that it thinks would be just great. There is absolutely no personal agenda.

Once again, if I'd heard this claim a few months before the affidavit, or read the transcript, I would have accepted it without question. Now it just sounded to me like gibberish. De Ruiter's non-denial denial was like Richard Nixon telling *The Washington Post* (on November 17th, 1973): "I'm not a crook." Was de Ruiter's insistence on having "no personal agenda" an unconscious confession? Had anyone accused him of having a personal agenda? His claim that he was just "living truth to enjoy and be as" certainly wouldn't get him very far in any courtroom. His claim that he was "not polygamous" was equally tenuous: polygamy is a social act, not a philosophical concept. (Technically, he was correct, since he didn't marry the von Sasses; but I was fairly sure de Ruiter was doing more than splitting hairs here.)

It may be hard, reading all this, for anyone who wasn't there at the time, and who hasn't a sense of de Ruiter's presence, to understand how so many people could be fooled by such obviously disingenuous behavior. The answer, I think, is that, whatever else de Ruiter is, he's not obvious. And I'm not sure he's disingenuous, either. If he had been practicing the kind of mealy-mouthedness favored by politicians and Mormons, I doubt so many people would have been fooled. What seems more likely is that de Ruiter himself was unable to understand his actions outside of his own "truth"—those terms which he alone defined. Such willed blindness creates a powerful spell over others, because in such a case, de Ruiter wouldn't be feigning innocence (as Nixon was): he would genuinely believe it.

But in the end, his argument was circular and in defiance of all logic: since he was absolute honesty and goodness, whatever he did must be honest and good. Yet his explanations for his behavior invariably pertained to realms beyond the understanding of anyone besides himself. What he was saying was, "It only *looks* like I'm an asshole. If you knew how good I really was, you wouldn't question my actions." At the same time, since he was justifying his behavior with circular arguments, apparently deep down he *did* have some doubts about it. On the same recording, de Ruiter talked about the end of his marriage (my italics):

> Up until about three years ago, what characterized our relationship is that I would accommodate her, and *I didn't do so to cope*. I did so because that is what I knew. So *there was a constant bending, her way*, and not standing in on insistence. And that is also why she loved me most was because of that. *If there was ever an issue, I would soften....* And once it was clear for me to no longer be accommodating, then I couldn't give her what she wanted. *I could only stay in what I knew. It wasn't pleasant for her*

and it wasn't nice. It doesn't feel nice. But it was genuinely good.

De Ruiter claims here that he was going into deeper levels of love and togetherness with Joyce, and that she was unable to follow him there. Is that a genuine explanation, or a clever "spiritualization" of something far messier and more personal? The message that's abundantly clear, either way, is that Joyce was not equal to his "fineness" and that she simply failed to understand the goodness that her husband was. In subtle ways, he painted her for the group as unequal to him, and therefore, in the wrong.

"Her experience was the whole relationship falling apart," he told the group. How else was she supposed to experience it? He wasn't just "going finer," into a deeper, more "impersonal" expression of his love for her; he was sleeping with two other women and lying about it! Even if Joyce agreed that he could sleep with other women (either instead of or as well as her), their marriage as it had been was as good as over. Joyce got to be "wonderfully worth nothing" and was given a "genuinely good" opportunity to "surrender." The group condoned his treatment of her, because, John was "going finer," into a deeper "bond of being" where his love and care for Joyce was no longer expressed through "surface bodies." And though the relationship did fall apart, it was only because of Joyce's demands.

But there was one question de Ruiter never answered: if all that was happening was the result of his being true to what he knew, *why all the lies?* The foundation of his teachings was "core-splitting honesty." Yet de Ruiter wasn't winning any core-splitting awards with Joyce. De Ruiter never explained why he chose to conceal his extra-marital relationships from Joyce until the last possible moment. He never let on who or what he was trying to protect. And he never addressed how much of his "accommodating" her was really based in self-interest. If he was keeping her in the dark because she wasn't ready to know the truth, and because he knew how unpleasant things would get the moment it all came out, how was that different from a personal agenda? In the end, the best "spin" won. The official bio, as it reads in 2017, summed up *the entire affair* in four lines:

> During the year 2000, the de Ruiters' marriage came to an end. A formal divorce was granted on 20th December 2002. The settlement provided that custody of their children was awarded jointly to John de Ruiter and Joyce de Ruiter. Joyce remarried and accompanied her new husband to the Netherlands, living under the name Joyce de Ruiter-Kremers. John de Ruiter continued living in Canada, sharing his domestic life equally between the separate homes of two sisters. The personal aspect of these relationships has now come to an end.

In the officially revised history, only half a line is devoted to the existence of the von Sass sisters (though they were with de Ruiter for ten years); they aren't named and there's no indication that they were on the scene before or during the break-up with Joyce. Now flash-forward eleven years, to November 2010. De Ruiter is asked by an interviewer (Neils Brummelman) about his break up with Benita von Sass (who again isn't mentioned by name). Before that, Brummelman asks de Ruiter about abusive relationships, and is told that, in such cases, the couple have "been doing the incorrect thing all along and that's what enabled the relationship to develop like that." De Ruiter suggests, reasonably enough, that even in the extreme case of physical abuse, the responsibility is *with both parties*. When asked about his break with Benita, however, he takes a diametrically opposed line:

> You can have one individual within a relationship who's being real and true to what they are knowing more deeply within, that doesn't guarantee the other is going to be the same. . . . If there's too much of a gap between the degree of realization . . . that is going to bring a difficulty; not so much for the person who is more advanced . . . but for the individual who hasn't realized it . . . . Their partner is able to speak of things that are profound, more complex concepts can be talked about, and the other individual will have a hard time understanding that . . . . if there's any distortedness within or contraction within, then that distortion is going to carry into everything, *including what they're not understanding of the other, and what they are understanding*. Everything will be subject to that distortion. [My italics.]

As with Joyce, de Ruiter laid the blame for the relationship's failure squarely on the other party, and in the process, practiced some sneaky spiritual damage control to ensure he came out of the whole mess smelling of patchouli oil.*

---

* De Ruiter gave this interview while his legal battle (over the ownership of Oasis) was on-going with Benita and Katrina von Sass, and the unspoken message is: don't believe anything you hear from these women, because they are not at a high enough level to understand me. So why did Truth select such unworthy women for de Ruiter? If, as all the stories have it, de Ruiter picked Benita for her "amazing heart," where was that amazing heart as she set about eviscerating his empire? I can think of two answers: either de Ruiter was wrong about her, or ten years living with him turned her heart to stone. There's possibly a third: her amazing heart was what gave her the courage to stand up to de Ruiter and say no to him.

John's Secret Id-Entity?

"A clear conscience is usually the sign of a bad memory."
—Unattributed

One of the things I became most acutely aware of while writing this account was how de Ruiter tends to divide people into opposing camps, with very little dialogue between the two. Many people who've been exposed to his teachings and/or know people who have joined his group see de Ruiter as cynical and devious. They regard him as a liar and a charlatan with some powerful hypnotic or NLP skills, and that's the end of it. Then there are those who are convinced de Ruiter operates at a "higher level of being," outside of ordinary criteria for judgment. To them, my attempt to submit de Ruiter's behavior to psychological scrutiny will appear futile and irrelevant at best. My hope has been to allow for both points of view, an impossible goal, except that I myself have allowed (or been forced to allow) both to co-exist in my mind for periods of time.

However skeptical I now am about de Ruiter, I still have the memory of my initial experiences. Because of those experiences, I can't ever take an entirely skeptical view, if only because the idea of de Ruiter as a masterful conman doesn't explain the impact he had on me (including inexplicable phenomena such as his infiltrating my dreams). So ironically, my point of view is probably untenable to *both* sides of the fence, namely, that de Ruiter is both a powerful spiritual entity *and* a liar.

My impression is that this dualism (not either/or but both/and) is possible only if there's a corresponding division in the man himself. If so, my sense is that it pertains directly to his sexuality, which is where all the controversy first started. At least partially due to his Christian upbringing, de Ruiter apparently once had a very traditional view of sex and marriage, one that centered on a belief in monogamy. Within such a moral framework, any kind of sexual involvement with his followers would have been strictly forbidden. At some unknown time, that changed dramatically; and to a certain degree, the teachings (most especially the *style* of them) changed along with it. So how did that change come about? Joyce recalled how her husband amended his opinion about the spiritual teacher Barry Long, in what she believed was a slow preparation for revealing the truth about the von Sass sisters:

> Barry Long called himself a Tantric master. There is room for that with these gurus. For John and I, who come from a more traditional background, that set off alarm bells. But for many of these people it's not a real deal breaker. I knew that he had connected with Barry Long, or had heard of him, and I was reading Long's books and I asked John about him: "He sounds like you: maybe he is truth?" At that time, John was very clear in saying that evidently he wasn't, because of all the women in his life. That reassured me. But then, sometime later, he actually gave me some article written by Barry Long's five women, their experience with Long. He asked me to read it, and asked what I thought about it. I was shocked, I didn't understand why he was asking for my response. There was always this context of Barry Long. So when he finally told me about the women, it was one of the questions I had: "What are you John, are you a Tantric master?" And he gave me the slow, silent nod again.

Joyce believes that, when her husband was nudging her towards the idea of "Tantric discipling"—which he'd previously denounced as a transgression from truth—he had already embarked upon his clandestine activities with the sisters (and possibly other women too). Yet once the "scandal" broke, de Ruiter didn't explain his behavior to the group in terms of Tantric mysteries, and he didn't reverse any of his previous teachings on monogamy and sexual frugality (until that time, he had advised against sex before marriage). If anything, his teachings became *more* austere, at least in delivery style.* De Ruiter's explanation was simply that none of this was what it appeared to be and that he was only doing what he knew was true. At the same time, he was careful to imply that his behavior *was not something for others to attempt to emulate*. In other words: "Do what I say, not what I do."

If at that time de Ruiter "graduated" from a post-Christian mystic to a Tantric master, he chose not to discuss it with his followers. Possibly he considered the knowledge potentially harmful, either to himself (to his reputation) or to his followers, or both. They were not ready to know the truth because—as he frequently told Joyce—they would not understand it. It's also possible de Ruiter was still struggling to understand the profound new developments taking place. Had he let the devil possess him and found that the devil was a powerful teacher too?

---

* It should be noted that the *terminology* which he and his followers employ *has* become increasingly sexual, see for example the following exchange from April 2011 (italics in the original transcript): Woman: "I'm trying to stay sensitive to the stream of you coming into me, and seeming to have a movement deeper and deeper. . . . There is a longing to really let you all the way through, in, and meet you . . ." De Ruiter: "*Open* to the *fine interference* of intimacy of being. . . . Open to Intimacy of Being—being free to provide *fine*, most delicate *sweet* interference to your function; *tiny* little touches. (*Long connection)* If Intimacy of Being is the *most beautiful fine ... soft* tipped brush ... let it be continually, within, touching something. (*Connection)* So that there is *just, just* a wisp ... of shyness and embarrassment, that is *always just* there." (*Long connection.)* Emphasis in the original.

According to Joyce, de Ruiter *was* something of a hedonist, a tendency which apparently only increased with his material success. Although those around de Ruiter saw that side of him all the time, they were given to understand that it didn't mean anything to him because he was "coming from a different level." He lived in a different, more detached way, and since he had a profound connection to truth, his pleasure seeking was superficial and irrelevant. Joyce and others "granted him that right to live the split, the dichotomy, this schizophrenic kind of life," believing that "the vulgar was just playful for him."

Joyce was shocked when she read Benita and Katrina's affidavits, because she heard them voice the same complaints she'd had: his lack of willingness to help around the house or be involved, the secret late night visits: "I thought, he just repeated it. The four-wheel driving, the movies, there's nothing particularly impressive about John's private life, it's self-indulgent and he likes adventure, he likes fun. I see nothing 'fine' about him, except the way he walks on stage and sits silently. That may be 'fine,' but to me that is such an image."[11]

One of de Ruiter's teachings with which I am quite familiar is "let the shallow be shallow" and let "the deep" take care of itself. To attempt to make the shallow deep is a mistake, according to John, because the shallow can never comprehend the deep and will only try to use it for its own (shallow) ends. That philosophy might explain why de Ruiter sees no contradiction between his privately hedonistic lifestyle and his public teachings, which have always been highly abstemious, even puritanical. (Self-interest and even personal preference are to be sacrificed to what we "know.") But does it explain why he feels the need to keep his shallower, hedonistic lifestyle separate from his public interactions, even to the point of secrecy? As Joyce said:

> He always says that he enjoys things shallowly, that they don't mean anything to him. So I don't think he would attribute great things to his hedonistic lifestyle. He would just say there's freedom to do that. One of his lines is that, because he has fully died, he can fully live. . . There are two different kinds of behavior. One is just his enjoying life: he loves to four-wheel drive, he loves movies, he loves to sleep in. That's just John being free, there's no meaning attached to that. The other is a blatant contradiction to what you would expect, and then there's tremendous meaning attached to it, and that is [that he is] *being asked to go against what he knows*. [My italics.]

De Ruiter's justification for his shallowly hedonistic behavior in the past was that it was shallow and didn't mean anything. His justification for his "deeply" hedonistic behavior (i.e., his sexual infidelities) was more interesting: *he was being asked to go against what he knew, in order to prove his love of truth.* The upshot of this elaborate philosophical premise is that, even when de Ruiter goes *against* what he knows to be true, he is still doing what he knows to be true. He has all the bases covered. When looked at closely, de Ruiter's more mundane forms of self-gratification appear to be a lighter, more superficial case of the same process occurring, i.e., of his going against what he knows as true—or what he has taught as truth—in order to access a higher or deeper level of knowledge. Might such a strange, even pathological, rationale have signified a shift in de Ruiter's psyche that has taken him further and further away from his early Christian asceticism and moralism, into a more "Dionysian" kind of embodiment?

The question that seems pertinent at this stage is, what exactly does "going deeper into what he knows" *mean* for de Ruiter, psychologically speaking? Is he really engaged in integrating a darker, more Dionysian aspect of his psyche (adultery, lies, etc.), and doing it publicly? Judging by the messiness of de Ruiter's private life, he has been either unable or unwilling to acknowledge (own up to) some of his deeper impulses, and so they have spilled out, not only into his home life, but into his temple. This is apparent in his strategy of "spiritualizing" his more dubious activities by using his teachings to give them the right spin. The flip side of this strategy—the price of it—would be that his teachings become more and more "peppered" with unconscious rationalizations. And while his public persona has become increasingly "refined" and "Christ-like," his hedonistic side has, presumably, been enjoying full, horny expression in his private (actually secret) life.

His followers sometimes argue that it is John's *private* life and he has a right to keep it that way. The logical answer is that it's not private, and never was, when it directly concerns his followers. If de Ruiter's strange spiritual journey of going against what he knows in order to do what he knows is out of control, as all the evidence indicates, then it is causing collateral damage and other people (especially his followers) are in the line of that fire. And if de Ruiter finds it more and more necessary to exclude this stuff from his public interactions and shield his flock from whatever dark new impulses he is embodying, in *whose* interests is that concealment, finally?

*

Hearing about a guru who secretly takes on his disciples as sexual partners no longer comes as a great surprise. These days it's seen as proof, if proof were needed, that the guru is "only human." This isn't the conclusion de Ruiter's followers reached, however. If anything, today de Ruiter is seen as even more superhuman than he was fifteen years ago. It's possible that de Ruiter's sexual proclivity is seen (by his long-time followers at least), not as a negative, but as proof that he has attained a "higher level" of being and requires a higher level of sexual gratification.

Most people tend to associate spirituality with saintly virtue, but there are plenty of stories—in both legend and fact—that indicate the reverse, that sensuality increases in proportion to spiritual attainment. Biology is destiny. Why *wouldn't* an enlightened being with his very own flock of adoring subjects—many of whom are attractive and willing females—be drawn to sexual dallying? Civilization is only skin deep, and the most primal and fundamental drive in the male of the species is the desire to spread his seed and inseminate as many wombs as he can get into. Judging by the many tales of polysexual deities, the biological imperative has its corresponding expression in the more numinous realms also. Krishna had one hundred and eight *gopis*, Mohammed had his harem, Charles Manson his "family," and Castaneda his witches. It is a tradition for shamans to have many wives, presumably because, if their energy is raised and refined to a higher level than ordinary men, their appetites increase accordingly. Biology has nothing to do with morality, and sorcery operates by laws another than social.

So far, I had heard two opposing points of view, de Ruiter's and Joyce's—the man and his (ex-)wife. Was there a reading of the facts that reconciled the two, or at least laid the groundwork for reconciliation? One thing became clear in the course of writing this section of the book: outside of his (seemingly exclusive) relationship with Truth, Joyce was a particular kind of reality to de Ruiter. She was flesh and blood, down to earth reality. She knew all his flaws, weaknesses and soft spots. She would *always* see through his stage persona, and she was never going to fully buy into his transpersonal "reality" as Truth-Messiah. Maybe that was another meaning of de Ruiter's comment that Joyce "knew too much" (to need to see a miracle), maybe it was *because* she couldn't believe in his supernatural powers that she didn't experience them? If Joyce saw her husband as an ordinary man, to some extent that would have been how he experienced himself around her. "My experience of John was [of] a completely normal guy with nothing different about his sexuality," Joyce told me. "He's not a Tantric master. I don't know what a Tantric master is, but I'm sure John wasn't one." Not for her, at least. (Unfortunately, Benita isn't talking.)

As long as he was with her, de Ruiter would have had no way to avoid the parts that constituted his raw humanness, which are generally the parts we try most desperately to avoid (or have seen). When Joyce refused to submit to his final test (as he must have known she would), he chose to follow the primal currents of his unconscious soul (libido) that had opened up, and shut her out as unworthy. He chose to go against what he knew in his heart in order to be true to what he knew—in another part of him. Unable (or unwilling) to explain any of this left him no choice but to fall back on tired but trusty post-Christian vernacular, and to give account of himself that way.

Perhaps the only feasible solution to alchemical stalemate with Joyce was the bizarre vision of polygamy which de Ruiter hatched, a vision in which he *extended his goodness*, not just to one but to many wombs—disengaging from a futile and self-defeating struggle to define his wife's reality as husband and master, and instead taking on godlike proportions. By splitting himself three ways among three wives, he got to be the father, son, *and* the holy ghost.

The truth made him do it.

Notes for Part Three

[1] http://www.atticuscutter.com/writings/biography-of-john-de-ruiter/
[2] http://www.thepathoftruth.com/false-teachers/andrew-murray.htm
[3] http://www.isaiah54.org/finney.htm
[4] "The Disturbing Legacy of Charles Finney," by Dr. Michael Horton http://www.mtio.com/articles/aissar81.htm
[5] "A Wolf in Sheep's Clothing," by Philip R. Johnson. http://www.romans45.org/articles/finney.htm
[6] http://www.thepathoftruth.com/false-teachers/andrew-murray.htm
[7] https://en.wikipedia.org/wiki/Sikh#cite_note-22
[8] Hutchinson, *Saturday Night Magazine*, May 5, 2001. https://skent.ualberta.ca/media/the-gospel-according-to-john/
[9] Scott McKeen, "I Was Gods' Wife," *National Post*, Canada, May 16, 2000. http://www.religionnewsblog.com/14340/i-was-gods-wife
[10] Ibid.
[11] In his article "The Gospel According to John," Brian Hutchinson quotes "Susan Scott" (not her real name) on de Ruiter's increasingly self-indulgent lifestyle: "People started to spoil him and buy him expensive clothes.... In the beginning, we'd take him out to dinner, and he was so humble that he didn't want to order. Then after a while, when he went out he would ask for cigars or cigarettes." Hutchinson, *Saturday Night Magazine*, May 5, 2001. https://skent.ualberta.ca/media/the-gospel-according-to-john/

All links last accessed Nov 4, 2017.

Part Four
The Shadow of Truth

"Images of purity corrupt."
—Joel Kramer & Diana Alstad, *The Guru Papers*

"Everything that exceeds a certain human size evokes equally inhuman powers in man's unconscious. Totalitarian demons are called forth."
—Carl Jung

"What we do is to bring words back from their metaphysical to their everyday use."
— Ludwig Wittgenstein, *Philosophical Investigations*

Injured Other

Besides Joyce and Jason Gerdes, I didn't have much luck finding co-operative witnesses. A few other ex-Oasians had been willing to talk to me, but only off the record or anonymously. I had failed to discover much at all about de Ruiter's early childhood, where the really formative experiences occurred. Joyce had hinted about something dark from that time which John had shared with her, but was unwilling to go into it. (This was shared on an Oasis bulletin board by "God" in 2017, and involved alleged early and unnatural sexual experiences in the de Ruiter household.) I was aware of the danger of using psychological theories to "explain" de Ruiter which would inevitably be tainted by my own bias. Outside of enlightenment, there is no such thing as an unbiased perspective. We see only what we are able (or willing) to see.

Undaunted by that fact, I have set about to explore psychological, at times metaphysical, models of interpretation in an attempt to get to the "root" of de Ruiter's strange behavior. The extent to which I came up with accurate models is impossible to say, since the only person who knows for sure isn't talking to me. John de Ruiter claims to be a living embodiment of truth. That's a fact. So what if we take him at his word and analyze his actions and words through the lens of that extravagant claim? Isn't this the fairest and most balanced way to approach the subject, as well as the most interesting?

At the risk of seeming frivolous, during the course of writing this account I discovered that "John de Ruiter" is an anagram for "Injured Other." This discovery seemed to relate to two closely related facts that have come repeatedly to my attention. The first is that de Ruiter attracts a fair number of psychologically wounded people as followers (I include my wife and myself in that category). No surprise there: a guru offering a panacea of "okayness" at a reasonable price is likely to attract more than his share of injured others; but it seems especially so in de Ruiter's case and, applying the principal of "like attracts like," the suggestion is that de Ruiter is wounded in similar ways.

The second fact concerns the number of people I've encountered who seem to have been *negatively impacted* by de Ruiter. Again and again as I approached people who knew him, I encountered the same reluctance, inertia, or outright refusal to talk about their experiences; the impression I received was that their experiences were too painful, embarrassing, or distasteful for them to want to revisit. That doesn't necessarily mean they were injured by de Ruiter. From my own experience, I know that association with de Ruiter can stir up painful aspects of the psyche and open up wounds from the past. There's every chance de Ruiter would be blamed for that even if he *were* innocent. That's the case for the defense and it's a solid one. The last thing I want to do is join an angry lynch mob persecuting an innocent.

Then there's the case for the prosecution. There are the claims of all those people (Joyce, the von Sasses, Don Rousu, Hal and Candy Dallmann, and many of his ex-followers), some of whom I've been able to speak to and some not, whose testimony is unequivocal. They are the injured others de Ruiter has drawn to him and, in many cases, cast off like unwanted muffler bearings. The best one could say about these is that he failed to heal them. As a researcher trying to get to the truth, I am left with the impression that, like a runaway 4 by 4, de Ruiter has left a trail of mangled bodies behind him, and that he appears to be either blissfully ignorant or coldly indifferent to this fact.

The psychologist Carl Jung had a maxim: "When an inner process cannot be integrated it is often projected outward." Ironically, de Ruiter himself has said roughly the same thing: "If you want to know where you're at, look around you."

De Ruiter successfully persuaded his followers that, for him to embody truth with his every word, thought, and action, included having secret sexual liaisons with his disciples. He persuaded them that his "knowing" told him to conceal such activities, and that he had done so without ever being caught in a flagrant lie. Actually de Ruiter *had* been caught in flagrant lies, but he had a catch-all answer, which was that he was speaking from a different level so it only *seemed* like lying. He didn't admit to adultery because in his mind it wasn't adultery. He was not a polygamist for the same "reason." He stated that his conscience was clean, regardless of his actions. For people who trust in de Ruiter, this is regarded as enlightened behavior; for most other people, it resembles something less benign.

To de Ruiter, at his "enlightened" level, everything is a matter of your point of view. Words have different meanings according to context. De Ruiter has perfected *the art of defining context*, not only for himself but for others. He determines what the context is ahead of time, and what the words he chooses to use *mean*. From what I can glean from his followers, no one else properly understands the context he's created, which means no one can question him when he claims "not to have meant it that way."

When the former US president Bill Clinton was caught in a lie, he received ridicule for debating the meaning of the word "is." De Ruiter's evasion is performed at a more sophisticated level. "You mean *that* kind of adultery? I meant the *other* kind. *That's* the kind I'm not guilty of." As long as de Ruiter considers himself to be an embodiment of truth, he is also the final arbiter of justice. He answers only to himself, and when he is caught in a sin, he doesn't blame it on the devil. He blames it on Truth.

Dismissing de Ruiter as a charlatan is too easy and doesn't fit the facts. What fits the facts is that he is genuine *up to a point*. For one thing, de Ruiter appears to be uncannily attuned to people's unconscious, and he certainly hits the nail on the head much of the time (as he did with me). This can't be entirely explained away as "suggestion." Perhaps de Ruiter is a kind of *savant*, a channel for truth rather than an embodiment of it? An embodiment would have to be equally true all the time, which appears to be what de Ruiter wants his followers to believe. The problem with this—and it's not a small problem—is that, when he gets caught in a lie, he *has* to turn it into a movement of truth. His self-designation suggests a desire to *identify* with truth and be done with any other kind of identification. In the process, he has fallen into the oldest trap there is.

The Bully of Light?

"The potentialities of the archetype, for good and evil alike, transcend our human capacities many times, and a man can appropriate its power only by identifying with the daemon, by letting himself be possessed by it, thus forfeiting his own humanity."
—Carl Jung, *Aspects of the Masculine*

Perhaps the most provocative stories I heard about de Ruiter related to his violent treatment of animals while a boy or early teenager. My only source for these accounts was Joyce, who heard about them from de Ruiter. Joyce has asked me not to include these accounts so I am honoring that wish, without neglecting to mention it at all, as I believe it may be essential to understanding de Ruiter. I knew from my wife and other sources that de Ruiter had publically referred to his "coarseness" as a child and a teenager, but there was little if anything that remained on record. His public bio makes no reference to it.[*]

---

[*] Joyce also told me that John was not only a bully but was bullied, at least on

In the absence of any overt mention of de Ruiter's childhood treatment of animals, I combed the bio for hints or clues, however vague. The bio describes de Ruiter's "inborn drive to find things out," and how it led to a capacity for making "go-carts, homing-cages for his beloved pigeons" and fixing up "lights in unusual places around the house." De Ruiter's carpentry and building skills "gained him the nick-name of John 'Golden-Hands,' affectionately recalled by his parents to this day." Yet apparently, those same golden hands did some rather strange things to small animals. Perhaps it was from his "in-born drive to find things out," or another, grislier manifestation of his "fascination with dismantling intricate devices, from clocks to car engines"? If so, no wonder the official bio chose to omit it.

Since neither he nor his family members have spoken to me, I can only speculate about the kind of early childhood de Ruiter endured. What kind of early experiences turned him into a bully and a "prankster," or caused him to mistreat animals? Joyce felt ambivalent about sharing these stories from de Ruiter's past with me, and in an attempt to balance things out, she recounted another, less grisly story. John's father would wake him in the middle of the night to go and find baby pigeons in an old abandoned house. "Maybe he stole them from nests," she said, "I'm not actually sure. He had a little shed in his backyard where he raised them and he would chew food and use his tongue to push it down their mouths to feed them." I didn't find this story nearly as "sweet" as Joyce did, but it definitely caught my attention.

---

one occasion: "[There is] a specific story he told me, in the McDonald's restaurant in Abbotsfield, which stood out in my mind, it must be because of the way he told me. A classmate had his cowboy boot on John's head, nailing it into the ground, belittling him, insulting him. This was apparently so powerful to John that he shared it with me. He was probably trying to tell me how he was bullied, and how small and humiliated he felt."

Apparently stealing baby birds from their nests in order to raise them was something de Ruiter *learned from his father*. And although it might seem (as Joyce suggested) to contradict accounts of cruelty to animals, the two behaviors could both relate to a single need. A boy's desire to take out his frustration on small animals goes hand in hand with caring for birds, because the desire to hurt and the desire to heal are both responses to a wound. By caring for his birds, de Ruiter could assume the role of loving parent and give to them whatever nurture he lacked as a child.

He is still doing the same today: feeding his Oasis pigeons, from his own mouth.

*

"So his playing on your gullibility and trying to fool you with this, that and the other thing—maybe that stems from the same place bullying comes from, but it got turned from black to white, so he no longer bullies in the darkness, [by] trying to hurt, he bullies now in the light, to play. So it's almost like he never changed, he just took his stream and purified it."
—Jason Gerdes, 2010

I have already uncovered evidence for de Ruiter being a bully in his childhood, as well as for the possibility that he continued such behavior into early adulthood in more refined (or disguised) ways, via pranks and weird haggling methods. But is there any evidence he is behaving in a bully-like manner in his present, "enlightened" state? At first glance it seems not: de Ruiter appears very far from an aggressive or violent type. On the other hand, a bully is someone who picks on anyone weaker, who uses his or her superior strength to dominate, terrorize, and control others. Bullying can take many guises, some obvious, some not. Using the ability to be emotionally distant and detached, for example—as de Ruiter appears to have done with Joyce and others—is a way to maintain a superior position. In extreme cases, it could come under a wider definition of bullying.

One ex-follower described to me in detail how he felt psychologically bullied by de Ruiter; his testimony had to be stricken from the record, however, in a rare case of a witness discrediting himself.* I corresponded with another man who spent eight years in Edmonton as a follower and had a similar experience to recount. The image he used to represent his time with de Ruiter was of being "naked and tied up in a dungeon . . . slowly dying. But heaven forbid I was allowed to complain or even consider that something was wrong!" He recounted how de Ruiter treated "sincere questions from dear devoted hearts" about the possibility of leaving Edmonton and moving on by telling them that "to do such a thing would be a most heinous crime," comparable to "breaking the bones of their souls." This person's experience was the opposite: leaving, he said, was like "releasing the bones of my soul from those chains and that dungeon." De Ruiter had implied that to walk away from him and his teachings was something "that would haunt a person to

---

* While I was preparing the book for publication in 2011, this person went to great lengths to persuade me that he had deliberately exaggerated his accounts in order to "help" me with my own process (without ever explaining how distorting the facts was supposed to help). He had recently spent time in Edmonton, attending the meetings, and discipled himself to de Ruiter once again. As a result, he evidently felt some guilt and reframed his version of events accordingly. Very little of what he wrote made sense to me, but the gist of it was that he believed he had been "projecting" his fears onto de Ruiter when he first corresponded with me, and that as a result, anything he'd said was inaccurate. He has since left de Ruiter and mostly returned to his previous position. This kind of vacillation is common among people who try to leave de Ruiter, or to leave cults in general.

their grave. [A]nyone who has witnessed his 'ways' with people would agree that he wielded great power over those under his spell. In my experience this can become literally terrifying when one starts to ask the question of oneself 'should I stay or should I leave?'" Another long-term community member confirmed his account, recalling how de Ruiter told someone that to leave the Truth once you had found it, or to turn away from it, "would be like breaking every bone in your body."

Does this sound like a loving enclave for truth-seekers? Is this the kind of protection racket which de Ruiter learned from the Native American Len? If de Ruiter's first experience of absolute surrender to a male authority figure (after his father, at least) was of being dominated and controlled by a bully—*and if it had worked for him*—has he unconsciously imitated that model ever since?

The word "bully" has specific associations that certainly make de Ruiter seem like an unlikely candidate. But I hadn't thought of my brother that way either, until my wife showed me a psychological description of the bully-type that fit him to a "T." The article describes bullying as "the single most important social issue of today,"* one that tends to be "an accumulation of many small incidents over a long period of time." Each incident might seem trivial on its own, when taken out of context, but together the "constant nit-picking, fault-finding and criticism" has an accumulative effect. Often there is "a grain of truth (but only a grain) in the criticism to fool you into believing the criticism has validity, which it does not; often, the criticism is based on distortion, misrepresentation or fabrication." Simultaneous with the criticism, the article describes "a constant refusal to acknowledge you and your contributions and achievements or to recognize your existence and value."

---

* See Appendix Two.

(Compare this to de Ruiter's repeated admonishment to his followers that they are "wonderfully worth nothing.") Also, "constant attempts to undermine you and your position, status, worth, value and potential; being isolated and separated from colleagues" (something de Ruiter allegedly did to Benita and Katrina), being excluded from what was going on (as he did with Joyce), being "marginalized, overruled, ignored, sidelined, frozen out, belittled, demeaned and patronized, especially in front of others."

Another bullying tactic is "having your responsibility increased but your authority taken away; having unrealistic goals set, which change as you approach them; finding that everything you say and do is twisted, distorted and misrepresented." The piece lists the "tells" that identify a bully, a large number of which match de Ruiter's public and private persona fairly well (based on the testimonies I have heard). The article cites four types of bully, including "The Socialized Psychopath or Sociopath" and "The Guru."

Rewriting Reality: Using Language for Spiritual Indoctrination

"Concerning what you know, within, is occurring here: instead of thinking what you're thinking, *be* what you know I'm doing. ['*Long connection.*'] That will manifest in your thinking and it doesn't come from your thinking."
—John de Ruiter, 2010

While I was researching de Ruiter online, I came upon an article called "Why We Believe," by Bob McCue. The piece begins by quoting Jeremy Loome:

"The meeting has gone on for just a few minutes when a perceptible shift occurs: the audience is no longer fidgeting. In five minutes on stage, John de Ruiter has said nothing. Initially, some in the audience seemed uncomfortable or merely bored. But now, they seem enraptured." This only works where the majority of the participates [sic] are believers and use their influence on the minority to pull them in.... We all tend to mirror the behaviour around us. A newcomer to the Mormon temple is hence impressed by the unusual reverence all there display and acts the same way. This is an otherworldly experience, and purposefully so. Silence, stillness and reverence are unusual states for most human beings. And for most of us, this sense of calm, control and power is attractive. Persisted in for long enough, this will break down the sense of self—our consciousness—in the attractive way described above. We like being in the presence of power that is aligned with our interests. This makes us feel powerful by extension, and hence safe. Power in the human context is largely conferred by agreement. In de Ruiter's case, the group in audience with him agrees that he is worthy of their silence and reverence. *For him to maintain a long silence is to emphasize his power.* [My italics.]

The most striking thing about de Ruiter isn't his truthfulness (on the contrary), or even the scope of his knowledge or depth of his wisdom. It is his charismatic stillness, his *power*. I am fairly sure even his most devoted followers wouldn't deny that de Ruiter inspires awe in them. My wife has said that being in de Ruiter's presence was so intense that she couldn't think straight. I'd had the same or similar experiences. I hadn't ever questioned it; somehow I'd seen his raw power as proof of his goodness, or as *a virtue unto itself.* The question that occurs to me now is not *how* he inspires such awe, but *why*? Is it that he simply can't help it? We all want to be powerful, and when we see extreme power in another, *we respond with reverence*, adoration, even love. But do such feelings really serve those around de Ruiter, or do they only serve de Ruiter?

From all I've seen, many of his followers perceive no intrinsic difference between the man and his message, because both equal "Truth" with a capital "T." The man *is* the message, and as a result of that belief, many of his followers don't really care what de Ruiter does in his private life. His presence and his power are so dazzling that they are blinded by them. What does de Ruiter do to correct this situation? From what I have seen, not much. By keeping his private life and the darker aspects of his personality hidden, he has created a rich and fertile ground for multiple delusions and fantasies to grow in.

There is a point during de Ruiter's interview for the *New Dimensions Café* podcast (December 15th 2010[*]) when he is talking about the power of silence, and he says: "when you know something, a voice isn't required. A voice is required when persuasion starts to take place." It's a curious statement to make for a public speaker. Is de Ruiter saying no one ever opens their mouth except to persuade, or is he tacitly admitting that he only ever uses *his* voice that way? The word *persuade* is defined as "to induce, urge, or prevail upon successfully," or "to cause to believe." It is described as "a form of social influence. . . the process of guiding oneself or another toward the adoption of an idea, attitude, or action by rational and symbolic (though not always logical) means."

---

[*] "The Direct Route to Awakening,"
http://www.newdimensions.org/flagship/3385/john-de-ruiter-the-direct-route-to-awakening/

Whatever else he is, John de Ruiter is certainly persuasive. He also seems intent on extending his "social influence" by guiding others—not always by logical means—to "adopt ideas, attitudes, and actions" which he believes (or claims to believe) are true. The principle action which he guides people towards is *moving to Edmonton and joining his community*. The ideas and attitudes which he encourages in others are ones he has defined, through a unique and idiosyncratic use of language (though whether he lives by them remains unknown). In the business of *persuasion*, de Ruiter invents new words and applies old words in new ways: words such as "knowing," "okayness," "innermost," "person," "dearness," "pull of being," "clean," "straight," "coarse," "fine," "entering," "the more of you," "what you first are," together make up an idiosyncratic syntax, a dialect of the enlightened. It is "truth talk," and for his followers, adopting those terms helps them gain intellectual access to an otherwise mysterious space, "John-space." The effect of truth-talking is to feel closer to realizing and embodying the power and the knowledge which de Ruiter appears to possess—and which he offers, at a reasonable price, through a combination of profound psychic "connecting" and *verbal persuasion*.

People around de Ruiter enter into deep trance-like states in which they receive carefully worded communications from de Ruiter. Those communications take the form of instructions or advice; but within the context of hypnotic trance, might they also be viewed as commands?

De Ruiter presents seemingly novel concepts encoded either in entirely new verbal constructs ("pull of being") or unfamiliar uses of known terms. Because they are unfamiliar, these phrases are received by a person's consciousness in a different way than ordinary language. They don't carry the usual associations from life, but *brand-new* associations that relate exclusively to de Ruiter and the group consciousness. De

Ruiter's anomalous phrases are like zip files that are designed to be "unpacked" once they enter a person's unconscious. They are Trojan horses that bring with them an entire context, the context being, as far as I can tell based on my own experience and observations, "John-de-Ruiter-is-the-living-embodiment-of-truth."

As in the hypnotic method, de Ruiter's carefully-constructed phrases enter into the awareness and take hold there, nexuses around which an entire framework of belief and perception can slowly begin to form. The more those phrases are heard—and above all, the more they are used, in an attempt to adopt the system of "direct knowledge" which is believed to be their source—the more the percipient's consciousness and *way of being* adapts and mutates to accommodate and "match" the new language constructs. It is *recalibration*. As William Burroughs said, language is a virus. Insofar as they enter a system and are accepted by that system, words act as *reprogramming agents*. If they are allowed to complete their work, they eventually turn the entire system into an extension and imitation of themselves. In a word: *a host*. This echoes one of Oasians' favorite Johnisms: "You are not worth fixing. But you are worth being replaced."

One example I have seen for myself is how de Ruiter's use of language obliges the listener to practice a kind of "doublethink," such as in the phrase "be a nobody." One can't actually "be" a nobody—it is a cognitive impossibility, one that it's necessary to perform certain mental contortions in order to allow to take seed in the mind. Without those contortions, rational thought will reject it as non-sense. A great deal of what de Ruiter says *sounds* like nonsense but his followers find ways to make it meaningful to them. I did the same. I even reframed many of his teachings to make them palatable to others, people who weren't as open to de Ruiter as I was. For me, that practice of "doublethink" formed the foundation for a new "way of being," a way that was modeled after de Ruiter himself, and based on his system of knowledge (or my interpretation of it). Judging by my experiences and observations, it entails *rewiring one's consciousness* in order to make sense of—never mind practicing—the things de Ruiter says—his "hypnotic commands." His followers—speaking from experience again, my wife's included—willingly submit to that recalibration, based less on a full understanding of the commands received than *a complete, suprarational trust in de Ruiter himself.* Although that trust is often experienced as a deep "knowing," it may be more accurate to call it a suspension of rational thought, and possibly a kind of dissociation.

Is de Ruiter's secret manual called "Rewriting Reality"? He presents his own reality paradigm as Ultimate Reality, as a living truth which he then invites all comers to "enter." But what becomes of those who accept the invitation? (At least one of them wound up dying alone in a forest.) If de Ruiter, as his followers believe, is one with truth, then the program he is installing in their minds and bodies is a program of truth, and there is no cause for alarm. But if de Ruiter isn't one with truth...

When Confucius was asked how he would rule the world, he said, "First change the language." L. Ron Hubbard and Dianetics worked hard at redefining the English language to make sure its followers understood less about reality than when they came in, while believing they had a handle on *a new and greater truth.* If Scientology is anything to go by, embedding people with a new language matrix is the key to cult management. Most of us are used to allowing our thoughts to tell us who we are. If you want to redefine a person's reality, start with their use of language and thereby hack into their thought processes. Every time a John-ite uses a John-ism, they are affirming their allegiance and adherence to the "royal" decree. They are paying psychic tithes to the King.

Creating Dependency (A College without Graduates)

"I don't think John's stories necessarily all add up. I think he just makes it up as he goes along. . . . It's very codependent, these people need him and he needs them. And they need him desperately to be the savior they need him to be."
—Joyce, 2010

De Ruiter calls his organization a college. So where are the graduates?

At my first meeting with de Ruiter, he hit the nail on the head by speaking about my inner child, a concept I'd been exploring over the previous few weeks with my wife-to-be. When I told him I felt as though my continuous physical illness and pain was a kind of punishment, de Ruiter told me, "You are pledged to nonsense." He added that I was addicted to a false way of being (I forget the exact words but I know he used the word "addicted"). In response, I held the microphone to my lips and spoke four words more appropriate to an AA meeting than a *satsang*: "*I am an addict.*"

Later, I discovered that de Ruiter frequently uses the term addiction. At first I thought nothing of it. I come from a family of alcoholics. One of the principals of Alcoholics Anonymous is "once an addict, always an addict." Alcoholics are encouraged to continue attending meetings for years after they stop drinking, regardless of how much they believe they have conquered their addiction. By going along with de Ruiter's "diagnosis" and identifying myself as an addict, had I unconsciously signed up for a lifetime's attendance? If it hadn't been for the intervention of Charlie and the affidavit from God, I could be attending meetings still. I might even have moved to Edmonton, a step which makes it a *lot* harder to admit that one has been conned. For two whole years, I believed de Ruiter was my way "home." I was convinced that all I needed to do was nurture my connection to him, and he would bring me in.

In April 2011, a woman said this to de Ruiter while sitting in the Chair: "Years ago when I knew I couldn't be here, I was afraid of getting left behind, and I said to you 'Please don't forget me.' I want to ask you that again. I don't feel that I'll get left behind but if it's possible that you could connect with me when I'm there." De Ruiter didn't contradict the woman's "story."

If a follower sees his or her guru as their "ticket" out of the hell of themselves, they become as dependent, psychologically speaking, on the guru as any human being can be on *anything*. De Ruiter has called an addiction to truth "a true addiction." For those who equate de Ruiter with truth and are addicted to attending the meetings, who fear they will be forever *lost* without him, there is no reason to ever question that dependency. It is a *true* addiction.

That same seminar, de Ruiter said: "*Live* being on the drip, like what you see at the side of many hospital beds. . . . It takes only a drip. Live on the drip. Even in the most sobering things, there you are on the drip."

*

While many people are left cold by de Ruiter, others come away with an unforgettable first impression. As an example of the latter, here's an account of a first meeting with de Ruiter, from Catherine Auman, a Los Angeles psychotherapist who specializes in "Spiritual Psychology and Transpersonal Counseling":

> a blindingness
> light swirling and collapsing and I can't see
> "what's the matter with the light?"
> I almost cry out
> maybe something's wrong with my contacts,
> I think, but there's also a warmth
> and something funny happening with my breath
> like sex, but that's not right
> because sex is not happening.
> The Majesty, and I can't breathe
> and suddenly I see that haloes are not
> artistic convention but literal fact,
> although I am not a person who digs auras
> or anything like that. But the Magnificence,
> I hear myself gasping
> and all around him golden light
> The Golden Light, bigger than anything ever,
> Absolute Wonder so big-ness of it
> I would fall to my knees but I can't move.
> All there in the emanation of one ordinary
> Being, and after the longest time he says to me,
> "Now you're really seeing."[*]

For many people, de Ruiter's presence inspires awe, wonder, and a desire to fall to their knees. Such feelings create a sense of absolute certainty about what de Ruiter *is*. His words, on the other hand, being frequently so difficult to make sense of, create a state of doubt, even confusion. De Ruiter encourages people not to trust their thoughts and feelings, or even their

---

[*] This website is no longer online.

intuition, but only their *knowing*. The question inevitably arises then: "What *do* I know?"

During my trip to Edmonton for the October 2010 seminar, I had a conversation with my wife and her cousin while we were driving to a meeting, about the meaning of the word "knowing." I said that a *knowing* for me was simply something I knew for sure, such as the fact that I was going to die. My wife's cousin argued that it was something more like an inner sense of truth, and not based primarily on reason (or so I understood him at the time). My wife suggested an example of what a *knowing* was: *"John's goodness."*

I said nothing and didn't think anything particular of it at the time. Later, I realized how significant her comment was. My wife had adopted the term "knowing" from de Ruiter; when she volunteered to give an example of what a *knowing* was, the first thing she came up with was "the goodness of John." Is this the Oasis program in microcosm? In Bob McCue's piece "Why We Believe," medical experts who have helped people recover from cults describe a similar experience to dissociation, "in which the mind *withdraws from reality based on cues and no longer connects properly to such tasks as consciousness, memory, identity and perception*" (my italics). Such a state of dissociation—withdrawal from reality—closely mirrors de Ruiter's advice to his followers not to trust their thoughts and feelings or intuitional faculties, *or even their experience*, but only "what they know." Apparently he prescribes a form of dissociation as a necessary means to disengage from the "surface bodies," and to "drop" all the way into "the tiny bit you know is true." For some people, that might be an effective way to access a higher, deeper part of themselves. But for others, they may be just as likely to wind up confused and lost in an unfamiliar state; eager to make sense of their new perceptions, they would then be *highly open to suggestion.*

John de Ruiter causes profound psychic dissonance in people, by means unknown ("something funny happening with my breath, like sex, but that's not right"). Then, while they are in this state of "newness" and disorientation, he imprints them with the idea of his power and benevolence. ("Now you're really seeing.") This would not even have to be a conscious strategy on his part: since he is causing the profound "opening" to occur, naturally he is the first thing people latch onto as they attempt to find some "ground" within that disorientation. In fact, this kind of psychic imprinting (primal dependency) is something he would have to be careful to *prevent* from happening—unless he decided there were benefits in allowing it. *Cui bono* from all this shock and awe?*

Timothy Gallagher had a similar take on de Ruiter's methods of "programming":

> He rules through implication. He doesn't say things

---

* The nature of psychological imprinting was discovered by an Austrian scientist called Konrad Lorenz. Curious to discover why ducklings followed their mother around, Lorenz hatched some goose eggs in an incubator and performed experiments. He soon discovered that newly hatched goslings would run after the first moving object they saw, whether it was their mother, a human being, a dog, or a rolling ball. Just about anything the goslings saw moving away from them during those first few critical hours would suffice. After following whatever "captured" them for that brief time, they refused to follow anything else. Lorenz called the behavior "imprinting," because of how the goslings' first impression created a permanent imprint in their consciousness (a "way of being"). When a freshly hatched gosling followed its mother, it learned to recognize her and associate with others of its kind. But if it followed a football and accepted that as its mother, it might want to associate with footballs for the rest of its life. It would gain from footballs *a sense of self and of belonging*. Lorenz discovered this in a rather intimate fashion, when his goslings were imprinted by the scientist himself (or rather by his wading boots); hence he was often depicted as being followed by a gaggle of geese.

in black and white but he speaks directly and programs directly the subconscious of people that he talks to. Now that requires a really quite high skill level. And John has quite a high skill level in programming the unconscious. So through implication alone you get to believe that he is like Christ, or God. Through implication you see yourself as in some way flawed, or with much to learn. And John keeps feeding little bits so that you keep having to come back for more. . . . And so through implication, people feel that if they leave they'll be deserting God or they'll be choosing the dark side. Through implication, everyone is too busy tearing themselves into bits to actually look at John and say "What about you man?" And they're too busy shredding each other. There's this rather unpleasant network of support for "being in truth" together, but it's actually quite a strange set-up because they're self-policing in a way, so John doesn't get looked at because he wrote the program. He's the programmer.

From everything I have seen at Oasis, from my own experience and that of my wife, based on all the testimonies I have heard of people who have spent time with de Ruiter (many of them "positive"), I haven't heard a single case of someone who became awakened by de Ruiter and continued living their lives *independently of his presence*. Most people who have left the community did so out of a feeling of disillusionment, not because they had received the guidance they needed and were ready to leave the nest and strike out on their own.* In fact,

---

* My wife is a noted exception, because she remained loyal to de Ruiter even years after leaving. If she left Oasis, it was, she said, because she no longer felt the need for proximity. My impression was that she had embodied

people who leave the community are generally regarded as apostates.

If de Ruiter is seen by his followers as being beyond human, the idea of aspiring to his level of attainment becomes unrealistic. What does that leave except the option of worship? Any attempt to live by the teachings, to be effective, would have to be based on an *understanding* of those teachings, yet this is something very few of his followers seem to have. One woman who spent years in the group told me:

> I have found trying to live those teachings has . . . I put myself into a pretzel and then wasn't happy. I just couldn't quite do it. It is a bit of a trick to teach something that's unlivable, because then you can keep people forever. One thing I've also observed is that, in the beginning John was quite simple and easy to follow and lighthearted and fun, and over the years it's become more and more and more complicated, and that's something I have also observed with many teachers: that they start out quite easy, and in order to keep the students it has to become more and more complicated. I have observed that, it just gets more and more intricate.

Such confusion can only be compounded by the fact that few, if any, of his followers know the degree to which *de Ruiter himself* lives his teachings. What exactly does being a living embodiment of truth *look* like, on a day-to-day basis? If the women who've seen de Ruiter at his most private and personal are to be believed, not that good. De Ruiter's desire to keep that

---

his "way" and so she was "free to go." Perhaps she was an example of a true "graduate"? Ironically enough, the first time she returned to a meeting, it was because I brought her back.

side of his life hidden, complete with (alleged) security cameras and Rottweilers, may have to do with more than simple privacy. If word gets out that not even *John* is able to practice what he preaches, all his teachings are invalidated in a heartbeat.

*

"Outside of the Meetings I was becoming a train wreck on a personal front. My marriage felt psychotic, my emotional body was wound about as tight as a person can get and I was *zero* fun to be with and had *zero* love to give.... My world was fast turning into an inferno of self-hatred."

—ex-Oasis member

There is a lot that seems naïve about de Ruiter. Before he became a living embodiment of truth he was (apparently) a simple, blue collar guy with a fairly standard Christian background. Intellectually challenged at school (according to the bio), by most accounts he was never an especially sophisticated thinker. An ex-follower summed up his case in colorful and incisive terms:

> The thing about John is that like everyone he is a product of his inherited conditioning, his culture, his life experience and the influences (such as Benita) that he cultivated around him. So step back and you can see much: very strong and narrow Christian roots, perhaps add in the dour Calvinism of the Dutch heritage, spent time with some weirdo Christian extremists, not much education, chip on shoulder because back then he was a bit goofy socially and appearance-wise.... So his teaching is still laced with all that guilt and sin and Christian ideas of good and bad, right and wrong, much shaming.

Did de Ruiter's naïveté set him up for a fall? He speaks a lot about believing only what you know, yet judging by his followers he has allowed them to believe things based on less than real knowings. The belief that he is a living embodiment of truth, for example, or in his "goodness," is something surely no one besides de Ruiter can have a "knowing" about.

In the last fifteen years or so, beginning with his substitution of the word "God" with the word "Truth," de Ruiter carefully removed all traces of Christian influences from his teachings, while at the same time concealing certain parts of his personal history—such as his apprenticeship to Jesus and his claims to being the fulfillment of Isaiah's prophecy (and what really happened in Bethlehem). He went to great lengths to remove all video and audio traces of those early years, and even discontinued the first fifty or so tapes from his College of Integrated Philosophy product line.* For de Ruiter to alter his philosophical position on certain subjects is understandable. But why erase traces of his prior beliefs? Rewriting one's history—and covering up specific areas of it—is what politicians and celebrities do. What makes it even more puzzling is the evidence that de Ruiter has not actually strayed very far from his Christian roots, but only taken care to conceal them via his *use of language*. According to Benita's testimony, at home de Ruiter claimed to be the Christ, doing the will of God and battling Satan. If de Ruiter still holds such beliefs, why doesn't he admit

---

* The tape "What is Evil?" in which he talked of satanic forces mining the earth and infiltrating human consciousness, was asked to be returned by anyone who owned a copy. Copies were presumably destroyed. So far as I know, no explanation was given. However, in 2016, Oasis made this audio available again.

it? Apparently he has given his belief system a facelift to widen his appeal and conceal his more Messianic aspirations.*

If de Ruiter's desire to distance himself from his Christian roots led him to develop an elaborate language to describe the "way" which he embodies, this might account for how, over the years, his language has become increasingly complex, abstract, and obscure, with ever deepening layers (apparently) required to understand it. Yet very little of his teaching is *practical* in any ordinary sense. Some of de Ruiter's followers have spent decades attending meetings, yet, judging by their dialogues with him, they are still unclear as to what he is talking about. (Or what *they* are talking about, since they have learned to parrot his terms.) People sit in the Chair and humbly ask de Ruiter how they are progressing, or even *if* they are progressing.† Over the years, de Ruiter has drummed into his followers the idea that they can't trust their thoughts, feelings, bodily sensations, or even intuition, and to refer only to what they know. But since they can't use any of their "surface bodies" to experience a "knowing," they may be left with only one solid point of reference. Like children looking to a parent, they ask John how they are doing. And like children, they learn to imitate his behavior and copy the words they hear him using without necessarily understanding them. Maybe they're hoping that, by saying the words enough, they can at least look and feel like they are "getting it"? (That was what I did.)

De Ruiter creates his own system of communication and of understanding truth, and only he knows the exact meanings of

---

* See Appendix Four for a more in-depth comparison of de Ruiter' teachings with Christianity.

† A woman in the Chair, in April 2011: "Can you see when you look at me whether or not I'm really integrating *this* or whether it's just a concept for me? I think I am integrating it, but I don't know if I'm integrating it or not. That actually sounds like nonsense when I'm saying it."

the terms he's created. He is the master of this truth, placing everyone else in the position of trying to figure out what exactly he is talking about, and having to refer to de Ruiter for confirmation or denial.

Christianity offers a model of perfection, righteousness, and truth in the person of Jesus, then emphasizes our own insurmountable inferiority. It offers a life-long contract (at a bargain rate) by which we can keep to the straight and narrow via daily submission to the Church. A direct connection to Christ (outside of the Church) is not on offer; in fact it is considered *heresy*. In the same manner, de Ruiter becomes his followers' primary connection to Truth. It's a connection they feel lost without, maybe even more lost than before they found him.

A Golden Bubble: Spiritual Bypassing & "Okayness" as the Seeker's Opiate

"When someone is able to perform the art of touching on the archetypal, he can play on the souls of people like on the strings of a piano."
—Carl Jung

De Ruiter's meetings are akin to theatrical performances, complete with audience participation. They appear to have been designed to reinforce the idea of de Ruiter's authority and the crowd's acknowledgment of it. Such enactments appeal to a fundamental psychological desire shared by everyone, the desire to love unconditionally, without limits, checks or bounds: the desire to *worship*. So what does de Ruiter *do* with all that loving attention? The more I have fathomed the apparent corruption, delusion, and dishonesty that lurks inside every corner of de

Ruiter's life and ministry, the more I have wondered why it wasn't completely obvious to everyone. How had I managed to overlook the evidence for so long? The answer is that I saw the same evidence as I was seeing now in a different context—the context of "John-as-Truth."

If de Ruiter doesn't practice what he preaches, the obvious reason would be that what he preaches is impractical. This doesn't make the teachings worthless, or even false, just impractical. But the obvious danger is that people will twist themselves into all sorts of contortions in an attempt to *make* them work, and that all they will get for it is back pains. If our self-judgment and non-acceptance is severe enough, the levels of denial required could send people into realms of psychosis or dissociation. (There has been at least one suicide reported among de Ruiter's followers before Anina's mysterious death in 2014.[*])

De Ruiter preaches living without a personal agenda, but his actions tell a different story. De Ruiter has claimed to have removed the element of self-interest from his actions, and naturally that's what his followers aspire to. That becomes the model for "Truth." But when personal desires are denied (rather than surrendered), they simply go underground, into the

---

[*] Bryan Beard, one of John's followers, who threw himself from a bridge in 2000. "In the year 1999, when I met John de Ruiter, another follower called Brian, [sic] who moved to Edmonton from Vancouver, a blond long hair and good looking guy, who was in distress and depression, committed suicide.... He moved to Edmonton in hope of finding help from John. I remember when Brian [sic] once told me, in the old meeting building, that he was loving John but he was not receiving the support or balance he was hoping for. After he lived a few months in Edmonton, I received the news he committed suicide. I heard he threw himself from a Bridge [sic] into freezing waters."
http://raymondparkerphoto.com/a-eulogy-for-bryan-beard/ Another of de Ruiter's followers, Tyler, also committed suicide some time later.

unconscious. What that leaves is an *unconscious* agenda of self-interest.

In one of our conversations, Joyce told me about something she heard John say many times, "that this whole Oasis thing meant nothing to him. If anyone wanted to come into the meeting and tear it apart, it was fine with him. He loved to make that claim, and that would be the kind of claim that would impress me.... Well, in fact, that's not true at all." In the 2010 interview with Neils Brummelman, de Ruiter was asked why he bothered to counter sociologist Stephen Kent's charges that Oasis was the start of a new religion. De Ruiter replied:

> Some things are helpful to respond to because to not respond to something may create difficulty for others. Those who I have a relationship with on various different levels, I have a responsibility to take care of that relationship, and to be taking care of something that is in my care because I am in a relationship with them... [It] is all factored in as to what is it that I am taking care of...

Over the years, de Ruiter has taken care to conceal aspects of his life from public view, including possibly dubious areas of his business dealings or anything that might undermine his image as a "living embodiment of truth." That concealment has included discouraging members of the community from reading the affidavit or hearing Benita's version of events. To the outsider, such an agenda appears damning; there seems to be no possible explanation besides that de Ruiter is protecting his image by maintaining a deception. This leads to the conclusion that he is a charlatan who doesn't care about anything besides his own self-interest. I am convinced this is not an accurate reading. I think de Ruiter cares about his flock; I think it's even possible he cares *too much*.

To some extent, this book is an attempt to redress the de-Ruiter-encouraged Oasis bias by looking at those aspects of the truth which de Ruiter has decided are "distracting," irrelevant, and even detrimental to the completion of his mission. I think de Ruiter has been keeping his flock in the dark because he believes it is in *their* best interests, as well as his, to ignore the more unsavory aspects of his "work." I don't agree with his judgment; I know beyond doubt that for me, exploring all aspects of the picture has been essential for my own "graduation" from his college.

If de Ruiter's "burden from God [is] to act against his own message . . . so as to prepare him inwardly for his upcoming battle with Satan," then pretty much any amount of apparent "untruth" is covered by such a "clause." De Ruiter then has to consider the effects of *being seen* to act against his own teachings, on those under his guidance and care. It is easy to imagine the cognitive dissonance such apparent "hypocrisy" would cause among his followers. It might even lead to *a mass apostasy* in the community—a rejection of the teachings and a lost flock, wandering through the wilderness without their shepherd. It's also easy to see how disastrous that would be for de Ruiter personally. So then how is he to separate, in his own mind, his responsibility to the people under his care from *his own self-interest*? By not thinking about it at all, perhaps, and letting "Truth" take over the reins?

De Ruiter could hardly fail to be aware that, the more he tries to conceal or "spin" his marital difficulties and the rest, the worse it is going to look when it finally does come out. Maybe he is *counting* on a rebellion? Every parent knows a day must come when his children reject his authority and leave the nest, and part of establishing the circumstances for that coming of age ritual is *to appear to be preventing it.*

*

"Seeing more deeply contains no guarantee against one's mind becoming concomitantly more clever at fooling oneself."
—Joel Kramer & Diana Alstad, *The Guru Papers*

The concept of *guru* doesn't have any real precedent in western tradition. Although the meaning is similar to that of teacher, it actually derives from an adjective in Sanskrit meaning "heavy." So literally, the guru is "the heavy" (the "villain" in modern movie parlance). Since the traditional guru-disciple relationship entails one of complete dominance and subjugation, the closest equivalent in English would perhaps be King, Emperor, or Caesar. The term Hitler chose to be addressed as, for example, was *führer*, which has a similar meaning to guru. Outside of the political and military arena, the eastern method of surrendering to gurus—seen as enlightened beings and "god embodiments"—has no real equivalent in the western tradition because the only god-embodiment which Christianity allows for is Christ. (The closest would be a prophet, which is more of an Old Testament tradition.) Westerners aren't hardwired to surrender to a man, or to believe that any man besides Jesus can embody God. Being a prophet isn't enough to demand total subjugation either, which is probably why Charles Manson, David Koresh, and John de Ruiter all claimed, in their respective ways, to be the Messiah. A western guru who wants to inspire his (westernized) disciples to surrender unequivocally can do so best by persuading them he is an embodiment of Christ.

Everyone who comes to sit with a guru is driven, in one way or another, by a desire to transcend their family patterns—to be free of personality flaws, foibles, obsessions, and whatever else is causing them to suffer. The goal is to surrender to and merge with an enlightened being who has supposedly overcome his or her patterns and attained a "clear" (to borrow a term from Scientology) state of being. Whether this is possible is beyond the scope of this account. What I hope to understand is what kind of effects such a "spiritual" relationship between guru and disciple has, for both parties, if the enlightened being in question is not entirely free of his or her own patterns. What if the guru is driven by the same basic desires, albeit at a "higher" (i.e., deeper) level?

Joyce told me she suspected a part of her spirit would always be with John, like a prisoner. Jason Gerdes shared with me an interesting recollection along similar lines. He had attended a meeting at Oasis around 2001, during which a woman got in the Chair and began to plead with de Ruiter to "let her go." Gerdes claimed he could see a struggle in de Ruiter because he didn't want to admit he had power over the woman. He was telling her she was there "of her own volition," while the woman was implicitly saying (in Gerdes' words): "That might be your cover story, but deep down, somehow you're keeping me here and I know it. And I want that to stop and I want to be let go." Gerdes described a veiled conversation occurring on two levels; at the deeper level, he "saw this poor person just begging [to be set free]."

In 2011, I came across a discussion about de Ruiter on the internet from 2005-6. Among the comments was the following, posted anonymously in January of 2006:

> In some cultures, when one gazes into the eyes for long periods of time, especially if not intimately involved with that person, it's considered to be robbing the soul. Johnites Love for John to "merge" with them. This is where he basically invades one's

> energy field with his energy field. He *is* very effective, and in fact, very powerful at this. However, I observe that this is when people become Hooked! There becomes some kind of energetic connection that [the] follower may be unaware of, or sees no harm in it. But if they are connected in this way, then are they continuing to follow John out of free will, at this point? I heard someone once suggest that he'd put her under his spell. I'm afraid that this was literally true! It seems his strategy is to travel to other countries, connect with people psychically and get them Hooked, so they will leave family, home and everything else, and move to Edmonton, where they can be a stable source of income and energy for John. It's as if he harvests souls!

While this might seem a somewhat melodramatic point of view, psychologically at least there's truth to it. When a guru becomes an idealized father (and mother) figure for his followers, there is a danger he will become as psychologically, emotionally, and energetically *invested* in his followers as they are in him. Since any relationship is always mutual to a degree, the best way to gauge how dependent a guru is on his followers is by gauging the extent to which *they are dependent on him.* If there is shared dependency, the guru, like a parent who refuses to let his children grow up, would be invested in *not* leading his followers to freedom.

Judging by many of his actions, de Ruiter appears to have absolved himself prematurely of responsibility for his actions. He seems to be like a more evolved religious fanatic who believes he is justified in any manner of bizarre behaviors simply because "God told him to." History is rife with precedents for such behavior, and in almost every case, the assumed "divine sanction" becomes a license for misbehavior. Perhaps God does speak directly to some people and dictate their actions; perhaps de Ruiter is even one of them. But sincere belief isn't enough to make it so, and history bears out W.B. Yeats' comment that, as a general rule, it is the most deluded people who possess the fiercest convictions.

In my experience, sitting in front of de Ruiter, in the atmosphere of reverent silence which he creates, caused a kind of unfocused, dissociated state of consciousness in me. From that state, all my attention (along with the attention of the others in the room) was fiercely concentrated on de Ruiter. Combined with that concentration, there was a deep emotional hunger for some crumb of confirmation or acknowledgment from him. When he threw me a glance or his words happened to coincide with something I was "in" at the time, it seemed to have been aimed directly at me and I experienced an upsurge of blissful "recognition"—recognition of de Ruiter and how wonderful and "true" he was. When his words echoed some thought I was having at the time, that led to a "knowing" about a personal truth relating to myself.

Looked at more soberly, however, my "knowing" was actually more centered on de Ruiter's power, the depth of his wisdom, and the central importance he had in my life, than on any insights about myself. It was all about "John." I felt overwhelming love for him mixed with childlike wonder and awe. I also felt "okay" about whatever had been bothering or oppressing me before the meeting. All my personal concerns became trivial and irrelevant in the light of a deeper "knowing" which centered on John's goodness. After the meeting was over, however, I would often feel deflated. Once I was no longer in his presence, I felt hungry for more of that "goodness."

I found a similar (anonymous) testimony, from January 2006, at the afore-mentioned comments section on the internet:

> The "numbness" of mind you mention is interesting in that for many of his followers it manifests not so much as a deadened state of awareness, and more as an acutely focused one. They see/hear/smell/taste/touch nothing (or at best very little) of anything other than John and his "teachings." As such, I liken the phenomenon more to a drug addiction than a malaise. There is purpose, thought, reflection, emotion in the process that accompanies the addiction, but it is focused and realized only in or about John. All other phenomena in life are rendered meaningless under these conditions....

If, as I have come to believe, this kind of experience is common—perhaps even the norm—in the group, it strongly indicates that de Ruiter is creating and maintaining a codependent relationship with his followers. The meetings offer temporary peace for wounded people, who between them create and hold a space of "okayness" in which it is possible to "transcend" (escape) everyday fears and difficulties. Such fragile souls would inevitably become dependent on their keeper for their (spiritual) survival, even as they are, ironically, providing *him* with a deep comfort and sense of purpose and meaning, one which he would otherwise be lacking. It is cosmic codependency.

As the author and yoga instructor Matthew Remski writes:

> The teacher becomes a black hole of interpretation, and in that darkness we dream the sun. We look at the teacher's blank face, his empty eyes, and we search for ourselves, and are strangely comforted by no response at all. His power depends on you not being seen or understood by him in the way that you understand yourself. He floats somewhere on the

dissociation spectrum: his lack of concrete personality relieves you of the pressure of your own identity, and of relating to others. He absolves you of the burden of self-knowledge, ironically, just as the jargon tells you that you are being led towards it. He replaces the Golden Rule with the Golden Bubble.*

Individuation & the "Dark" Side of Spirituality

"Every increase in knowledge may possibly render depravity more depraved, as well as may increase the strength of virtue."
—Sydney Smith

John's first son and second child, Nicolas, was born soon after the events at Bethlehem. (De Ruiter was also the second child and first son of his parents.) Nicolas was born in 1988, and those first few crucial years of his life were the years in which de Ruiter turned his band of Lutheran renegades into his own ministry. By 1995—the year Nicolas would have turned seven—de Ruiter was giving *satsangs* in the bookshop and moving into full guru mode. His marriage with Joyce ended four years later, in 1999, when Nicolas was eleven and on the threshold of adolescence.

De Ruiter claimed that he first "knew" he would commit adultery (not his words, of course) thirteen years previously. ("About thirteen years ago, there was a clear arising from the being that I would be with another woman, which for my mind

---

* "His body is a golden string your body's hanging from: Leonard Cohen and the disgraced guru," Aug 2013. http://matthewremski.com/wordpress/his-body-is-a-golden-string-your-bodys-hanging-from-leonard-cohen-and-the-disgraced-guru/

was an incredible shock.") That would have been 1986, the year his daughter Naomi was born. It was also the year his involvement began with the Bethlehem church, when he was first getting clear confirmation of his destiny as a Christian leader. The following year, his heady "romance" with Bob led to the "realization" that he was the fulfillment of the prophecy, "the One." This was also the period in which he told Joyce he was "battling the Beast."

If we leave movements of truth out of it, it seems safe to say that, when a married man with three children embarks on a secret affair with two sisters, he is either unsatisfied in his marriage or having difficulties with the role of husband and father (or both). By the time de Ruiter met the von Sasses, his own daughter, Naomi, would have been ten and she would have entered puberty exactly as the marriage reached crisis point. Apart from the specific circumstances of a guru sleeping with his disciples, this begins to resemble more and more the common case of a man undergoing a mid-life sexual identity crisis as his own children begin to come of age. De Ruiter even turned forty a month before the crisis broke.

So what was happening for de Ruiter internally during these critical years? Was he finding that his own family "patterns" were interfering with his capacity to function as a husband and father, the first intimations of this crisis arising in 1986, when Naomi was born and "a new woman" entered into his life? It would be understandable if, rather than follow his own counsel and "lie down" in those patterns and let his weakness, vulnerability, and inadequacy show, de Ruiter sought a "high level" solution outside of the marriage and came up with a spiritual get-out clause. By becoming sexually involved with some of his disciples (there is no way to know how many or how soon), de Ruiter may have been attempting to "heal" his wounded masculinity just as many men do—by proving his sexual prowess. In this case, the wound was only perpetuated, firstly via the women—Joyce, his daughter, the von Sasses and however many other women in the group—and, less obviously, onto his sons and the men in the group, who received a distorted example of male sexuality hidden beneath a royal cloak of dissembling.

When de Ruiter reinterpreted his deviant sexual behavior as an irreproachable "movement of truth," he publically disowned those patterns that were driving him and left them for his loyal servants to pick up. While the men were seeing, with their own eyes, the proof of their King's woundedness, they were simultaneously being told a different story, a story which ensured they remain loyal to their King and look to him as a model of upright masculinity, while deep down in their bones, they would have known otherwise. This would be especially true for John's sons, who initially turned against their father and sided with their mother, but who have since joined his "camp," to sit on the left and right sides of the Oasis throne.

By putting forward this spiritual cover story, the message de Ruiter gave was that it was *not okay* for a man to let his wounded sexuality show. Even as that pattern-distorted primal id energy rose all the way into full expression in de Ruiter's private life, the outer show of royal fineness and purity became ever more "refined." I think it also became increasingly corrupting because, while the corresponding wounds were opening up in the psyches of all John's male followers (as their id energy began to stir within them), they were denied the "low-down" necessary to understand what was happening to them. Their captain had lost his compass and, worse, was acting like he didn't need it. And as the Dionysian goblins ran riot through the kingdom, the knights of Oasis were being fed the same old New Age Christian line about "movements of truth" and "bonds of being." Behind the razzle-dazzle of the Truth Empire, a shadow was slowly engulfing the land.

*

It's important to point out at this stage that my experience of de Ruiter has not been wholly negative—or even especially harmful. While it's true I lost my way for a while and gave up my autonomy and sense of self—and while it is true that my marriage just barely survived the upheaval which seeing the truth about de Ruiter caused for us—recognizing this has been a learning, and liberating, experience. Yet while it would be wrong to say that de Ruiter had a detrimental effect on me, at the same time, I think this is only true because I recognized the ways in which he *was potentially* having such effects. A junky might well say the same about heroin, or, to be fairer, a psychedelic experimenter about LSD. One or two trips can be beneficent. But pretty soon the unhinging begins.

The truth—and the way of being—which I *believed* de Ruiter was embodying allowed me to connect to a new depth of understanding in myself. It wasn't *all* lies. It was only that the stream I was receiving was laced with something else besides truth. After, it was up to me to sort the seeds of my experience and figure out which were real.

In de Ruiter's imaginative explanation of his "high-level adultery," at the December meeting in 1999, he said this:

> I knew that I would do what I knew was true. Regardless of what it would cost me and regardless of what that would cost others. . . . I knew that I would give in to what I know even though it would do something, that for all appearances, I would no longer be beyond reproach. . . . I am surrendering to what I know regardless of what it looks like,

regardless of how that assaults all of my patterns, all of my patterns of what a relationship is, what a relationship is confined to. And for all of those patterns it was ultimately devastating. But I would never hesitate in responding to what I knew, regardless of what kind of death that would introduce . . . . That is just an ultimate cost, personally, for Joyce, for my kids, and for those that come here being touched by truth and trust in me. . . . It is because of knowing what I would respond to regardless of what it would cost to me and to others. It is just a supreme love of what I honestly know.

What de Ruiter describes—his "supreme love" of doing only what he knows is true, regardless of the consequences for himself or for others—is the way of no compromise. It's a notion that has a great deal of romantic appeal (especially to men), and I have tried to live by that same philosophy myself. In the process, like John, I justified all manner of harsh treatment of others—as well as myself—in the name of "truth." Based both on my own experience and de Ruiter's example, there is a world of difference between living for truth and living for others; in that context, living for truth might be the most "selfish" thing a person can do.

The idea that de Ruiter is so profoundly in love with truth—*his* truth—that he would willingly sacrifice not only his own comfort but other people's too, is a powerful one. It isn't only a religious concept, because it closely matches existentialism and certain, more progressive schools of psychology. The road of individuation is a lonely road. At the same time, what de Ruiter lays claim to is a form of enlightened selfishness that appeals to a very deep part of us. It appeals, for example, to the wounded child that has been abandoned, rejected, or betrayed, the child who brooded for years in his bedroom, late at night, and swore through lonely tears: "*Never again!*"

In 1998, de Ruiter said: "Following your conscience is the surest way to get away from truth." He has advised his followers to let go of moral structures, because in the end only they can know what is right or wrong for them at any given moment. When I was twenty-four, I suffered heartbreak and reacted by giving up a large inheritance and traveling to North Africa to live a destitute life on the streets, begging and stealing for food. I didn't tell anyone where I was going, and I assured them I might never return. In a way, that was the *easier* path for me. It was the path "I knew to be true." It was also what my patterns made me do when triggered by unacceptable loss. When I told my family I was leaving, I saw sadness but no recrimination, and no one questioned my decision. Perhaps they knew nothing would sway me from my course, but I think it was also a response to my "core knowing" that it was not a matter of personal choice but of psychological survival—of "destiny." It was both a selfish and a selfless act. There was "nothing in it for me" except the knowledge that I was doing what I knew was true. But I was also disregarding everyone else's feelings, to the point that it was just as if those other people didn't even exist for me. I acted compulsively as well as "heroically," because from my own point of view, there wasn't a clear difference. That was my hero's quest and it was necessary for my individuation. It entailed the abandonment of all my loved ones, and I had no qualms about how my decision would affect them. As I saw it, like de Ruiter, *I literally had no choice*.

Myths and action movies of the kind enjoyed by de Ruiter (and myself) make heroic enactments seem simple and straightforward, and the hero (whether Braveheart or Neo) is heroic in all the usual ways. In real life, doing the right thing is more complex and ambiguous. It isn't a simple matter of meeting a series of external challenges but of exploring the psychological wounds which prevent us from growth, from becoming wholly and authentically ourselves. It's about facing our deepest fears. Who's to say what sort of unpleasantness the "hero" might be sucked into, as he follows his lonely road of truth? If his one-pointed determination is ruthless enough, he might even end up becoming the villain *without ever realizing it.*

Based on my exchanges with some of his ex-followers, I'd say this viewpoint is gaining some ground among people who have got close enough to de Ruiter to begin to sense his hidden agenda. Tim Gallagher told me in 2015:

> In actual fact, he's quite potentially malevolent. There's almost a mechanical quality. If it serves him it's fine, if it doesn't . . . . And so there are people in the group, and he selects them according to their usefulness, I think, their wealth, their good looks, their connections. There are lots of ordinary people that he doesn't give a fuck about. It took me a long time to realize that that's how it was. . . . By talking in absolutes he appeals to Germans, and the group has got a lot of Germans and the Germans do a lot of organizing. Who's he picking up these days? Germans and Israelis. He keeps going to Israel repeatedly. . . . But also they're the two most guilty nations on the earth. And I think he has them read like a book. He's just hoovering up useful assets for himself, so that, if you ever want to come against John, you've got to go through a defense shield of Israelis and Germans. . . . I think he's very clever.

In his community-cum-cult Oasis, de Ruiter offers a space for anyone who wishes to "enter" into the devastation of "absolute surrender." There is very little mention (since his confession in 1999) of the damage which he has wrought, in his ruthless and one-pointed pursuit of goodness, upon home, family, and loved ones in the name of a transpersonal truth. De Ruiter welcomes with open arms his fellow walking wounded. They wander dazed and thankful from broken homes to join him in his icy fortress of solitude. It's a familiar pattern, and however consciously he might be involved in his own healing process, underneath it all de Ruiter appears to also be a wounded child, seeking his father's blessing and the loving warmth of his mother. Isn't that the subtext of every heroic journey?

The temptation de Ruiter appears to have succumbed to is the temptation to render his actions symbolic and so inflate them out of the messy realms of the personal, and into the clean, cool light of the archetypal. Yet it *is* heroic, because it is also symbolic: de Ruiter is taking on the fiery patterns of the ancestors and a whole, sickly Christian tradition of disowned shadows and sexuality as expressed over centuries of religious persecutions, civil injustice, and domestic violence. If he believes he is taking on "the sins of the world," who knows, maybe he is? Isn't that what every man needs to do to assume responsibility for his own life?

As a child, John was given the name "golden hands," most probably by his mother. The name suggests healing and transformative, solar (masculine) energy. (I noticed over the years how de Ruiter continues to use the word "golden" as a term of *praise* to denote what is of the highest.) The nickname came from his apparent ability for building things, yet the stories in his bio which immediately follow the mention of "golden hands" are of little Johnny *breaking things down* to their constituent parts. Apparently de Ruiter is at least as much a destroyer as a builder; that's the dark side of spirituality, and without it, no teaching is complete. Maybe he even broke things apart *in order* to rebuild them? This is a pattern that played out during his apocalyptic stint at the Bethlehem Lutheran church, when he created a rift in the ministry and, from that wreckage, assembled his own church.

While his mother praised him, John's father pushed him to be a carpenter and a cobbler, and no doubt hoped he would use his golden hands to earn an honest living. Did Cornelius de Ruiter (who was affectionately known as "Cor") ever give his son his blessing, I wonder? Judging by de Ruiter's rejection of the simple lot of carpenter/cobbler, he had no desire to honor his father's wishes; and if de Ruiter did not respect his father, it was likely he never felt that his father respected him, either. Is it just coincidence that de Ruiter's supreme virtue is what he termed "core-splitting honesty"? What's in a word?

Enter the Dragon: Archetypal Possession

"The Defendant explained to me that part of his 'burden from God' was to act against his own message and to violate his own marriage so as to prepare him inwardly for his upcoming battle with Satan. He spoke in soft convincing tones, claiming to be a kind of willing victim suffering God's will. He claimed this preparation was further 'profound evidence' of the truth of his 'calling' from God to be the 'embodiment of truth,' and that what 'may appear or may be suffered on the outside' is not 'in reality what is happening on deeper and profound, unseen levels.'"
—Benita von Sass, from the affidavit

There is something about a man who believes he is Christ/God/Truth/the Messiah that—short of a simple diagnosis of insanity—doesn't permit itself to be nailed down (pun intended). It is like trying to hold onto a live fish: the only way to keep it still is to kill it. What follows are the things I was able to deduce about the fish, before I gave up and threw it back into the ocean.

To be enlightened suggests to be filled with light and devoid of darkness. In psychological terms, it implies that the unconscious has become fully conscious and all of a person's "shadow matter" integrated by the psyche. Until such a level has been attained, however (assuming it's possible), that shadow matter will *always* find ways to express itself. If de Ruiter has publically assumed the Christly role of a living embodiment of truth, evidently he is trying very hard to be (seen as) "good." At a certain point—or in other areas of his life—he might be compelled to take on the opposite pole, and become a "living embodiment of untruth." The most obvious way that kind of polarity would manifest would be in public and private expressions, and at a surface level that seems to be the case.

While de Ruiter's "guru" persona is overtly benevolent, he appears to have treated his wives with a degree of cruelty at odds with such benevolence. That's the shadow. What is damning about de Ruiter is not that he is capable of cruelty and scheming, but that he attempts to conceal (and dissemble) his private behavior rather than let it form part of his total persona. He has done the opposite of owning up to it, and this suggests he is trying to *dis*own it. The worst thing to do with shadow qualities is to try to conceal them, because it is only by bringing them to light that they can be "dissolved," i.e., integrated. The goal isn't goodness but *wholeness*.

Any kind of teaching—including one that purports to be "the living truth"—is inevitably in-formed by the person it comes through. If de Ruiter's enlightenment experiences are trauma-based, then all his teachings and the transmission that comes through him is going to be shaped by that trauma. Although he might appear to be embodying truth/Christ energy, he is really only embodying *a close imitation of it.* It might *seem* like the real thing, but in fact it would be a clever counterfeit.

Bob Emmerzael claimed that de Ruiter was establishing truth "by *what he is being* and what he is teaching." According to someone at Oasis, de Ruiter said, at some point outside the meetings, that while he was embodying truth on stage, it was quite different when he was living his day-to-day life in the world. So if de Ruiter at the meetings isn't the same person as de Ruiter in his home life, does that mean some kind of supernatural transfiguration occurs whenever he enters the meeting space? His statement can be interpreted to mean that he is a channeler, but channeling is something de Ruiter has publicly derided, and a far cry from being a living embodiment of truth. (Anyone can be a channel: it is a kind of voluntary possession.) A person might channel Christ—his words—but can they embody Christ energy without being one with that energy? If enlightenment is about being fully in the moment, where is the logic behind only being the living truth *some* of the time? It implies that this is a *role* de Ruiter *assumes.* Why is it more "important" for him to be true at meetings than in his day to day life? Because he is getting paid for it?*

If some of his followers recognize Christ in de Ruiter's performance, it proves, at most, that Christ is within them and that de Ruiter has a knack for bringing it out. But a talented hypnotist can make someone think they are a chicken; that doesn't make him capable of transmutations. Is it really so different with de Ruiter? Giving people an experience of Christ consciousness doesn't prove he is Christ. And if that experience is dependent on being close to de Ruiter, then what is its value, finally?

---

* It is also at odds with de Ruiter's alleged claim that, if he ceased to be true to what he knew, he would die.

Judging by Benita's testimony (allowing for some degree of misunderstanding on her part), de Ruiter believes his cosmic task is to permit the darkness of "untruth" to enter into him and to have *expression through him* (by violating his marriage and acting against his own teaching), as part of his truth-embodiment mission. That is his "burden from God." There is a psychological equivalent to that process, somewhat at odds with de Ruiter's more theological one, and it's called "integrating the shadow." The difference is that the Satan which de Ruiter is preparing to battle is not an external, cosmic presence but a disowned aspect of his psyche. It is his own shadow, an archetypal force which he summoned forth, through his own action and non-action, as a result of over-identification with Christ and denial of all that is "satanic" within him. By allowing himself to be possessed by Satan for "the salvation of the world," de Ruiter would really only be showing his true colors—those suppressed distortions—as *an ordinary human being*. For those who have allowed de Ruiter to become the living truth, however, such an unveiling of reality might well seem like the end of the world.

The idea of archetypal possession is akin to being possessed by one's own unconscious, which is where archetypes reside (Freud's term for them was "archaic remnants"). The deepest and most powerful aspect of the unconscious is the shadow, which is the sum of everything a person rejects or disowns in themselves. A very obvious example of this is a Christian preacher who considers sex the devil's tool and preaches hellfire sermons about how sensuality leads to damnation, while secretly abusing altar boys. Such devious, unnatural, and secret sexual activity is a way for his shadow to express itself without the preacher ever having to admit he is "damned." (Bar the devil from coming in the front door, and he sneaks in the back.) De Ruiter's case is both more extreme and subtler. He identifies with Christ (extreme), but his notion of sin entails any act of *self-interest* that does not serve "Truth" (subtle). Nonetheless, the same dynamic applies: whatever he rejects in himself is pushed into the shadowy regions of his unconscious, and it is *that shadow material*—or the corresponding archetypal energy—*that possesses him.*

What follows is a long description from Tim Gallagher from our talk in 2015. There are many correspondences with my own impressions of de Ruiter, impressions which initially I included in this work but then took out for fear that they were simply too "alarmist," too reactive, and too melodramatic to do anything but confuse readers. I knew I had a bent for "paranoid" readings and so I thought it best to curb that bent as much as possible. Tim, on the other hand, was with John for many years, starting in 1998, and had only come to his conclusions via a very long period of contemplation and direct personal involvement with John. Hence I felt his testimony had considerably more weight. Here it is in full:

> With John I felt that he may represent a nonhuman intelligence. My intuition was that he was representing like an extraterrestrial dimension. This sounds crazy but one of my very first experiences was of this, when I first came to Edmonton. I had a very clear vision, like a fully lucid vision, that John was from another dimension but he wasn't as he appeared and my blood ran cold. I ignored that, because I saw that as my own internal opposition to the truth, and I talked myself round. But recently I've come to realize, what he pursues is the feminine. He pursues the juice of the feminine. It's a bit like the energy of the earth itself, in a way. He kind of pretends that he embodies that, but I think he completely lacks that. That's why he has use of the juiciest women he can get his hands

on. That's one aspect. But I also think he represents an agenda which is not an ordinary human agenda, and he has never disclosed what that is. He is coming from a strange place but he doesn't trust us with sharing that so he himself cannot be trusted.

But that's a lot of my own intuitive perception. He's not a straightforward, run of the mill conman. He has huge insight, he has huge access to various levels of mental perception, I think. . . . When you first see him he sends out a lure, like a shiny coin almost, but it's "*the* truth" and it's this feeling. And that draws you out, and draws you further and further out, and what he's done (I mean, this is my imaginarium of it), he is using the energy of everyone who invests in him, a bit like a bank. And what he's done is he's created a construct, but he himself hasn't really got that energy. He's using everybody's energy to weave the construct, and then the contract becomes binding for those who have invested. I call it the crystal maze. It's almost like a dimension within a dimension and it's not an ordinary happening in the earth. It's quite strange. And there *is* an energy that's held in there, but I think it mostly belongs to people who've invested in John. I think there's a very powerful trance state that means that you can't think critically anymore, you can't question John's authority. You just withdraw if you feel threatened, and also that you can become quite hostile to a person that you sense is not on board.

*

"The *ambiguous* or *narcissistic delusional guru* is often extremely charismatic, persuasive—even hypnotic, and can be a gifted orator. They may be able to 'channel' a true *emanation of being* at certain times, such as when they are teaching, and hence they are good at impressing people and manipulating their 'belief' in them (although this comes ultimately from the *astral 'luminous attractor' entity* that is using them as its instrument).

—"Levels of Enlightenment"

The question I kept coming back to during my first attempt to write this book was, did de Ruiter really believe he was the Christ, and if so, what exactly did that mean? I came up with four possible interpretations of such a belief:

1) De Ruiter is the Christ.

2) He is deluded and/or insane.

3) He is lying for opportunistic or unknown reasons.

4) A combination of all of the above, namely, de Ruiter is possessed of certain Christ-like qualities, but has over-identified with them to the point of deluding himself that he actually *is* Christ.

During the first phase of writing this book (2010-11), I received an email from an ex-follower of de Ruiter which included a long article (quoted above) called "Levels of Enlightenment." This person shared her experiences of de Ruiter, chief among which was the overwhelming impression of being in the presence of Christ energy. She told me that she had had numerous awakening experiences during her lifetime, including what she believed were visitations from "the Christ." The moment she sat in John's presence, she said, she instantly recognized the same presence. Despite all her doubts about him, she said that whenever she sat in his presence during meetings, she had powerful experiences of deep recognition and of "union with the divine beloved." It was "the finest vibration" she had ever experienced with any teacher, she said. At the same time, she told me that she had enough private conversations with "John the person" to know that the presence coming through him in meetings was completely different from de Ruiter the man (even if de Ruiter would have people believe otherwise).

She described how, when she first arrived in Edmonton (after having avidly listened to and applied de Ruiter's teachings for many years), she was shocked to find that some of the most "senior" students (working in administration), people who had been with de Ruiter since the 90s, were some of the most self-righteous, cold-hearted, unloving, and controlling "religious conservatives" she had ever met. (She also mentioned that his two wives—presumably the von Sasses—weren't the least bit interested in his teaching, and wondered if they knew something the others didn't.)

When I first corresponded with her, I was somewhat resistant to her contention that she had experienced genuine Christ/Truth energy in de Ruiter's presence. At the same time, I was curious to hear more, because her experience almost exactly matched my wife's, who also believed something "divine" worked through de Ruiter but was separate from who he was *as a man*. The difference between this woman's perception and my wife's was that my wife didn't experience any conflict over it, or at least wasn't admitting to it. I shared some of what I had written about de Ruiter with my correspondent, and she remarked that I was apparently still somewhat emotional about the subject and that, as a result, I was assuming an overly "dualistic" point of view. I was suggesting that de Ruiter had taken the Christ energy for his own use and so become a kind of "Antichrist" figure; I believed it was easy enough to explain de Ruiter's numinous effect on people as simply deception. "Even the elect would be fooled," etc. The trouble was that I was reverting to a suspiciously Christian line, that de Ruiter was a false prophet and a servant of Satan, etc., etc., a limited view, at best, however emotionally satisfying it might be. The idea of archetypes being "good" or "evil" is a religious viewpoint, not a psychological one.

De Ruiter was raised by Catholic parents. His formative experience at the age of seventeen centered around some kind of awakening-cum-Christian conversion, after which he spent going on ten years practicing the faith, albeit in unorthodox ways. It wasn't until his mid-thirties (around 1995), when he met "Boots" Beaudry and began to pick up some New Age terminology, that he shed his Christian garb and remolded his persona to suit a wider audience. Nonetheless, according to Benita's more recent testimony, he continued to use Christian terminology behind the scenes, such as when he spoke of "doing the will of God." If Benita was to be believed, he had identified himself *as* Christ. Christian belief only allows for the notion of Christ *as a person*, a divine being who came once and who would come again at the end of time. "Christ consciousness" is a New Age concept that is incompatible with orthodox Christian belief. De Ruiter has implied on several occasions that he is a higher manifestation of truth than anyone currently on the planet. Does that mean he believes he is the fullest living embodiment of Christ consciousness? And does that make him (in his own mind) Christ *in person*? If de Ruiter believes something of that nature, does his belief come with the corresponding mission, of judging the quick and the dead, ushering in the Apocalypse, and so forth? What if he should fail in his mission? Is that even a possibility? And what would de Ruiter be willing to do to ensure that he *not* fail? Are there any means that would not be justified in his mind by such an end?

Asylums are filled with individuals who believe they are Christ or that they are supposed to have *been* Christ before they lost the plot. They are usually diagnosed as schizophrenic. Joyce described a period in his twenties when de Ruiter believed he was becoming schizophrenic, roughly the same period he first claimed to have encountered "Jesus" while driving his truck. De Ruiter managed to escape being locked up in a psych ward, however, by being careful only to share his Christ-calling with people who would *support him in his belief* (starting with Bob Emmerzael*). Through such a pragmatic (and quite sane) strategy, he was able to create a mini-consensus in which he *was* Christ, or as close as made no difference. This is a luxury few schizophrenics enjoy. Over time, de Ruiter learned to keep his more radical beliefs quiet, donned the relatively respectable guise of "author and philosopher," and went on to give "seminars" in place of messianic sermons (or messianic sermons disguised as seminars).

As Tim Gallagher humorously put it to me:

> I think he's familiar with all kinds of... I wouldn't say it's just consciousness, I almost feel like saying technologies because I just don't know what the point of him is, or what he thinks he's doing. And the thing is he's not transparent. If he were to tell you, "I'm from Zargon, and back home we like to find people that are a bit less intelligent than ourselves and have a good laugh and I've woven you into a crystal maze and you're never going to get out. And I want the sex energy of you coz it connects me to the earth which is what I want because I actually want to suck the life out of the earth. How do you feel about that?" It's like, "Well actually yeah, I kind of felt something like that was happening John." It's not just an ordinary conman, because his abilities are quite sophisticated.

---

* It is possible that the belief in John-as-Christ originated with Bob, since apparently the idea came into full form during their late night sessions together. Bob Emmerzael might even have been the sower (or at least waterer) of the seed of de Ruiter's messianic mission.

I have heard de Ruiter assure his listeners that his drive to spread the gospel of Truth is devoid of a personal agenda. But even if he *does* believe in his divine mission (whatever it might look like in human terms), is that actually the case? If there was a period during his "awakening" when his sanity was in jeopardy, persuading others that he was Christ might have been the only means to escape the terrifying possibility that he *was* insane. There is a fine line between divine calling and lunacy, and if an insane man convinces enough people to believe his delusion, then to those people he is no longer insane but divinely inspired. What could be more of a personal investment than getting to be the Messiah?

By identifying himself as the Christ, de Ruiter would be getting to *be* that for as long as he could persuade others to believe it. But if the experience of awakening to the truth, and later his visits from "Jesus," came to him not spontaneously and unbound but as a response to some deep need within him, the likelihood is that he was tricked, and that the entity that identified itself to him as "Jesus" was nothing of the kind. It would make no difference whether he realized his mistake later on, the "pact" he made with such an entity—i.e., whether some extraterrestrial overlord or simply his own unconscious—would be *binding*: He would have no choice but to continue to let the archetype possess him and move him.

By his own admission, de Ruiter is only doing what he knows—but what is that? He has soared unimaginably far and fast through the heavens since that first lift-off. If his instruments were even a tiny bit off in Bethlehem, by now he could have landed on the wrong planet entirely—or be drifting aimlessly through space.

Most bizarrely of all, he might not even know it.

Part Five
Don't Ever Buy Nothing
from a Man Named Truth

"Ancient dogma decreed that no man can see God, which is true. God is not an object. We can only see *as God*, but then, when we do, God is all we can see... He is the robber, the desperado, the saint, the slave, the king. Each of us defines him, and each must then experience his or her definition of him."
—Joseph Chilton Pearce, *Evolution's End*

Off to See the Wizard

"When you follow a teacher that doesn't have an expanded will, then that is giving power to that density of will within that teacher that will not let it go at *all* costs. That then makes a teacher a *somebody*. Where there is an expanded will, there is no somebody. Unless you *know* that someone is mastered by truth, you can listen to them and hear them, but don't follow them."
—John de Ruiter, 2000

When I set out to analyze and understand de Ruiter, I knew I was entering a rabbit hole. I knew that all the psychological or even metaphysical theories in the world wouldn't be enough to make sense of him. One of the biggest difficulties was that de Ruiter can't be judged, or understood, as a discreet entity, because, as a guru, avatar of truth, and/or cult leader, he has become the center of a collective body called Oasis. The King and the people are one, and the only way to really understand de Ruiter is to see him as part of a larger system made up also of his followers.

Whatever his motives might be, there's no getting around the fact that de Ruiter is on a bid for worldly power. If a carpenter enters his workshop in the morning and by night comes out with a table, it's safe to say that he *intended* to build a table. It didn't simply "happen" while he was pottering about the workshop. So it is with de Ruiter and the Oasis Empire. He and his followers can talk all day about "movements of truth," while the skeptics can argue that it's pure self-interest at work; both are blinded by preconceptions, and neither is correct, because neither conscious self-interest nor transpersonal Truth is in the driving seat, but *unconscious patterns*. Truth moves in mysterious ways. My challenge (and presumably de Ruiter's, and that of his followers too) is to understand how the various, opposing agendas—the unfolding of truth and the will to power, Myshkin and Machiavelli—can combine into a single "movement."

On March 23rd 2011, I flew to Edmonton with the intention of meeting John and telling him about the book I was working on. I timed the trip to coincide with a gala event at Oasis to raise money for the Oasis garden, to the tune of $50,000. The event was an auction of items and services provided by members of the group, as well as a raffle, the first prize of which was "a day in the wilderness with John"! It seemed like an opportune moment to make an appearance. I also wanted to meet several people in Edmonton to interview them for the book: Barrie Reeder and Hal Dallmann from the Bethlehem Lutheran church, Jason Gerdes and possibly others, as well as to visit the courthouse for updates on the von Sass/de Ruiter case.

I arranged to attend a meeting with Jason Gerdes on the only night he had free. It was Jason's first time at the new building, and he hadn't seen John in several years. It was a long and very dull meeting, over three hours, and although we both put our names down, neither Jason nor I got to speak, because the meeting was taken up entirely by an Indian man and his wife. During the first part, I stayed focused on de Ruiter. I was watching his breathing because I'd read at a forum that his breathing was shallow, an observation that was presented as proof that he was "obviously a fake." So far as I could tell, his breathing was normal. The Indian woman was gushing adoringly, and when I looked at John on the screens, his expression seemed sad. A bit later, when I looked over at the left screen, it looked as though his right eye was melting off his face. He looked heavy and stricken.

I felt no awe, only compassion, some gratitude, skepticism, a trace of pity, and a smidgeon of hostility (as it happens, these were all feelings I'd felt towards my father). I felt mild curiosity but it was almost as if it didn't matter who de Ruiter was anymore. His words no longer seemed profound, and I began to wonder how hard I'd had to work in the past to generate the feelings of awe I'd experienced in his presence. It was as if I'd followed cues from de Ruiter and the rest of the group. Maybe I'd wanted so much to *get* it that I had pulled the necessary feelings and associations from within myself. And then, once I'd got it, no one could have told me I hadn't.

Being there, I had a visceral sense of reclaiming my own power. It was as if I'd left it with the guru for safe keeping. I wasn't there to ask for it but to take it, and it was happening just by the fact of my sitting there. I had flown all that way to discover that I no longer wanted anything from John, perhaps even that I had nothing to say to him. In the past, I had sat in front of him and tried to match his power, to receive it or honor it or surrender to it. Now I was aware only of my own power, and of how much I did not belong there, with these people. The guru was just another person, doing his thing. After the meeting, Gerdes commented on how unhappy John looked.

The next day, I went to the Queen's Bench courthouse to look for new affidavits, but the only extra information I found in the case file was a transcript of Benita's testimony. There were a few interesting facts, including that Benita had apparently been working on John's "book" (I presume his biography). It also listed Benita's home address. According to the file, the case had been dismissed by the Judge the previous year, and there had been an appeal which had also been discontinued, on August 18th (Joyce's birthday). That didn't gel with what Peter von Sass had said to me, on several occasions, that the case was ongoing, which was the ostensible reason why neither he nor his daughters would speak to me. I went to another section of the building and confirmed that the appeal had been discontinued, possibly with a settlement.

The next day I had a meeting with Barrie Reeder at the St Peter's Lutheran church. The meeting lasted three hours and went fairly well. At one point, Barrie threatened to break my neck if I repeated what he was about to tell me; he sounded like he meant it. I told him there was no need for threats and he mellowed and assured me that he'd only sue me. He then revealed something fairly unremarkable around the whole Rousu/Dallmann/de Ruiter affair, including a few clues which helped me to correct the picture I'd been building, based mostly on Joyce's recollections. Reeder suggested some questions for Dallmann and asked me to call him, Reeder, after my meeting, in case Dallmann didn't give the full story. Towards the end of the encounter, Reeder knelt before me, put his hand on my shoulder and prayed for the success of my enterprise and other things. I wondered if Reeder's death threat, followed by his blessing, was an indication of what I could expect from de Ruiter.

I got a ride to Oasis with a lady named Kali, from Boulder, Colorado. Kali had finally moved to Edmonton after eleven years of following de Ruiter. She had sold her farm in the country now that her daughter had finally grown up. I felt sad for her. When we arrived the café was jam-packed with people in elegant evening dress. I wore a cream linen suit I'd found in England, in a thrift store, before I attended my brother's funeral. I got my raffle ticket and drink coupon and exchanged words with an Englishman wearing a silver crop circle around his neck. He knew of my writing and various identities, and spoke in complex sentences that meant nothing to me. He seemed to be trying to show off his intelligence, and I slipped away as soon as the doors opened. I was curious to see how they had turned the "church" area into a party space. All the seats were gone, and in their place were several round tables covered in black cloth. The room was candlelit and tastefully arranged. On the various tables were the donations of followers that were being auctioned, strange items, ranging from a buzz saw to a Jester's costume. I wondered if the buzz saw was an in-joke.

I floated around waiting for John to show up, exchanging pleasantries with a few of the followers who recognized me. I had brought a small digital recording device to record my encounter with de Ruiter. Normally, my preference is for total transparency, but I had weighed the pros and cons and decided I could justify this subterfuge in the interests of keeping a complete record of the event. I drank a few glasses of water and then saw that John had arrived with Leigh Ann. They were wandering around in their usual regal fashion and I followed them with my eyes for a while. Presently, a short lady joined the couple and I decided to take the next opening. When I saw the royal couple was alone again, I cashed in my drink coupon for a glass of champagne (some Dutch courage) and resolved to approach them. They were walking slowly around the edge of the room, appraising some large paintings rested against one of the walls. They had their backs to me and I had to come right alongside them and speak to get their attention. My heart was pounding.

"Hiiii," I said, a long drawn out sound.

John and Leigh Ann both turned and said "Hi." John said it was nice to see me. He sounded sincere enough. I asked him if he remembered me from Bristol and he said yes. He made a comment about my wife not being there and I told him that she had stayed at home. I asked how they both were and John said they were very well. I started to explain why I had come there and had a moment of disorientation when I realized I didn't remember where I was! I stared at Leigh Ann and said: "Where the hell am I?" before I regained my senses ("Edmonton!"). I pushed on by saying that I had come expressly to talk to John and was hoping I'd be able to see him outside the meetings. He said nothing so I added that I knew he was flying to Australia soon, but that I hadn't contacted him ahead of time because I thought he was "a very abstract kind of person" who liked to do things spontaneously.

After a pause, de Ruiter said that it wouldn't be possible because he was leaving tomorrow. Leigh Ann asked how long I would be in Edmonton and I told them a few more days. I said that I had many things I wanted to say to John and that I didn't know where to begin. (No response.) I admitted that it was probably not a good place for it, however, since he was there in a social mode and (no doubt) wanted to keep things light. That prompted a small nod from him. I mentioned that I'd written him a song ("Little Johnny Golden Hands") and that I had brought my guitar, hoping I could play it for him. He remained silent so I ploughed on. I explained how, in the two years I had known him, "my whole life had turned upside down." Leigh Ann smiled approvingly.

"Particularly in the last few months," I said, "I've been going through a lot of confusion around yourself, and I think that I came here to just see where I was at with you, and I came to the meeting on Thursday, I'm not sure if you saw me?"

John nodded and I added that I was with his old friend Jason and wondered if he'd recognized him. John nodded in a noncommittal way. I said I'd wanted to speak to him on Thursday night but hadn't had the chance, adding that "just being there allowed me to see things more clearly."

De Ruiter acknowledged that—I think he said "good"—and I sensed that he was about to excuse himself. I said that I didn't want to be a burden and impose on him, but that I wished we could have some "quiet time," even if it was just half an hour. There was a pause, during which de Ruiter did not show a flicker of interest.

"The feeling that I get," I said, "is that all these people are here looking to get something from you, and nobody's actually giving anything *back* to you."

In retrospect, my comment was a bit ironic, considering that hundreds of people had come to give up their goods and services to him. I was fumbling to find the right words, while outwardly I remained confident and calm. A woman on stage started to make an announcement. She began with a loud "Hello!" De Ruiter told me that he wanted to listen, smiling faintly. I stood by silently while he and Leigh Ann listened to the woman talk about the event. I didn't hear a word she said; I was simply waiting for the next opportunity to speak, acutely aware that I would only have a small window of opportunity. The three of us stood there for a couple of minutes and then the woman's microphone started to fail; de Ruiter remarked on it, and the announcement gradually wound down due to the technical fault. I was sure they were preparing to make excuses and leave.

"Maybe I won't get another chance to speak," I said, "so I perhaps should just . . . cut to the chase, as they say." (I had hesitated because the expression seemed faintly aggressive.) "Since I last saw you, I've written a book. . ." De Ruiter's face remained blank, devoid of emotion or interest. I told him in a few short phrases about the book; still there was no response. I reminded him of our encounter in Bristol when I had asked him if I could tell his story and he had told me that somebody was already telling it. At that point, he nodded. I told him that I'd had no idea back then that I'd end up writing my own book about him.

"But since I came in October," I said, and trailed off. I was remembering the affidavit, the train wreck of de Ruiter's relationship with Benita, and everything I'd been through since then. How on earth could I sum all that up?

"Things have come up," I said. "I don't want to go into detail, but anyway I've written this book and I'd very much like to get your input, coz it's obviously incomplete without your side of it."

De Ruiter still made no comment.

"I know that you don't talk about your personal life very much," I said, "and you like to keep that separate from what you do; but for me that hasn't been possible. For me to know you and understand you as a man, as a human being, has been absolutely essential for me, because until that time you were like this abstract, godlike being that I couldn't even relate to. That was very disempowering for me. I tried to match you, I tried to be like you, it didn't work. So this has been a process of me discovering your human side, as far as I've been able to."

When de Ruiter still didn't say anything, I mentioned that I'd been speaking to Barrie Reeder that morning.

After a pause, he asked, "Barrie who?"

I said the name and mentioned the Bethlehem church, and de Ruiter gave another noncommittal nod. I wasn't sure why I'd mentioned Reeder and by way of explanation I said that speaking to people who had known him in the past was helping me to understand him better. I turned to Leigh Ann then and said: "I don't know if many of these people see John as a human being."

Leigh Ann said that they did. I said I didn't know, and she replied that the people who lived there did. I was skeptical.

"I feel as though all these people are worshipping John," I said. "So that's like a prison. That's what I feel."

I stared into John's eyes and there was a pause of maybe thirty seconds or more. Whether or not I was staring at de Ruiter the whole time, I didn't come away with the slightest clue as to what he was thinking. Finally he said that he couldn't take too long and that he needed to be "milling about."

I nodded and told him that I had wanted to let him know, and that if he was interested and wanted to talk to me about it, I wasn't sure I would be coming back to Edmonton, but there were other ways we could communicate. Leigh Ann said I could send an email to the college. I suggested leaving my info and if John wanted to contact me, that was probably the best option. There was a pause, after which I said, in a plaintive voice, "I very much want to help, John. I know that probably sounds kind of absurd."

John looked at me and for the first time he seemed aware that I had actually said something. He said that it didn't sound absurd, but that for him to be "coming out upfront" and spending time with me was not something he normally did. Circumstances would have to be "more extraordinary," he said. He then added something vague about responding to "all the different things" that came his way. I felt his uncertainty as he fumbled for the right words. I was aware of being gently fobbed, and that our meeting was at an end.

"I wanted to present myself here," I said, "so you could see me, look me in the eye, and then you would know, what's the right thing to do. I can't know what the right thing is for you. I can only know what it is for me; for me it's to come up and speak to you, tell you straight up what I'm doing: I'm writing a book and I hope to publish it. It's about you, it's a sympathetic portrait, but it's . . . it's a human portrait."

There was another pause. De Ruiter's face remained blank and disinterested. He said that he would probably see me around, back here or in Europe. It was half a question so I told him he probably wouldn't see me in Europe. I added that I'd be there tonight if he wanted to speak to me, and I'd leave my contact details. After a brief technical exchange about how best to contact him, I touched him lightly on his left arm, thanked him for listening, and said, "Enjoy the night."

He said, "Bye for now" and they walked away.

In the last instant, as our eyes broke contact, I felt a tiny wave of hostility pass between us. It was so subtle and ephemeral that I couldn't say at the time if it came from him or me, or both. But in that moment, I fancied that, behind all the civility and politesse of our meeting, two ancient sorcerers had squared off in the temple. There was also something I had become aware of during the meeting, which apparently I had been too awestruck to notice the last time we stood face to face. De Ruiter was an inch or two shorter than me.

Render Unto Caesar

"The hidden function of the sacred has been to get people to sacrifice to it."
—Joel Kramer & Diana Alstad, *The Guru Papers*

After the encounter with de Ruiter I ran into Lars, an attractive young man whom I'd met and liked on my last visit (he looks a little like Matthew McConaughey). Lars was on the opposite side of the room to where I'd encountered John, and we stood and chatted for a while. I brought up John, and as I did I saw the royal couple "milling about." They were coming towards us and it looked as though de Ruiter wanted to speak to Lars. If so, when he saw me he changed his mind, and they both floated by, smiling and nodding. "Speak of the devil" I said to Lars, who seemed a bit disconcerted. I told him I'd been having some doubts since the affidavit and Lars mentioned that he was on the "committee," a group set up as a "buffer" between de Ruiter and any doubters in the group, so that (according to Lars) John could concentrate on the teachings. The way it worked was that anyone who had questions could present them to a committee member, and they would be brought up at the next committee meeting.

Lars said several times in reference to the affidavit, "They are just allegations." I countered that, even if they were false, they were still coming from the woman John had chosen to spend ten years of his life with, a fact which raised questions in itself. Lars didn't agree and seemed uncomfortable with my line of reasoning. After a while, I could see he was looking at me with mild suspicion. When I asked him about Benita's statement that de Ruiter had claimed he was taking Satan into himself in order to overcome evil, Lars didn't seem interested. His replies began to make less and less sense to me: he was saying that he didn't think there was any need to go into "all of that stuff" and yet his reasoning struck me as more emotional than rational. I could see he didn't want to continue our conversation, so I wandered off at an opportune moment.

Later, I was talking to a friend, Niels, in the café, when we were joined by a blonde, muscular guy in his late twenties (at a guess). He spoke to us about being in the Chair recently and how de Ruiter had hinted at his moving to Edmonton. The young man (who lived in New York) didn't feel "the pull," however, and he had approached de Ruiter in the café about it later. He told us that de Ruiter had pretty much told him that he had a *knowing* that the young man was supposed to move to Edmonton. The encounter had left the young man feeling as if he was "screwed" if he didn't come. He said that de Ruiter had been applying pressure on him and that he found it disturbing. It didn't seem right or fair to him, for John to do that. I told him that, based on the many accounts I had heard, de Ruiter often applied pressure to get people to move to Edmonton, as well as to prevent them from leaving. Niels agreed with me and we had a three-way conversation, after which I played my "Golden Hands" song for the young man. He was disturbed by it, but also moved. While I was playing, two small blonde girls came and listened, gazing at me with shy smiles. Maybe they were standing in for the von Sass sisters.

If that was the high point of the evening, and possibly the whole trip, the auction was definitely the strangest part. Once all the donated items had been sold off, "human resources" were next. Tree clippers, masseurs, and other local professionals stood on the stage while the crowd bid for them. One person I saw on stage, a tree clipper, was tall and thin and wearing a white suit like my own; with my less than perfect vision, he could have been me. Later, I saw him in the café and for a brief moment I thought he was the actor, Kevin Bacon. It was a disconcerting coincidence, because when I'd seen him on stage I'd had the thought that the whole thing was like a "meat market." It had also reminded me of ancient Rome, with slaves being auctioned off. I wondered if the gala was really about raising money or if it was a symbolic enactment of the Oasians' devotion to "Truth"—or to their Emperor.

I talked to an Israeli man afterwards and he admitted that he hadn't wanted to come to the event. He said the whole thing seemed weird to him. When I agreed, he backpedaled by saying that it wasn't de Ruiter's idea, that he just "went along with it." One person had an idea and then others took it up, he said, and that created "a movement." His reasoning sounded flimsy to me and I replied that John always had the final say about such things. He responded that John liked these kinds of things because they "undid structures," by which I suppose he meant they confounded expectations. (He seemed to be implying that the crass commercialism of it appealed to de Ruiter; a bit like Osho with his Rolls Royces, perhaps?) I countered by saying that the gala was actually strengthening structures, because it was extending de Ruiter's empire. His response was that it was to do with integrating the spiritual with the worldly. It was a fair point, except that few people there seemed to acknowledge how "worldly" the Oasis Empire was. The party line was that it was all for truth, but I already knew that the only way to square that circle was by equating de Ruiter with truth, as his followers did. I wondered if there could be a much deeper integration going on that few of them suspected. Having offered up their belongings and auctioned out their services, the Oasians were throwing everything they had into the truth pot in order to increase de Ruiter's worldly power, for "truth to be established." While we were talking, the man's wife came over and told him to come away from me, referring to me as "that silly man." She already knew I was not part of the team, because of something I had said to her earlier.

I got a ride back with Kali and we had a pleasant chat on the way. She said she'd been sorry when I was shut down at the Birds of Being forum. "Do you have to be stupid to be John's follower?" she asked, somewhat indignantly. She told me that, even though some of them had been there for decades, she didn't know many people in the group who had had any kind of "shift." She had been there thirteen years and still hadn't experienced a shift, she said. She seemed to be reaching out, not quite daring to voice her doubts clearly.

By the time I got back it was around midnight and I felt uneasy, as if I had done something wrong, as if I had betrayed de Ruiter in some way. I spoke to my wife and she pointed out that "defying the father" would naturally feel like the wrong thing to do. Although I had been at least outwardly friendly to de Ruiter, there was definitely some unrecognized hostility there. I knew he must have noticed it, because I had. It was as if I had sent a message to him: "I don't recognize your authority anymore, and right now you're an obstacle on my path." It was true, in a way. He had become an obstacle to my individuation. The only way to get past that obstacle had been to face it head on.

Part Five: Don't Ever Buy Nothing from a Man Named Truth

Candy's Story

"He's not the Messiah. He's a very naughty boy!"
—*Life of Brian*

The following day I called Bob Emmerzael on the telephone, having found his number online a week earlier. I waited until Sunday to increase the chances of catching him at home. He picked up and I introduced myself and told him I was writing a book about de Ruiter. I talked for several minutes while Bob listened silently; my heart was beating fast and I was short of breath. Bob seemed open and friendly, and eventually I relaxed. Our conversation lasted about half an hour but Bob didn't say much. He asked me about myself and I began to feel hopeful that he would be willing to talk. I gave him a condensed history of my life, leaving out the period when I'd believed I was one of "the two witnesses" described in Revelation, and later on when I'd fancied I was the One. Emmerzael said that he wasn't interested in cooperating with an "exposé." He informed me that he had left de Ruiter around seven years before and that they hadn't been in communication since then. He said that leaving had been his "initiation," and that he'd left because he didn't feel the direction de Ruiter was going in was "right for him" (Bob). Very tentatively, I asked if it was only because de Ruiter's change in direction wasn't right for him, rather than it not being right for de Ruiter. After a pause Bob replied, "No, I don't think I would put it that benignly." I waited for about thirty seconds and then Emmerzael said that he didn't want to say any more. He gave me his email address and I thanked him for his time and hung up. The conversation made a strong impression.

The next day I took a bus to meet with Hal Dallmann and spent some time traipsing through the icy backstreets before I found his house. When I arrived, Hal was out of sight and his wife, Candy, seemed surprised by my arrival. Hal emerged from the living room looking dazed and I wondered if I'd woken him up. He had a gray beard and he was overweight. He led me into a little office while his wife stayed with another woman. I asked if it was okay to record our conversation and he agreed. After our talk, we moved to the other room and sat at the kitchen table with Candy and the other woman, who apparently knew a lot about de Ruiter and wasn't deterred when I said that we would be discussing some "sensitive material." Candy sat opposite me. I talked for a while about my experiences with de Ruiter and why I was writing the book. Candy was especially curious to hear how I had fallen under de Ruiter's spell and how he did what he did. I asked her if I could record our conversation but she was against it, so I took notes instead. Candy was probably in her fifties, but she was fresh-faced and attractive, with clear blue eyes and a warm laugh. She struck me as a sincere person and I didn't get the impression that she was bitter about the experiences she was describing, though she obviously thought poorly of de Ruiter.

She described how she had been through a period of crisis in the year or two leading up to 1986, when de Ruiter first arrived at Bethlehem. She had been very "vulnerable," she said, when de Ruiter approached her and told her there was something he knew about her that he wanted to share with her. He was offering "some kind of healing," she said, and since she felt in need of healing she agreed. She and Hal met up with de Ruiter in one of the offices, but de Ruiter wanted to see Candy alone. Candy was wary at first but Hal reassured her. De Ruiter took Candy down into the church basement, where apparently Rousu had a larger office. He sat opposite her and began to speak. With little or no preamble, Candy said, de Ruiter "virtually told me I was a whore."

At the time, Candy had an adopted daughter who was "on the streets" (I presumed she meant soliciting, though she didn't spell it out), so when she heard de Ruiter's accusation, she immediately felt responsible. On the other hand, she assured me that she had always been faithful to her husband and never even looked at other men. When she told de Ruiter the same thing, he told her that her goodness was "a cover up for [her] harlotry." She had "the heart of a harlot," he said.

Candy was extremely upset and over the following days she underwent a crisis of faith and experienced "anger and hatred towards God." She described it as being "under the oppression" of John. It was only when de Ruiter accused her husband of something of which she knew he was innocent that she "came to her senses." Once she experienced righteous anger on her husband's behalf, she realized, "who does [de Ruiter] think he is?" In the meantime, she had told Hal what de Ruiter had said, and he went to the elders and complained. They believed this was the reason de Ruiter was asked to leave the church (or at least a contributing factor). If the Dallmanns' account was accurate, it was possible that, when de Ruiter leveled charges at Dallmann and spoke with Reeder about Dallmann, it was with the aim of strengthening his own position at the church. That was one interpretation, at least, but it was far from clear, especially since no one seemed to remember the exact sequence of events.

Candy described how she would "feel guilty when John preached." "He would lay guilt on you," she said, "make you feel guilty about yourself, and he was the one who would lead you *out of yourself*." It was an odd choice of phrase. When I made a comment about how de Ruiter might have been corrupted over time, she replied that he had been corrupt from the beginning. Predictably, Candy then said that de Ruiter had "a whole horde of evil spirits" and Hal concurred.* I found myself taking their statements more seriously than I would have in the past. I was in an odd position, because in the past I had been judged by small-minded Christians and branded as a "witch" or sorcerer, and my response had been only contempt. Now I found myself sympathizing with the Christian point of view!

Candy's account seemed like a minor incident, but the context (it happened at the major turning point in de Ruiter's career as a spiritual leader) suggested otherwise. Candy described John as "laying guilt on people and *being the one to take them out of themselves.*" Maybe that was still his modus operandi as a "non-dualist" teacher and guru? My experience had certainly been similar: I had felt more acutely than ever my "uncleanness" and lack of "straightness" as a result of taking on de Ruiter's teachings, and I had seen him as the way "out" of my "sinful" state of "sovereignty." I was also beginning to suspect that—as with most men—de Ruiter's attitude to women was a key to understanding him. Reeder—who had been very fond of Joyce—told me he had seen de Ruiter treating her very badly, bullying her and so forth, and he seemed to think that it was indicative of his treatment of women overall.

Candy had been very well thought of at Bethlehem, and as both a "minstrel" preacher and a young and beautiful woman, she had a powerful influence on the congregation—perhaps especially the men. De Ruiter's closest ally in the church, Don Rousu, had allegedly become romantically infatuated with her around at that time, and there was some suggestion that she had been mentioned in some apocryphal prophecy about a "light-

---

* Dallmann mentioned a curious detail: John used to listen to Bible tapes speeded up, believing he could absorb the information even when the words were unintelligible.

haired woman minstrel who would lead him [Rousu] astray." It's possible de Ruiter felt threatened by Candy, and hence a need to degrade her. According to Reeder, many of the other women at Bethlehem were practicing direct revelation at that time, and direct revelation was *de Ruiter's specialty*. Allegedly, de Ruiter not only disparaged Candy, he cast aspersions on all the women there by stating that only one of them (Sandra Budinsky) was "clean." When I asked Candy about de Ruiter's view of women, she said it was "disgusting." Yet he was counseling women at the church, even though the accepted rule was for male preachers to counsel men and for women to counsel women. So how did that happen? I left the Dallmanns' with more questions than I'd arrived with.

Later that same day, I took the gumshoe initiative and paid an impromptu visit to Benita's house. It was on the outskirts of town and it took three buses to get there. Having tramped through several feet of snow in my sandals I eventually found the house and rang the doorbell. A fit-looking teenage boy with blonde hair opened the door. It was Benita's son, Felix, whom I'd read about in the affidavit. He was friendly and when I explained what I was there for, he said he was sure his mother would want to talk to me. She wasn't home, however, and he didn't expect her any time soon. I asked for a telephone number and after some hesitation he gave me his cell number and said I could call him later, once he'd told Benita about me. He asked if my book was going to be positive or negative and I told him it would be the truth. "So probably pretty negative then," he said. He said then that he considered de Ruiter to be a conman, adding that he had spent time with him growing up and that he liked him. He called him a "manly guy" and indicated that they had done the usual father-son stuff together. He was sorry that his mother and his grandparents had "wasted ten years of their lives on this guy." I tried to get him to talk about his experiences but he obviously didn't feel comfortable so I gave him my number and email, thanked him and left.

When I called a few hours later, Felix was cool and sounded suspicious. He said his mother didn't want to talk to me and when I asked if she would at least give me her reasons, he said, "What's in it for her?" He said that I was obviously getting money to write this book, so I set him straight about that. I told him that it might be in everyone's interests to get to the truth about de Ruiter, but I knew I was wasting my breath. Felix was not just cagey, he was hostile, presumably because of whatever Benita had said to him. I guessed she was angry I had shown up at her house uninvited and spoken to her son. I felt doubly deflated, because a couple of hours before that, I had received an email from Bob with a single line, stating that he was not interested in talking to me.

The next day was my last day in "Demontown," and I went back to Queen's Bench and managed to get the details of the new case against de Ruiter. Apparently Benita, undeterred at having her previous case thrown out by the judge as being "in poor taste," and at having her appeal denied, had armored up and launched a new attack. Her charges against de Ruiter this time were "oppressive, prejudicial and unfair conduct which includes, but is not limited to, departure from proper accounting principles, failing to file and manage the company, failing to file annual returns, failing to account, failing to advise, failing to have annual meeting and engaging in conduct not authorized by the shareholders." This time she was asking for $3.5 million in damages or a share in the property (not including minerals), $2 million in "punitive damages," and an "injunction against defendant enjoining him from aggrieved conduct" (whatever that meant). At the very least, the documents established roughly what de Ruiter's estate was worth: somewhere in the ballpark of

$5.5 million. That begged one more question: why had Oasis needed to mount a gala auction to raise a measly $50,000?

That was my last task in Edmonton. The trip had proved both a success and a failure on various levels, pretty much exactly as I had expected. I had paid around $1000 basically to look de Ruiter in the eye, tell him what I was doing, and say, "Do what's right." It seemed like a fair deal.

A Thorn in His Side

(Brian:) "I'm not the Messiah! Will you please listen? I am not the Messiah, do you understand? Honestly!"
"Only the true Messiah denies His divinity."
(Brian:) "What? Well, what sort of chance does that give me? All right! I am the Messiah!"
"He is! He is the Messiah!"
(Brian:) "Now, fuck off!"
"How shall we fuck off, O Lord?"
—*Life of Brian*

Having completed a first draft of the book in early 2011, I put it aside, uncertain about the implications of publishing it. Despite everything, I still hadn't reached a satisfactory understanding of de Ruiter. Maybe I never would. A couple of months went by and I sent out a proposal to a few publishers. I received several rejections, and for a short while I thought I wouldn't publish. Then a few minor incidents convinced me it would be worthwhile, and I started looking into self-publishing. I went over the manuscript and reworked it, and got to revisit my experiences one more time. I was struck by how I still found myself swinging back and forth between appreciating de Ruiter, and thinking of him with that same underlayer of admiration, possibly affection, and viewing him as a corrupt and dangerous individual. It wasn't simply that I couldn't make my mind up. It was as if I was literally in two minds.

I read through my own writings and the accumulative evidence overwhelmed all my doubts and I felt secure in the knowledge of what de Ruiter was. But as soon as I stopped looking at that evidence, the old perspective started to creep back, a devil whispering in my ear, trying to convince me that I needed to look again, look deeper, that John was good and true and none of the evidence mattered. It was exactly the kind of "reasoning" his followers used, and although it no longer worked for me, it was still going on internally. I was like a person in love who couldn't accept evidence of infidelity. To whatever degree, I was still afflicted. I was the lover spurned. After preparing the manuscript, I abandoned plans to publish. It wasn't time.

Candy had said that de Ruiter put her "under the oppression," made her feel guilty for *who she was* and then let it be known that *he was the one* who would lead her *out of herself*. ("I am the door, the way, the light.") In Candy's case, de Ruiter knew her weak spot and targeted it, bringing about the corresponding crisis for her. Conviction of sin creates guilt or an awareness of existing guilt, and that paves the way (prepares the "mark") for receiving a way out. It is the oldest spiritual-political game there is: Problem-Reaction-Solution. The tactic backfired on de Ruiter, however, and he wound up getting expelled from Bethlehem. When he left, he took with him a group of followers who *did* come to see him as the way, the truth, and the light, and who were willing to enter into the door that he was opening to gain respite from their guilt-wracked selves. They were all Christians, and this was the same period in which de Ruiter informed Joyce he was the Messiah. The net result was something that distinctly resembled a man assuming the role of

Christ for some very desperate people, placing them in perpetual service—or psychic servitude—to his person.

*

On the one hand, de Ruiter has created a great deal of mystery about what enlightenment actually is; he has talked about repeated "deaths" and a never-ending "cost," and so on. On the other hand, he has made it clear that, whatever it is, enlightenment *is not for everyone*. It is "only for those who are tenderly okay with endless suffering." In his online bio, de Ruiter describes the two-year period prior to his final awakening as "a state of what seemed to me to be never-ending pain." Yet, in a 2012 interview, he said, "I didn't have anything of the suffering or pain or difficulty. Things just opened up very unexpectedly."[*] Minor discrepancies in de Ruiter's story or teaching can be overlooked, but this is hardly minor, so why the drastic change of tune? On other occasions (for example on the tape "Bob's Story," already quoted) he has stated that he only became enlightened due to the purity and cleanness of his heart, and to his willingness to surrender and pay the price. Enlightenment, for de Ruiter, *has* to be earned. To all appearances, de Ruiter's system is a reward and punishment system—just like Christianity.

De Ruiter has said, "If you want to know where you're at, look around you." It's the tenet of existential psychology as well as mysticism, so what happens if we apply it to de Ruiter? Since we can't look inside his mind to find out where he is at, if we look around him, what do we see? If de Ruiter truly believes he

---

[*] 6:50 minute mark.
http://www.youtube.com/watch?v=qkqKmpzczjo&list=PL520C86D59C00F79A

is a Messianic stream of pure goodness, and that his devoted followers have got it right, shouldn't his outer life reflect that?

Whether de Ruiter is consciously allowing the darker aspects of his (and the collective) psyche to materialize, through his action and inaction and through the Frankenstein's monster that is Oasis, or whether he is truly possessed by that darkness, the end result is the same. And in either case, it will all come out in the wash of John's personal Armageddon.

Throughout the process of finding (and eventually exposing) the flaws in de Ruiter's edifice, one thought has continued to play around in the back of my mind: *I wanted to help him.* Maybe it was only because that would be the final, uncontestable proof I was his equal, and even the better man. But there was also genuine compassion, even if only for moments at a time. As de Ruiter self-inflated on the ether of his archetypal calling, his avatar-sphere moved inevitably into the path of thorns, and I *was* those thorns. I was the horns he had tried to surgically remove and the tail he kept tucked away inside his tailor-made trousers. Tenderness and tact combined with ruthless honesty, I was only telling my story, and he was the false hero inevitably revealed as the heavy to restore balance in my own psyche. After that, he became what he always was: a supporting character who temporarily succeeded in stealing my thunder.

By wanting to be like de Ruiter—most especially by believing it was what my wife wanted in a man—it was inevitable I'd wind up competing with him. Whatever test John represented to me—a test not of faith but of knowledge and discernment—and however close a call it was, I can now say without hesitation that, by knowing him, I gained a stronger sense of my own truth. Knowing him and falling prey to the illusion he generated—the illusion of spiritual superiority—was a unique opportunity for me. I am able to say that, now I have passed through the disillusionment of seeing his humanness. As long as I saw de Ruiter as a god—or a superior man—I remained lost inside my own infantile projections of the father I never had. The moment I saw he was just a man like myself, I came of age. I couldn't have done it without him; and yet, the final realization, paradoxically, is that I never needed him, or *anyone*, to define my reality. The greatest truth John taught me was that he was, for me, untruth, because any truth not sourced within myself is only a shadow of truth.

Part Six
Coming into the Now

"It's extraordinary to consider that the mystique of Roshi's oshos may have been built on their ability to mystify the obvious and pardon the unpardonable—a skill easily confused, it seems, with the skill of describing, as zen longs to, the indescribable."
—Matthew Remski

"It is obvious, therefore, that in order to be effective a doctrine must not be understood, but has to be believed in. We can be absolutely certain only about things we do not understand."
—Eric Hoffer, *The True Believer*

"Hell Proofing will take us to the brink of insanity."
—Oasis member

Meeting Machiavelli (2013 update)

On the night of August 8th 2011, I had one more in a long series of significant dreams about John de Ruiter. By that time, I was living with my cat in Guatemala, having separated (temporarily, as it happened) from my wife partially due to my efforts to uncover the truth about de Ruiter. I had finished the initial draft of this book, and after several fruitless attempts to find a publisher, I had filed it away and pretty much put the whole thing behind me. Or so I thought.

In the dream, de Ruiter was holding a meeting inside a large stadium. He began by giving an almost superhuman demonstration of his physical grace by moving a bunch of cups and plates that were on the stage using a single, seemingly impossible movement of his arm. A couple was sat in the Chair to speak to him, a sort of "professor" and his wife. They were madly in love, both with each other and with John, and they started kissing passionately in front of him. I could see by observing his facial expressions that the "professor" was quite deranged. Via some kind of deductive process, I was able to ascertain that his derangement was a direct result of exposure to de Ruiter's teachings. De Ruiter was either oblivious to this fact or simply indifferent.

The next segment of the dream entailed my discovering (via the input of a woman in the group) that de Ruiter had drawn a large circle around the gathering and was drawing people's energy to the very outer edge or circumference of the circle. He was then able to siphon their life-force through an opening in the circumference of that circle, a bit like drinking from a coconut with a straw.

In the final and most disturbing part of the dream, I saw the unhinged "professor" entering a castle. He had been given a mission by de Ruiter to locate some rare animal part (something like a pig's bladder). In fact, this was just a ruse, a fool's errand designed to get rid of the professor once and for all because, due to his derangement, he had become a liability to Oasis: living evidence of the harmful effects of de Ruiter's teachings. The professor entered the castle and just kept on going until he walked all the way out the other side, off the edge of a cliff, and into the ocean.

I heard and saw de Ruiter conferring with his oldest son, Nicolas. "What a dumb motherfucker," he said, and then laughed diabolically, like a B-movie villain. I was astonished to see his dark side so palpably and undeniably expressing itself. All his softness and gentleness was revealed in an instant to be nothing but a cloak for deep malevolence. Even though this was exactly what I'd suspected, I could hardly believe my eyes and ears.

The dream then became less of a dream and more of a kind of psychic state. I was aware of eavesdropping on a very secret conversation and of the danger implicit in doing so. It was as if I was present in some ghostly, disembodied form. I pictured myself walking inside the castle, ahead of de Ruiter and son; at the same time I knew I mustn't materialize enough to be visible to them or the gig would be up. In order for de Ruiter not to be alerted to my presence, I had to remain mostly in another dream—and this other dream was playing in the background, all but drowning out de Ruiter's words. Even so, I was able to hear them by an act of intense concentration.

His son congratulated de Ruiter on having successfully destroyed the professor. John said, "But there is one who will not be prevented." I knew immediately (even before he said it) that he was talking about me, and I felt a thrill of danger, but also of specialness. Finally, I was being acknowledged as different from all the rest!

With his words, de Ruiter seemed also to be acknowledging that he would not be able to prevent me from exposing him. It was almost as if he was admitting defeat ahead of time.

"He will not be bought," he said. "He will not even be moved by the flow of kindness."

I understood by this last that I wouldn't be swayed or placated by John's apparent (or even genuine) "goodness." As long as there was even a tiny element of corruption in what he was doing, it would be that which I would zero in on. I knew this was true, and I had no problem with it. I did not see my implacability as unkindness.

*

Two more years passed (2013) before I returned to the manuscript, ostensibly to get it into shape and make it available, if only to get it off my hands. Since it no longer mattered much to me either way, I reasoned that I was sufficiently over my "issues" to make the judgment call. I pared down the book to a little over half its original length, jettisoning some personal material and a whole lot of psychological/occult theories that were too speculative by half. Going over the text one more time, perhaps the strongest feeling it stirred was one of distaste and discomfort—not for de Ruiter but for the job of mapping his inconsistencies and failings as ruthlessly as I could. Halfway through, I realized that, in a strange way, and despite all his apparent attempts at concealment, obfuscation, and mystification, de Ruiter was something of a sitting duck for my pen. He was like the emperor in the children's story, making my job, perhaps, as simple and straightforward as pointing guilelessly at what no one else could admit to seeing.

My first ever memory of my father is an archetypal one, like something out of the Old Testament: him lying naked on the bedroom floor, passed out from drunkenness. It's a snapshot of a whole forgotten narrative, a picture that tells a thousand stories—but also, just one. My father was not an upright man; he was painfully exposed in his weakness, though not by choice. Perhaps the same is true of de Ruiter?

For me to "expose" the man I once saw as the greatest and purest example of manhood I ever knew is no mean feat, and it is also a thankless task. There will be no kudos or congratulations, and almost certainly no financial compensations (I could even wind up getting sued by Oasis). The only conceivable reason to do it is because I have to. I have to testify to what these eyes have seen, the original wound that wounded me, in the very deepest part of me, at the core of my masculinity. To say I'm sorry wouldn't be right, and yet I *am* sorry, not to have written this, but that it was necessary to do so. This work is filled with sorrow. It's about a man of sorrows who was born at the wrong time and who couldn't admit it, who built an edifice out of nostalgia for a past he never knew, and who today rules over an empire of dreams.

If that man is a distant echo of my own father(s), and if I am the last living remnant of him, then the picture I have drawn of de Ruiter's image is like a fun-house mirror image of myself, the way my life might have gone, or still might, without the awareness, insight, and guidance which "injured others" like de Ruiter and my father provided me with. At the end of this long journey, now this book is almost done, what can I say with any certainty? What do I *know*?

That whatever I have against de Ruiter, it is nothing compared to what I have in common with him. Maybe they are even the same thing.

Part Six: Coming Into the Now

Wounded Anina

Anina Hund (name truncated at the request of her family) was first reported missing on March 23, 2014. Her disappearance was reported by CBC news as follows:

> The 32-year-old went into work on her day off, but hasn't been seen since. She left behind her phone and ID. Her 2005 blue Toyota Echo is also gone. Her roommate Caroline Hendley reported her missing to police. "It almost feels surreal," Hendley said on Tuesday. "This is not something that happens in real life.".... Hendley said her roommate's disappearance is completely out of character. "Something has really happened to make this happen for her," Hendley said. "This is not something she would have chosen to do. This is not Anina."[1]

Less than two months later, on May 12, Anina's body was found. It was reported by CBC news on May 15.

> The body found near Rocky Mountain House on Monday has been identified as that of Anina Hund, say police. An autopsy completed on Thursday confirmed the identification. EPS detectives say there were no signs of foul play. They are not treating the death as criminal. The body was found by RCMP search teams in a forested area just off the road several kilometers north of where Hund's car was found in March.

It was just over a year after the news broke that I first heard about the incident, via one of the sources I had contacted while first working on this book, Phil Stretch. Phil emailed me with the principal facts around the case and sent a PDF of a letter that had been distributed by Anina's family the previous month, which includes the following passage:

> [W]hen the search for Anina began, probably two days after she went missing, John called Anina's Mum on her mobile—in the middle of the night. John had just travelled overseas to the Netherlands. He spoke very fast and seemed alarmed, and repeated several times insistently that it was a crime. We were astonished at this decisive declaration and tone. Later we tried to make contact with John again, knowing that she was always in close contact with him and that emotionally and spiritually he would be the first to know what would have been going on with her before she disappeared, or even after. Anina admired John and lived her entire life to follow him, and trusted him to 100% [sic]. She did not take counsel on important life issues from anyone but him, which she communicated to him and others openly. The direction she took in all the steps of her life were guided directly by his words.

Phil also pointed me to the College of Integrated Philosophy's official response:

> A year ago we all learned of the passing of our friend Anina Hund. She was an intelligent, thoughtful and caring person, who was deeply loved by everyone at The College of Integrated Philosophy. Recently, some individuals circulated speculation about Anina, relying on selective extracts from her diary. Several of Anina's close friends have voluntarily come forward with the facts pertaining to Anina's diary extracts. These facts are that Anina's writings describe nothing

other than waking dreams and visions. She described these visions to her friends during the last year of her life. The information given by Anina's friends corrects the misleading conclusions made in the letter supposedly composed by the Hund family. Out of respect for Anina's memory, and the others affected, everyone is encouraged to ignore this false speculation. The truth is consistent with what we always knew about Anina.

This "disclaimer" was also posted at Birds of Being on April 29, 2015, under the title of "Clarifying recent events and remembering Anina." The first response was a couple of lines from "God" (my source for the affidavit) about suicide, after which a woman named Vistara wrote this:

> I am concerned that Anina is being made to appear delusional and/or unstable in her ability to discern dream or vision from reality and she is not here to give her own voice to the events (or "facts") that led to her suicide. I am also concerned that—according to the Oasis statement—friends of Anina are coming forward to reinforce this characterization. I'm sure that there are many who consider themselves to have been a friend of Anina, but at least in my conversations with those I know were her close friends, the image that stands out is of a woman who prized clarity and who was known to process difficulties privately but who has also shared her struggles with her closest friends (and with John). None of the folks I've spoken to recall that she was disturbed by "waking dreams." The alleged excerpts from Anina's diary, if they do point to a real event that she was struggling to make sense of, are very troubling. If John did have a physical-sexual

encounter with Anina before she died, that is very troubling for a number of reasons, least of which—even if it was inadvertent—is putting a devoted follower into the position of having to sort out an extremely complex event without being able to share details with/gain counsel from close friends (for obvious reasons); most problematic being the abuse of power such an act involves and the possible subsequent concealment of it.

The excerpt from Anina's diary in its entirety was provided to me by Anina's sister Anna in 2017:

2 March 2014

I need to write down my clarity to give knowing momentum, to move in the right perspective and to hold to it. I need to take care in my conclusions not to mix levels. John showed me what sexuality is for.

. . . .

John said in the last meeting before he left and before we moved in sexuality together that it's to stay in what we know, in our heart, not to separate because of pain or pleasure. It was like a stretch to stay in the knowing while having sexual pleasure. It went on for hours. I think I did stay clean in it, I was noticing the depth while the physical experience was going on. And it's touching on patterns, on beliefs that it is not OK to have sexual experiences. I have thought that being clean means not having sexual experience, while this showed me that sexual pleasure can be clean.

Then the focus is not on the experience, not on being physically satisfied, that's a tightness push and grab. The focus is on the deeper levels loving as they move as pleasure in the body and touch sexuality.

When it moved to an orgasm, at the point of physical release it was all still and full of meaning. It was like meaning still, not moving. I was receiving and liking it, I was gone in it. The satisfaction was in meaning.

He taught me to stay with moving as a being in sexual pleasure. He also answered my questions I shared with him about what sexuality is for.

That it doesn't suit my desire to have a partner is not the point. I also can't draw the conclusion that I have such a relationship with John, that I will continue to make love with him. I wondered whether he just can't be contained to one relationship, whether he makes love with people while he is on the other side of the world. What he did in no way jeopardized his marriage. It is not personal. I know it is OK, not wrong. Don't draw conclusions in yourself. If you stay open the experience will move right through you without anything being held on to for yourself. Part of me wonders why John entrusted such teaching to me when it is likely to have me spinning. But I am able to not spin. I am able to be clear. He said I am really learning. Don't mix levels. With John you will never have less difficulty. He will always give you more. There's nothing in it for you, you can't have anything from it, you can't own it, have it for yourself or keep it.

Don't worry about the future. Just respond to what is opening now.

I certainly have an interesting life.

Stay clear, keep your hands off it, don't draw conclusions, don't think about it or worry. You are able to not take that awakening into yourself. If I experience lack in my life it is not due to any circumstance. It is because I am not being all the meaning I have awakened to. I need to be all that I have awakened to. There's only one way and that is

> forward, further in, deeper. Open, keep opening and you will be more. I have stripped my life of distraction (apart from skiing) and now I feel empty and really see what I have been all along—lesser meaning, using life to fill it with less. When all the distractions come to an end and you realize how dull you've been. Live for everything you have awakened to. Skiing was nice, but also empty and dull because I was not being what had opened that night.

On May 14, 2015, the College of Integrated Philosophy posted an hour-long recording of a meeting with de Ruiter and members of his group to discuss the matter (edited).[2] Despite a feeling of irritation and disgust at having to re-immerse myself in the Oasis-pool, I listened to it three times in 2015, in order to try and adopt a balanced and impartial view of the latest (at that time) de Ruiter scandal.

The aim of the meeting/recording seems to have been to contain a potentially explosive situation. The situation in question was the death of one of de Ruiter's group and the subsequent actions of her family, who were at that time disseminating material highly suggestive of unethical, possibly illicit, behavior on de Ruiter's part, as being relevant to, if not instrumental in, Anina's death. Clearly de Ruiter had both a responsibility to address these matters and a personal interest in doing so. One of the things I listened out for (as always) was which of these (responsibility to the group vs. personal interest) the meeting seemed to be most serving.

As always with John, it was far from easy to determine the meaning, much less the intent, of much of what was said. He categorically denied any physical relationship between him and Anina (21 minute mark); he also implicitly denied calling up her parents in the middle of the night (68 mins), though the subject isn't ever raised by any of the attendees. (In 2017, Anna told me that de Ruiter didn't call them in the middle of the night after all, but in late evening, and that because of their grief and exhaustion they had believed the time to have been later than it was.)

Other significant points raised at the 2015 meeting are as follows. Towards the start, de Ruiter is asked about trust. A woman refers back to the period in 1999 when the truth came out about his affair with the von Sass sisters and his having lied to Joyce. She wants to be reassured. John tells her that, when the "self" hears things it doesn't like, it naturally moves towards distrust. He warns against drawing conclusions that aren't backed by justified reasons. The woman wants to know what would be a justified reason for mistrust. He responds (at the 10-minute mark):

> Something that's based on fact and also is in direct connection to all of the direct knowledge that you have, concerning your relationship with all of the direct knowledge that you have with me and concerning me; and if it's, if the pointing of mistrust separates you from that direct knowledge, then you're no longer being informed, because the most important information in you is being separated from, and the surface information that relates to how you feel in yourself is being adhered to.

The woman responds with, "I trust you, I trust you, I trust you absolutely, and I know your trustworthiness." She then asks him if he was untrustworthy in any way in the past (1999). De Ruiter evades the question by asking the woman what her framework for trustworthiness is. He then presents the possibility that behavior which she would consider untrustworthy "could be true" (i.e., a movement of truth), but that she would be unable to get past her mental and emotional resistance to see that.

De Ruiter then uses the analogy of being *lost in the wilderness* and compares the immense pressure of the situation to her current state of not knowing what to believe. He says that thinking clearly is impossible in such a situation, and that the best thing to do is to "take a little snooze."

At the 25-minute mark he says: "I am carrying everything. I really know and understand where I am going in all of this, and how this is all unfolding in our community."

A bit later he says: "My first responsibility is to everything. When it is to everything, that really changes the level and the flow of information. That changes how I manage the flow of information."

At around 41 minutes, John says, "It is important not to draw a conclusion until you know. And when you do know, *then you must conclude.*"

After this admonition, a young man takes the mic and mentions how, on a walk with Anina, she confided in him that John "had showed her how to make love." His reason for bringing it up is apparently to point out that she did not seem to be having any difficulty with the experience.

De Ruiter tells him, "That requires some qualification," which evokes laughter from the group. The young man replies that all he has is the context, but that to him it was clear that Anina *was not speaking literally.*

"OK," de Ruiter says. "You said that it was clear to you that what she said wasn't physical and literal, that it wasn't physically with me and literally with me."

"Exactly," the young man says.

De Ruiter says "OK" again, apparently satisfied, and the exchange ends there.

Next up a woman says the following:

"What I'm really getting is that, even while you've really clarified some things with what, um, Joel was saying, and we have already heard this anyway, but, while that's a conclusion *that's based on fact so now we must conclude*, prior to that . . . . I needed to make room for being with the possibility that it could be true."

At this point, and at the risk of leading the reader, I want to point out that de Ruiter's denial of having had a physical relationship with Anina, combined with Joel's assumption[*] of the same (which had to be coaxed out of him), are very far from equating with facts, and neither would be admissible in court as anything but hearsay. Admittedly, this meeting is not a trial; but even so, if de Ruiter is really interested in keeping his flock focused on *what they know*, oughtn't he to have corrected the woman's assumption at this point?

Instead, de Ruiter lets her continue speaking for a time and then offers a psychological challenge. The gist of it seems to be that, separate from the question of whether or not there is any truth in the idea of de Ruiter having sex with Anina before she died (his categorical denial of which the woman accepts *as fact*), is it possible, he asks, for that scenario to be "of truth"—i.e., sanctioned by the truth. After some coaching, the woman admits that it *is* possible, that this scenario could be a match for what she knows of John (even though she staunchly rejects such an idea), and also be "of truth," i.e., right and good.

"If the real, in-truth possibility exists," he tells her, "you cannot overrule it." (Note that John is not discouraging anyone present from overruling the real, in-truth possibility that he *did* have sex with Anina and is lying about it, on the contrary. But he

---

[*] The previous speaker was the first male voice on the recording, so it's probably safe to presume he is "Joel."

is encouraging them to allow for the possibility that there might be goodness there *if* he had done so.)

The woman responds that she can allow that it might be true and that there might also be "a goodness in that."

"Is it possible for a being of truth to be that way," de Ruiter asks, without you using history to inform you?"

De Ruiter's approach here is curious. On the one hand, he is explicitly dismissing Anina's accounts of having had sexual relations with him as "dream and vision," and allowing his followers to take that denial as established fact. At the same time, he is encouraging them to seek a place in them which *can* admit the possibility it really happened but also admit that it could be true and good—i.e., no reason to mistrust him. Yet he omits to mention that, if it *were* true, it would also mean he had lied about it and was lying about it *right there and then*. This is *an entirely separate* issue from that of a hypothetical sexual dalliance with one of his followers. Really, it is just as if he is asking: can you accept that I am lying to your face now, and still consider me good and true? And the answer he gets is yes!

From de Ruiter's performance with Joyce and his followers back in 1999, it's clear that he plays fast and loose with the facts when it comes to serving what he insists is *a higher level of truth*. Facts in de Ruiter's world shift and mutate according to need, whether his own or those of his group (or whoever he is talking to). It's not all that hard to imagine him changing his tune at a later date—if facts surface that oblige him to—and professing that his categorical denial of having had sex with Anina was what the truth moved him to say *at that time*, because of the delicacy of the situation, and that now he is being moved to reveal deeper levels of what was moving through the group at that time, now they are ready to hear it.

It's as if de Ruiter is giving *two versions* of events: first an overt denial for those who aren't ready for the full truth so they can keep their shrines intact; secondly, an implicit admission, meant for those who are either already in the know or who are ready *to* know, ready to be complicit with both the sexual liberties taken and the duplicity that surrounds and protects them.

At least, that was my impression, in 2015, and the best way I could square John's circular logic and make something halfway coherent out of a tangle of contradictory signals. In possible support of this reading, a couple of posts from the Birds of Being thread may be worth quoting. This is from Kevin A, from May 8, 2015:

> I have come to learn over the past week that there are indeed things that most of us do not know with regard to John. This leads me to wonder how many other things there are, and in all honesty, I find it disturbing. I used to be willing to let it all pass by, being comfortable in resting in what I saw was unquestionable. I am past that point now, and I am willing to know and I want to know in order to be more engaged in and more aligned with my own choice, my own knowing and my own clarity.

And "danny boy" from May 10:

> If John does engage in tantric teachings with students, while that may be difficult to align with inner cultural beliefs and projected ideas about a pure teacher/father figure, it is not inherently wrong in and of itself. It is a profound opportunity to question such things, withholding all judgment and conclusions, but letting it disturb all the inner sediment and observing closely how it all comes to rest in a different order. . . . What I do have as an ongoing

> disturbance is the idea of a teacher or organization concealing events. . . . I haven't yet found a reason to conceal in matters such as this. As a sub note the reason I started following this topic was to read a copy of the letter written by Anina's family. I had contacted Anina's sister to get a copy of the letter that they had sent to people but was told that she can't send it out anymore. Apparently Johns [sic] Lawyer had just warned them that if they continue to share the letter he will take legal action against them.

*

De Ruiter's lawyers did indeed threaten Anina's family with legal action and successfully silenced their attempts to hold John accountable for Anina's death. At the same time, they were discouraged from looking further into the actual cause of it. The mystery around Anina's death is simply this: how and why did she die? Was it accident, suicide, or foul play? And yet it isn't necessarily an either/or question, since it's reasonable to propose a spectrum between suicide and accident that includes semi-accidental suicide, an unconscious death-wish, for example. It's also reasonable, necessary even, to allow for a spectrum between suicide and foul play, such as when someone is driven, seduced, manipulated, or coerced into suicide by the actions of other parties.

Even the law (sometimes) recognizes this: Charles Manson was convicted of murder when he was never placed at the scene of the crime. His influence on the actual perpetrators (his "Family") was seen as great enough for him to bear the burden of responsibility for their actions (though the actual killers weren't considered exempt). Is there such a category under law as "induced suicide"? If not, there probably ought to be. And to begin to address the question of whether Anina's death was accidental, suicide, or the result of foul play, we may first need to allow that it could have been all three, to some degree at least.

According to Anina's family, the police have filed the case away as unsolved. There was no actual inquest into her death and hence there is no official cause of death (besides a reference to hypothermia). At the College of Integrated Philosophy, there was an observable effort to steer people away from the conclusion of suicide. Ostensibly, this was to protect Anina's memory; but it may also have been to protect de Ruiter and the College's reputation and public image. When a follower of a spiritual teacher commits suicide, it reflects poorly on the teacher and his methods and on the community as a whole.

The verdict of accidental death, which the College implied by refuting the possibility of suicide, has come under question due to the fact that Anina's body was found naked. Everyone who knew her said she was well-organised and always well-prepared for winter conditions, and that she would never have set off into the country without the right equipment, much less without her phone and ID (which she left at her work place). The verdict of suicide, on the other hand, has been questioned because Anina did not seem unusually distressed or unhappy in the days leading up to her disappearance. Regarding the first point, this is known about hypothermia:

> Hypothermia can kill at an amazing pace when cold temperatures and strong winds cause the body to lose heat quickly. Shivering starts first in order to produce body heat from the rapid muscular shaking. When the body's temperature drops to or below 35 deg C/95 deg F, dizziness and disorientation kick in, then the shivering stops. The body now only maintains heat around the vital organs—brain, heart and lungs, and shuts down blood circulation to the arms and legs. Heart rate becomes slow, intermittent and weak,

and the blood vessels widen. *This makes a person feel hot and want to remove all their clothes before they finally slip into unconsciousness. Ultimately, the heart stops. Stories are told of climbers being found naked and dead up on a mountain, with their clothes folded neatly a short distance away. This is because the person becomes confused and hot.* Their brain tries to bring order to the scary and unfamiliar situation, although this can be potentially lethal.[3]

So far none of this points to foul play. Yet when de Ruiter called up Anina's family a mere two days after she was last seen, he seemed convinced a crime had been committed. This is how Anna wrote down her impressions soon after the call:

> 25th March 2014, about 9 p.m.: Call from John de Ruiter . . . . He expresses his compassion (without using this word) for our state of being devastated about Anina's disappearance. The fast pace of his speech was astonishing for us, since we experienced that he usually talks extremely slowly during his meetings with the community of followers. . . . I said that we are afraid that Anina may not be living anymore. I communicated that we felt sure that she did not commit suicide, but that we think it's a crime. He immediately agreed with emphasis. He argued that it was noticeable that she had left her purse, mobile phone and coat behind (the coat was new to us). . . . He then reported that he had talked to Anina on Friday evening and that she had appeared well, grounded, emotionally stable and full of light. He repeated that he is convinced that she was in a good condition/frame of mind and that he thus is convinced that she did not commit suicide. He stressed that if she had had thoughts in this direction,

> she would have surely communicated these with him, since she was in regular communication with him. . . . He concluded that even if Anina would be found and it would appear to be suicide, he would not believe it. . . . This telephone call of John evoked many thoughts in us. We were astonished about the fact that John phoned. And we were struck by John's conviction that Anina was dead. He did not appear to give the possibility that she lives, any chance.

Another thing in support of the "foul play" explanation is the fact that, as I also learned via Anna, Anina's car was found completely clean of any fingerprints. I addressed the possibility that Anina might have had the car thoroughly cleaned (if she was preparing to commit suicide) and then worn gloves. Anna assured me that no gloves were found in the car or with the body. She did say she'd been told that apparently cold temperatures can prevent fingerprints because the fat on the fingers is too hard, but she thought it unlikely there wouldn't have been any fingerprints at all, from warmer seasons.

What has become abundantly clear to me while talking to Anna is that, for Anina's family and for those who loved her, it has been extremely difficult to reach closure with her death. To lose a loved one at a young age is hard enough; to not know the circumstances of the death makes acceptance all the harder. Another thing that is I think inescapable is that, at the time she died, Anina's life was deeply involved with John de Ruiter and that many of her most essential beliefs, feelings, and decisions were influenced by that relationship. This doesn't make John to blame for her death, or even necessarily accountable. But it does suggest that her death can only be fully understood within the context of her relationship to John and of what she believed about it, and about him. It's also perfectly reasonable to want to know what transpired between them, both openly and privately, and whether the sexual nature of it was entirely in Anina's mind, whether it had a literal, physical basis, or whether it occurred in some strange twilight zone between the two.

This question becomes much more pressing (and elusive) now de Ruiter has publicly admitted (in 2016) that, due to some mysterious "Calling," his relationships with his followers does sometimes include a sexual component, and that this *has* been going on in secret for many years. He has acknowledged that the effects of "the Calling" on women he is "called" to be sexual with can be highly disruptive to them and cause intense distress. There is also the tacit acknowledgment that the sexual component of "the Calling" might sometimes (or even always) begin at the level of an "energetic" encounter, or what de Ruiter and many of his followers have tried hard to dismiss, in the case of Anina, as "waking visions."

*

Some of the questions that are relevant to understanding Anina's death are as follows:

Was she in a fully physical sexual relationship with John and did he lie about it?

To what degree did this sexual relationship (whether fully physical, energetic, or entirely fantasy) contribute to Anina's state of mind at the time of her disappearance?

Was Anina alone when she drove to the place of her death?

Was she alone when she died?

Was force involved?

Was coercion involved?

Was her death related to de Ruiter's teachings in some way?

Did de Ruiter know about her death at the time it happened or soon after, and if so, how?

Part Six: Coming Into the Now

Anina's family has written a report about Anina's death that includes a passage about her involvement with de Ruiter:

> The family was very skeptical when Anina moved to Edmonton in order to join up with John de Ruiter. On the one hand she seemed to have herself in better hands and she became calmer and could better control her upsets and anger (emotions in general) than before. However, her ability to be spontaneously joyful was quite cut off and weakened. Furthermore, her family noticed that her manner of speech changed oddly. She spoke in exceeding magnitudes of "love" and "sweetness" and "purity of heart." This she accompanied with smiles of a dreamlike seriousness. The family had the impression that she had drifted off into an unrealistic and artificial world. She walked differently. One had the sense that she was floating, that she was aspiring to become light, delicate and soft. Anina wasn't able to explain her strange rapture or ecstasy to the family members and their questions were only answered with statements that included words so strangely formatted that the sense or meaning of them became incomprehensible. Her answers to their questions were lost to them. The family had the impression that due to this, serious conversations were massively distorted because instead of using typical and generally understood language, she exclusively used the same vague and obscure vocabulary which John de Ruiter used. Whenever the family mentioned this to her she would smile and state that they wouldn't be able to understand anyway, as they were not "enlightened." It appeared to Anina's family as though she were simultaneously living in two worlds. . . . Anina had several pictures of John de Ruiter placed around her room and wore a picture of him around her neck in a

locket. Her behavior gave one the impression of her being in love with this person. When she spoke of him she would explain how "sweet" he is and would giggle just as women who are in love generally do. This caused great worries for the family as she normally spoke of him with regard to him being an admirable philosopher and not a lover. In actuality he organized meetings of hundreds of followers in Edmonton and other countries. It was obvious to the family that she was not in a partnership relationship with him and that this would likely not ever be the case. John de Ruiter was at the time divorced and lived openly together with two different women. Later on these women left him and he re-married again. . . . The John de Ruiter group is organized in such a way that it represents a "world unto itself." All of the members have duties to perform and it is expected that they will help in the building or the garden without pay. Anina did all kinds of work; cleaning toilets, helping in the café and working in the office. She took an extra day off work each week in order to help John de Ruiter even more. Meetings with de Ruiter regularly took place two to three times per week and as per Anina's family, cost approximately $10.00. Anina participated in all meetings as do 300-400 other followers. . . . The young woman who was in fact healthy, even though having a slight tendency to a "Rubenesque" figure, suddenly began undertaking radical treatments, primarily in her struggle to lose weight. These injured her quite severely and she began having health issues mainly in her intestinal tract. At one point she was near anorexia.

This report, if accurate, indicates that Anina was suffering from an emotional and psychological pressure to live up to (her idea of) de Ruiter's teachings, even to the point of self-negating, self-harming, or obsessive behavior.

In the final days before publishing this work, Anina's sister, Anna, gave me a list of incidents leading up to Anina's death which she felt may have indicated Anina's state of mind in her final weeks. The list included the following:

- One of the last people to see Anina alive was her house tenant (she owned a house but didn't live there). This was around lunchtime on Saturday, March 22, 2014, and Anina met up with him to extend his rental agreement. He later told Anina's mother that Anina had been unusually giggly, even "giddy."
- On March 21, Anina had made an appointment with members of the Oasis College for 10 a.m. She arrived two and a half hours late, although tardiness was very unusual for Anina.
- The day before, on March 20, Anina phoned her mother. Usually they talked every Saturday, but on the Saturday Anina disappeared (March 22), her mother was travelling to Dresden. On their last conversation, Anina's mother found Anina to be happy, even elated, due to a conversation she'd had with John. Allegedly, John had told Anina about "a new opening in her brain." If true, this is a very significant detail because (as we will see in the next chapter), in 2017, de Ruiter stated publicly that one result of the "Calling" (i.e., his having sex with female students) was that it caused an opening in their brains.
- Based on notes Anina's mother took when she talked to Caroline Hendley (Anina's landlady) soon after Anina disappeared, Caroline said she came home on

Thursday, March 20, at 9 p.m. and, since there was no light on in Anina's room, assumed she was already asleep. Caroline found this strange, as Anina never went to bed that early. "There was something she was working through," she told Anina's mother.

- Caroline told Anina's mother that, a week or more before, after a Friday meeting at Oasis, Anina had come down from her room, sat in front of Caroline in the living room, and gazed at her intensely. Caroline asked Anina if something was troubling her. Anina said she couldn't talk about it. "I just wanted to connect with you," is what she allegedly said, before returning to her room. Caroline then heard Anina sobbing desperately.

Anna's opinion is that this incident may well have occurred on the Friday of February 28, 2014, two days before Anina wrote her diary entry about John showing her what sexuality was for, on Sunday March 2.

Anina's family believes Anina would have risked everything to live up to her convictions (convictions mainly sourced in insights she had via de Ruiter). After reading her diary entries, they felt that her commitment to her values was "stronger than her will to live," that is, if the life was one that didn't live up to her convictions.

Curiously enough, while I was mulling over the Anina mystery, I listened to an interview with Meagen Gibson about the Andrew Cohen documentary, *How I Created a Cult*. In it, Gibson described the rigorous spiritual discipline which Cohen imposed on his followers, at the Foxhollow community in western Massachusetts. She gives an example of a group of women who were failing and desperate, going down to a lake in November and performing their "prostrations" in the icy water, with no one monitoring them for safety. They were in the lake for an hour, she says, until they were turning blue and their teeth were chattering so hard it seemed they would break off. Gibson recalls the testimony of one of the women:

> Then there's this moment when the pain stops and you stop shaking and you're so relieved, and you're actually kind of, like, your thoughts become very calm, and everything becomes very calm. Now in hindsight I realized that's hypothermia, you're actually getting close to being in a lot of danger; but then you think that you're actually breaking through to something. You think you're breaking through some sort of ego mental incapacity or some sort of mental wall that's gonna get you through to this experience that Andrew's been hoping that you're gonna make. They were pulled out of this lake unconscious. . . . They said that they knew when they were doing [it] that it was possible that they could die, but if they died it would only mean that they had failed Andrew, and that they had failed to become this spiritual person that he was asking them to, that it was *their* failure, not the fact that they were being asked to [do this].[4]

While it might be premature to speculate that Anina's death had a similar spiritual motivation behind it, all the evidence points towards something besides ordinary suicide, much less accidental death. Anina's family's report continues:

> In the months before dying Anina told her mother that John de Ruiter often spoke about death. She had spoken personally with de Ruiter about life, before and after death. As she herself reported, he told her that one can achieve more during one's life with respect to awareness and realization but that this

would still be possible after death too. Many months following her demise Anina's family read sentences in her diary that she had written only three weeks before her death, which appeared strange to them.

On 28 January 2014, John de Ruiter's Twitter account tweeted this: "When you lay down your life for what you are after you've died, you're clean." As is typical of John-speak, this powerfully loaded phrase lends itself to more than one interpretation, but it appears to be an admonition to give up your life to "what you are after you've died" in order to be "clean" (free of sin) in life. For someone who views John's words as coming from the mouth of Truth itself, it is a powerful injunction to sacrifice everything in order to be true, to be clean. Laying down her life is exactly what Anina did; and as a result, she literally became what she would be after she died.

Ignorance is Strength: Oasis 2017

The final prompt that led me to release this book came in early 2017, once again via Phil Stretch, who sent me a copy of a statement posted at a private Facebook group by one of John's female followers called Randi Dalgaard Jensen Lee. Lee described being approached by John, with John's wife Leigh Ann present, in a very formal manner, and invited to become John's lover. What follows are excerpts from her statement:

> September 2016. John and Leigh Ann invited me to visit them at their house in Edmonton. I joyfully gave thanks for the invitation and arrived at the house on Saturday the 3 of September at one pm. The three of us sat down, at the coffee table in the living room and

after some time talking about our recent experiences at Nordegg, John said the following. J: "The reason why I have invited you here today, is to tell you that for some years now, the calling has moved me to be with other women sexually and now The calling is moving towards you." The following 3-4 hours, before I left in a taxi, the three of us talked about what had been put on the table. John and Leigh Ann shared with me that they had been surprised, that the calling had moved towards me, since it was the first time, it moved towards a woman that did not live in the group in Edmonton. I was sitting in Johns [sic] living room and my heart was pumping so hard it felt like it would come out of my chest at any moment. At one level I felt confused and on another level it made sense to me that John and specific women could benefit from this particular experience together, to learn particular lessons. I did my best to ask the questions that I felt was [sic] important, to ask in the situation I found myself in. Here is what I remember myself asking. Not necessary in this order.

I asked what John making love to other women is for? Is it connected to the deep and Johns [sic] reference to "building in the deep"? How long had it been taken place? How many women do you have and can I know who they are? How does Leigh Ann feel about it (the question was to Leigh Ann personally) where would it take place and how? Why have you not opened this up to the group in Edmonton and the world? How would it affect my relationship to another man and can I marry again? . . . J: "A little over 3 years ago I put together a committee of people from the group. They know that the calling is moving in this way." John also talked about how our sexual communion was not tantra and that it would change everything and I would be able to embody all of my awaking in this. "The world is not ready for this. People will not understand. I, John, will seem like a cliché. Many in the group in Edmonton [are] not ready for this. Not everyone will understand. You can have a husband again, but he would have to understand, what we are doing and he would have to agree, that I, John, come first in this. If you agree to this, I want you to, write to me how your sexuality moves. In as many details as possible and as often as you can."

John repeated this more than once. I didn't think to ask what the purpose of this is. I was told that if I responded to this, I had to see my doctor and have tests to make sure that I didn't have any sexual diseases. Before I left, John and Leigh Ann said that If anyone asked me directly, about this, *I should not lie directly but be creative with my answers and distract [their] attention on the subject.* . . . The following days I realized that a part of me was in a bit of a shock. I know that John and I are deeply connected. I don't know what I had expected when I got the invitation. Intuitively something felt out of alignment. [Emphasis added.][5]

Randi took some time to think about it and after several days let John and Leigh Ann know that her answer was no. They were surprised and let her know that they were "strongly opposed" to her "being open to others about this issue." Randi remembered being told by John, "Talking to other people about this is not a decent thing to do and you have broken an honor code." Soon after, John began the process of official "disclosure" about his secret sexual congress with female followers over the past years. He thereby confirmed Benita's claims in the affidavit (that he was sleeping with four married women in the group). The form the official disclosure took was in a long interview John did in the Oasis building with his followers present, on March 4 and 6, 2017. The interview was meant to appear spontaneous and in the spirit of inquiry, but allegedly the questions were scripted by Oasis, with de Ruiter's input. Like other meetings, it was filmed and put at his website, viewable for a fee. In the first part, John says the following:

> In my moving with a woman physically and sexually, my reason for that is so completely other than anything to do with this world, anything to do with myself, and also anything to do with what I am as a being. Drawing me right back into the ancient and the bigger picture, in moving that way, physically and sexually with a woman, I'm very directly transmitting what it is I'm responding to, what it is that I'm absorbed completely into, and what it is I'm bringing here. In sexuality, the physical movement, making sexuality physical, for reasons that are completely other than, means that I have to in some way communicate and transmit, convey, from the innermost outwards, what I'm absorbed into, what I come from, and for reasons that are completely other than. Inasmuch as there is response in the woman to what she's resonating with, and knowing within, through whatever levels in her she comprehends, she realizes and comprehends, initiates *an opening in her brain*, all centered in on the resonance of what she knows. Essentially, I'm moving in a way that reproduces what was produced in me through the calling and my response. In the case where this is taken place and she would return to her husband, she is able then to transmit and communicate the same... As she moves toward her husband and responds to

> her husband, she naturally moves all of that depth that she absorbed into, and now of that, she pours, extending the same to her husband. [Emphasis added.]

Translation: John is transmitting some extra-dimensional energy of consciousnesses into the women he has sex with, filling them up with it regardless of how much they are able to process or integrate whatever he is doing, and they are then passing on this transmission bug to their partners (whether or not they know about their wives' involvement with John). When the question of secrecy came up, John's response showed that, while he had developed his dissembling skills since 1999—the last time he really had to "fess up"—his basic line of defense was the same.

> If there's oneness within the self, then what could look like secrecy isn't secrecy because secrecy on the level of the self and from the perspective of the self is duplicitous. Within oneself what is also then on the level of secrecy is the split between the conscious self and the subconscious self. Wishing for the subconscious self to be relegated to a place not seen or experienced because it interferes with our comfort zone; it interferes with our experience of ourselves, our sense of self; it interferes with what we are able to see of ourselves which is just our conscious self, and protect that from everything that's deeper in ourselves, kept secret and not integrated yet. So in that way, anyone who is not really being in the heart is keeping duplicitous secrets, having a shadow side that must not be seen. And if the shadow side breaks through, for whatever reason, there's a serious recovery program to cover all of that up again. Where there is a oneness within the self because awareness is

> being one with what it knows on the level of the heart
> ... the principle of secrecy is over and gone. ... So
> it's really awareness in manifestation within the self,
> oneness taking care of meaning. There what can look
> like a secret holding or secrecy is not secrecy, where
> there is oneness lived within the self, there is no
> secrecy. What's being embodied there is the principal
> of being of openness.

In other words, it only *looks* like secrecy to you because that's all you know; and while *you* are lying and being duplicitous, even when you are telling the truth, *I* am telling the truth even when I am lying, because my heart is pure, and yours isn't.

To this masterpiece of spin, the "interviewer" responded with an even greater piece of thought-stoppage:

> In the context of our group, I've felt over and over
> again that, in a way, the less I know the better
> (*laughter*), because then I am constantly pushed back
> to a level which is not the level of information. If I had
> all the information available to me, I would probably
> use it at the simplest level of myself, because that's
> what my self is used to doing. And then I could readily
> draw conclusions, have opinions and beliefs, based on
> that. But if I don't know the facts in that, then I'm
> returned to what may be a deeper resource or a deeper
> level within myself.

Translation: Ignorance is strength.

*

Some thoughts and questions I had while sifting through the Oasis wreckage in 2017.

Is part of John's M.O. to stop thought by tossing out garbled and non-grammatical sentences?

How long has he been "moving" unto women in secret? Did it really begin with the von Sasses, or does it date further back, perhaps even to the Lutheran days?

Was there always a consistent spiritual rationale for it, or has it been evolving in tandem with the impracticality of concealment?

Sexual initiation and transference is an ancient concept. But while something is transferred, it isn't necessarily something *good.* This concept goes all the way back to Genesis. But what is genuinely being offered, and what is stolen by sleight of snake?

Insofar as the evidence points to it not being "good," what is John transferring? Ancestral poisons?

John offers the Fruit of Ancient Knowing. Nordic ET speak with forked tongue. John also says the "human being" is "the weakest form of all." A tip of the serpent crown for those in the "know"?

What's beneath the surface is always wider and deeper than the point that is sticking out. And the pointiest point here is a dead damsel, found naked in a forest, partially devoured by the Dragon, her distress cruelly ignored.

The key to the disclosures, like everything else John does, is control. Perception is there to be managed. Speech is only ever used to persuade, never simply to express. If there were ever the slightest admission of guilt, or even accountability, from John, the whole crystal maze would shatter in an instant.

The bigger the lie grows, the more fervent the belief becomes. We can expect to see bigger lies, and more fervent belief, as the pressure to conceal the Mirage of Dark Oasis builds.

There's a crucial distinction between going against social conditioning (morality) and going against Truth, even if the first is a slippery slope that eventually leads to the second, as John's trajectory suggests. The quote I am perhaps most dependent on for understanding John is Joyce's:

> There are two different kinds of behavior. One is just his enjoying life: he loves to four-wheel drive, he loves movies, he loves to sleep in. That's just John being free, there's no meaning attached to that. The other is a blatant contradiction to what you would expect, and then there's tremendous meaning attached to it, and that is [that he is] being asked to go against what he knows.

I wonder if John's son Nicolas (who managed to get a hold of an early draft of the book) will zero in on this? It will be telling if he doesn't, just as it is telling that John never addressed Benita's account about battling Satan. If it was completely bogus, which I don't believe, then I suppose ignoring it might be the smart move. But if she just got it "a bit wrong" then it needs explaining exactly how and what the correct interpretation is. Was John ever questioned about it? As far as I know, it was tacitly assumed to be "off limits." Something the birdies were better off staying in ignorance of, as per the Oasis Truth-Ministry's maxim.

At this stage, everything points to a secret teaching that is being revealed like a slow drip via John's covert activities: by his fruit shall ye know him, but only once you have fully ingested it, and it's too late to say no.

I am left in a raw state of apprehension wondering just how deep and dark, and how destructive, John's Secret Life might be in its "defying conditioned ways of being" (Nicolas) and its disregard for "cultural norms" (Ibid.)?

*

A parent often keeps certain knowledge from his children out of a desire to protect them, believing that "ignorance is bliss," or at least that what they don't know won't hurt them. The problem with this reasoning is that—as de Ruiter must be aware—children do know when something is wrong in the home, and withholding information can be a kind of "crazy-making." If, for example, a child's parents are in the midst of a messy divorce, for the child's "benefit" the parents may agree to maintain a pleasant surface relationship and keep the child in the dark. This way, so the reasoning goes, the child can continue to believe that everything is fine, at least until the divorce is finalized. But for whose benefit is this deception? The child cannot fail to be aware, *at some level*, of the discord between the parents. Since it is not being included in the reality—since it is being fobbed off with a false version—whatever discomfort and distress the child experiences, it now lacks the necessary context for *understanding*. The result is that the child can only attribute the distress it feels *to something within itself.*

Members of the Oasis community may have a visceral sense that something is wrong; but since they are not being included in the behind-the-scenes reality, since they are being treated as children who are not ready to know the truth, they have no way to process that awareness or to speak about it openly. Based on my own experience, anyone who does express doubts about de Ruiter or his teachings is perceived as having lost his way and in need of "help." The fault *must* be in them, it cannot possibly be in de Ruiter or the teachings. This will cause a growing rift in the community between those who are starting to question "the official version" and doubt the father's infallibility, and those struggling to maintain the status quo and override, not just the evidence of their senses, but their own *inner* sense—their "knowing"—that something is rotten in Oasis.

It's inevitable that the child will eventually find out about the split, and quite possibly from someone outside the family. How is that child going to feel when it discovers, not only that the parents are splitting up, but that it was never consulted about it? As well as a catastrophic break in the child's reality, there will be an additional sense of betrayal. I'd wager this is what de Ruiter is risking with his own policy of silence. Or is he perhaps counting on it?

*

In April 2017, certain allegations about John's past were posted by "God" (as far as I know, this thread was quickly deleted). In response, one of John's long-time followers, posted about his experience within the Oasis community. He wrote of "the difficulty of pain and the shunning after his divorce from an 'Inner Circle' member," as a result of which "I did lose my sanity for which I am on medication." The person stayed in the group because of their love of John. They gave "permission to the Deep to do in us what is best . . . When this starts it will not make sense and there are no time limits but there will always be just enough light to walk in. Hell Proofing will take us to the brink of insanity." They wound up their comment by comparing life at Oasis to "Border Control. It had the effect of confirming for each of us personally what we are in or not yet a part of."

On October 14 2016, the same person posted on a thread about the infamous Milgram experiment in which volunteers roleplayed being guards and inmates. The experiment allegedly brought out such violence and cruelty in the participants playing guards that it had to be aborted. The follower posted at the thread: "This can happen even amongst us and within our social structures and so called Inner Circle. It is, within the self-deception of being right at others [sic] expense."

The phrase "hell-proofing" used by this follower has now entered the Oasis lexicon. Similar, though not quite the same, is the belief that de Ruiter is making those who are selected for his "Calling" "bomb-proof" by stirring within them every kind of discomfort and distress via his "interventions." Apparently, this sort of "proofing" means being subjected to so many miseries and humiliations that nothing can faze you afterwards. Is this de Ruiter's (via Len?) secret teaching method, to put people through hell so they will be hell-proof on death? If so, it is not a million miles away from the modus operandi of extreme Christian flagellants. De Ruiter's Christian background seems to have led to an appliance of extreme Christian methods combined with equally extreme *anti*-Christian principles (such as an immersion in sin in order to attain grace).

As more and more is revealed about de Ruiter's secret "teaching" methods, his followers would appear to have three choices:

1) to disbelieve the revelations (this becomes impossible if and when de Ruiter himself confirms them)

2) to believe them and face the possibility that de Ruiter is a corrupted source of wisdom. This leads to cognitive dissonance, disillusionment, and the desire to either challenge de Ruiter, and face ostracization, or simply to leave the group.

3) To believe the revelations and find a way to incorporate them into their all-essential belief in the goodness, purity, and truth of John's "Calling."

The third option is in many ways the hardest of all, but at the same time, for those deeply invested in John and the community (and who know too much to dismiss the truth of the allegations), it may be the only one they can bear to consider. Taking this option requires a steadily evolving process of letting go of morality, conscience, cultural conditioning, and a felt sense of right and wrong. This is what is being referred to as "hell-proofing." The question then arises: where is the limit to how far some Oasians will go with this process?*

Historical Precedents for Spiritual Power Abuse

"In my experience, these guys never just have one weakness. The guru who is fucking everyone he can is also lying continually—covering up, covering over, maintaining appearances, saving face. It's not just the women who are violated in the lonely and debasing interviews of sanzen, although that would be bad enough. It's everyone who came to this man for guidance in any matter, because as he's sitting there listening to you pour your heart out about your life and relationships and terrors and practice, he's also busy wondering if he's covered his tracks well enough, or how he's going to score the next piece of ass."
—Matthew Remski

During the above quoted "interview," John introduced an entirely new element to his personal history when he referred to an awakening experience at the age of twelve, during which the sky opened up before him and gave him his "calling" (a relatively

---

* Meanwhile, some voices at Oasis, (a.k.a. the College of Disintegrating Philosophically) claim that de Ruiter has been warning that the end times are coming and encouraging "survival training" in the wild, among other extreme-behavior prescriptions. It's worth remembering that, even in the early days, John used to take men into the bush for "recreational riding" and the like. Jason Gerdes remembers, long before John was a guru, John taking him into the wild and deliberately getting them lost. He also recalls bringing guns along in case of bears and, once they were there, how John began calling for bears. One person who has left the group commented: "This apocalyptic bit hits me because the last tendril I had to break was of exactly this fantasy that somehow had been planted in my psyche (which might have been ripe soil from a catholic upbringing) that John would save me come the breakdown of society."

new buzz word at Oasis). While many Oasians seemed to take this radical act of reinvention without batting an eye, others were becoming increasingly disturbed by John's freestyle, fast-and-loose approach to truth. It has become apparent that, for Oasians, the truth is whatever John says at any given time, even when it contradicts former statements and reveals them to have been lies or concealments. One former follower (Matt) pointed out to me that an ever-changing story about awakening was also characteristic of the Mormon founder Joseph Smith.

> Joseph Smith, the founding prophet of the Church of Jesus Christ of Latter-day Saints, claimed that as a 14-year-old boy he had a vision of God the Father and Jesus Christ. The official account of this first vision found in Mormon Scripture (*Pearl of Great Price, Joseph Smith—History*, 1:14-20) was not recorded by Joseph Smith until 1838, 18 years after the supposed event. However, for years before this, Joseph, and his close associates did talk about his early visionary experiences. These earlier accounts contain significant variations from the official First Vision account.[6]

The article then lists ten different versions of Smith's "awakening" presented in the thirty-two year period between 1827 and 1859 (Smith died in 1844). Of course the parallels with Smith also extend to the practice of polygamy that has always been part of Smith's church, even if it has come into disfavor in more recent times.

Another group with distinct similarities to Oasis is the Agapemonites, or Community of The Son of Man, a Christian sect that existed in England from 1846 to 1956. The name comes from the Greek: *agapemone*, meaning "abode of love," and it was founded by the Reverend Henry Prince in Spaxton,

Somerset. The community took its sexual practices from the theories of various German religious mystics, and its primary object was "the spiritualization of the matrimonial state."[7] The Agapemonites also predicted the imminent return of Jesus Christ and, according to newspaper accounts, Prince's successor, John Hugh Smyth-Pigott, declared himself to be Jesus Christ reincarnate, a.k.a., the Second Coming.

The Agapemone community consisted mostly of wealthy unmarried women, and both Prince and Smyth-Pigott took many "spiritual brides." Later investigations revealed that these "brides" were not solely spiritual and that some even produced illegitimate children. In 1860, Prince lost a lawsuit brought on behalf of Louisa Nottidge by the Nottidge family and the group vanished from the public eye. It finally closed in 1956 when the last member died. Three years later, John de Ruiter was born. (Just kidding; though the parallels *are* striking.)

In the very early days of his pilgrim's progress, when his Ministry was still forming, John somehow managed to gain access to the Lutheran women as a spiritual counselor, even though this went strictly against the rules of the Church. How did he manage it, and what was his aim in doing so? If his counseling involved shaming women, as he did with Candy, placing them under the "oppression" of sexual guilt and leading them "out of themselves" and into him, is that the M.O. he eventually perfected via Oasis and which he is only now making public (and only because it has backfired), in 2017?

There is nothing startlingly new or radical about this, seen from the outside at least. The history of spiritual teachers abusing the trust of their followers, generally though not always female, by sexually exploiting them is, if anything, more the rule than the exception. Here are a few recent examples:

Michael Lyons, "a self-styled Buddhist guru who used his 'mystical' charms to rape and sexually assault women" was sentenced to ten years in 2010 for "a decade-long reign of terror." Lyons "attacked hundreds more middle-class victims in Britain and America" via an international spiritual cult. His followers, "some of whom believed he could cure cancer, funded his lavish lifestyle as well as introducing him to new potential followers." Lyons' "group of slavish female followers treated him 'like a god.' He was driven around in luxury cars, toured the world with trips to Miami, Washington DC, London, Paris, and India." One of his victims testified that, while raping her, Lyons "was saying that I was proud, and that I had to be crucified to find enlightenment. He told me he was showing me real love."

> Behind the slick, smiling exterior, police believe, is a dangerous sexual predator whose real number of victims may run to more than 100 worldwide—many fearful of speaking out in the wake of his exhortations that to do so signalled emotional weakness. In fact, this was just one of many bogus doctrines espoused by [Lyons]. Such was his web of deceit that it is hard to know what part of him is genuine. Wherever he was in the world Lyons proved himself an impressive wooer of young, often vulnerable women. As Mr. Giles relates: "His victims tend to be highly intelligent with an interest in spirituality, but at a point in their life where they are searching for answers. They are introduced and recommended to Lyons by the Friends of Mohan. They see these successful happy women and the promise of a solution to their problems and are lured in." . . . Yet, astonishingly, even the five charges of rape and three of sexual assault eventually brought against him was not enough to persuade some of his followers to turn their back on him during his trial. Many gave

evidence in his defence, calling him a "genuinely spiritual man."⁸

Another example is Gregorian Bivolaru, a yogi from Romania, where yoga was forbidden until 1989, the time of the Romanian Revolution. After the revolution, Bivolaru founded the Movement for Spiritual Integration into the Absolute (MISA), a non-profit association with a socio-professional, philosophical and educative character. MISA's aim was to increase the spiritual level of people by spreading yoga knowledge and practices. Yet according to a human rights activist, Seppo Isotalo, "It has all the characteristics of a cult: one truth, one leader, and it isolates the dissident." In 2005, Bivolaru was charged with eight counts, including sex with a minor (later retracted), tax evasion, and illegally crossing the border to escape prosecution. Bivolaru asked for asylum in Sweden, claiming he feared persecution in Romania. On 15 April of the same year, the Romanian Police issued a second warrant in his name, in which he was accused of "human trafficking and other charges related to organized crime." An official document recounts that "under the cover of courses for initiation in the yoga practices, the investigated persons attracted, manipulated and exploited the participants (of whom many were minor) to their own personal interest, thus endangering their psychic development."⁹

Tilak Fernando, a Sri Lankan guru said (by Stephen J. Dubner, quoting Joseph Banks, publisher of *New Frontier* magazine) to be "adept at performing *siddhis*, feats combining physiological and psychological processes to produce paranormal results—'when you have those abilities and mix them with fraud or sleight of hand, you have a very powerful package.'" Fernando's typical student, once again, is "a vulnerable woman, often with a psychological or physical ailment, an addiction, or a history of abuse."

> "He finds your emotional hook," says a former student, "and then it doesn't matter how intelligent a person is." To one student, a masseuse, Tilak explained that his sex with her was really "a sacred transmission of the light." The masseuse tracked down other women who had left Tilak and found that he had told them what each wanted to hear: that sex with Tilak would make her attractive to other men; or that sex with Tilak would heal the scars of an abusive past; or that sex with Tilak was the way to achieve enlightenment.[10]

Then there's Michel (born in South America as Jaime Gomez), the Los Angeles-based guru who ran a community of roughly one hundred people called Buddhafield for over twenty years beginning in the 1980s. As was revealed in the 2016 documentary *Holy Hell,* Michel saw himself as a Christ figure. He charged $50 for weekly hypnotherapy sessions called "cleansings." The primary incentive for the group was what Michel called "the knowing . . . the most intimate connection to God possible," granted only to the most privileged disciples.

> No one wanted to leave before they'd experienced it. [Participants] liken "the knowing" to an LSD trip: colors swirl, trees sway and divinity presents itself. . . . Using the spiritual teachings they'd been fed, members fixed deep meanings to the experience, often calling it, at most, "God" or, at least, "intoxication." If it was ineffective, Michel claimed that person wasn't spiritually prepared to receive "the knowing." . . . Barring fleeting skepticism, no insiders questioned Michel's rules. They'd found tranquility.

> "There was truth in all of it," Coquet said. "There were lies and weird manipulations, but they were based on something we really believed in." And for a long time, no one would rather return to normal society, anyway. "This [was] such a great way to live, to see life from this way," Allen said, describing their justification.

Michel also prescribed celibacy, "citing the release of energy that comes with an orgasm as an inferior high." At the same time, Michel (who changed his name to Andreas and moved the group to Austin in the wake of David Koresh and Waco) "was manipulating male Buddhafielders into sleeping with him. Advised never to say no to their teacher, disciples—gay and straight—would receive spiritual awakenings during 'cleansings' and then convince themselves to give their bodies to Andreas. They were effectively being raped, but it carried the guise of consent. No one talked about it. 'You're just a sack of meat to this person,' one man says in the movie. 'That's when I began to hate him.'"

As the truth came out, many people left, while others remained. "Those who actually left were forced to 'disconnect' from the group, just like in Scientology. (Buddhafielders were sometimes ordered to maintain ostensible friendships with these people to keep tabs on them, should anyone choose to contact the authorities.)"[11]

I could go on and on, and before long I would probably have enough to fill another book. But the point is clear enough even from these few examples: there is a template for sexual exploitation and abuse of power granted to spiritual leaders via an assumption of their specialness, their divine *fiat*. Naturally, every group is made up of followers who believe—who *know*—their leader-teacher-guru is different. They may believe their guru is different for not taking sexual liberties, at all, and for being above such desires (only to find out that he isn't); or they may believe (either from the start or later, once the truth begins to come out) that their guru is different because what he (or, less frequently, she) is doing is not "ordinary" sexual behavior, at all, but *extra*ordinary, transcendental, and geared towards the bringing of truth, "the ancient," or some higher-deeper dimensional reality into form, that it is actually sexual "initiation," "cleansing," "transformation," and that these "alchemical" practices have to be kept secret due to their sensitive and radical nature, because people, with their culturally conditioned prejudices, will inevitably misunderstand unless they experience it directly.

Casualties of "Truth"

"When you know that you're listening to meaning, then you're letting meaning directly access you and alchemize you. You're letting it fundamentally change you in a way that is without return. You're letting meaning in and you're letting meaning have permanent effect. You're letting meaning rewrite your body, your nervous system. You're letting meaning in and you're letting meaning rewrite in your body what matters."
— John de Ruiter

There is an unconfirmed anecdote I once heard about John. He was on holiday somewhere and was seen hiding behind a tree when he spotted someone he didn't want to interact with. He stood concealed, waiting for the person to leave before finally emerging into sight. This is a story I'd love to confirm, because, when it comes to showing how a Master's feet are made of clay— that the emperor has no clothes—the devil is in the details. But even more than being a wonderful illustration of how, in many ways, *ordinary* a man John de Ruiter is, the anecdote seems worth including, for all its "apocryphal" nature, because of its beautifully concise symbolic meaning. The word "true" originally meant "steady, firm," and comes from Old English (West Saxon) *tríewe, tréowe*. This fairly long etymological line seems to end with *dru*, meaning "*tree*." Hiding behind the tree of truth to avoid embarrassment! Isn't that de Ruiter's *modus operandi* in an acorn?

The aim of this chapter is to continue the process of "cracking the John-deRuiter-code." Simply stated, I am going to look more closely at John's own words to try and better determine the truth about his methods, motivations, and goals. This entails referring to his use of language and juxtaposing it with what is currently known about his behaviors, public and private, in the hope that his modus operandi can be seen for what it is. Language is a powerful tool for mystification, and my hope is that it will eventually be possible to crack the code of John-speak in such a way that the spell can be broken once and for all.

The evidence I will be referring to is from two meetings John gave at Oasis, Edmonton, on March 4 and 6, 2017. This is when John spoke publicly about having secret sexual meetings with some of the women in his group. It happened after the disclosure was made by Randi (who turned him down), despite John's instructions not to speak about it. The original disclosure, then, was not made by John, making John's disclosure more of an attempt at damage control by appearing to be responding to it. In the process, he made the rather tenuous claim that his secrecy was all about "timing," and that now it was finally time to speak out about it. This is a transcript from an exchange at an evening meeting on November 28, 2016, when John answered a question asked by Nathalie O' Tool:

> Without development in myself and my being together with the development of this group, disclosure becomes callous, disclosure loses its value. So disclosure for me [*unclear*] is balanced between together with development and timing. I love the development that's there and the timing. The development is profound and rich. The timing has the clarity of a ringing bell. A really little bell. Doesn't need to be bigger. When it's clear, it's clear. The level of disclosure and development I'm holding a lot. It's not at all too much. And it is all good. I have the development, I move the development and I know the timing. . . . The capacity for responsibility is development. Everyone is here for what I am, what I bring and where I come from. I know it and I carry it. To fall through can be understandable but I haven't.
>
> *Q: How can we best be in this?*
>
> From the inside out, as always. By quietly standing in what you really deeply have. Which is what direct knowledge and clarity you have. To not cast either side, not even a little bit because of any upheaval in yourself. Because of any pain, hurt or cost in yourself. When it comes to anything deeper than yourself, doubt destroys.

Even before this, the first occasion John spoke about his sexual involvement was at a "working lunch" at Oasis, with about fifty Oasis employees present. Though it was apparently filmed, it was (also allegedly) heavily edited and not made generally available. From what I have heard, John was apparently so vague that people had to ask him what he was talking about and whether he was speaking about physical sex or not. This is especially relevant in light of Anina's death in 2014, because her diary entries refer to some sort of sexual experience with John, which John insisted, then and now, was a dream or vision that did not take place physically. The general vagueness that surrounds all of John's statements seems to be especially pointed (and deceptive) when it comes to accounts of his sexualization of his female followers. In retrospect, John's sexualization of women, if I may use the term, begins at subtler levels, in group meetings and presumably private ones too, during which John appears to have been "grooming" some of his followers in preparation for a future, fully physical sexual encounter.

In the first official disclosure interview of March 4 (around the 51-minute mark), John admits: "I didn't realize these purposes [of having sex with his female followers] at the time, that I do realize now." He indicates later that he didn't fully realize these purposes until that very day—i.e., once he had to come up with a convincing explanation for it. Yet John's secret sexual seductions of his female followers (most of whom were probably married) date at least as far back as 1998, and probably further still. (In 1999, John told the group that he first had a "knowing" he would sleep with another woman besides his wife thirteen years earlier, in 1986.) So if we're to believe John at all, he has been in the dark about his reasons for doing this for somewhere between twenty and thirty years. At the same time, his followers are assured it was only ever a movement of Truth, or, as he currently languifies it, "the Calling."

So if John didn't realize the purposes of choosing to have sex with his followers, does this also imply that he had no clear idea of the consequences of doing so, for himself or the women (and for those followers who were allowed to know about it, and, for that matter, those who weren't)? In 2017 he stated: "It definitely did catalyze my movement into the deeper levels, my movement into the Calling, my movement into the bigger picture and the backdrop, my movement into greater reality, other dimensions and other realms, because that's all I really had as a real resource to draw from, for me to move in this way... in a way that I would never otherwise move." John claims that secretly having sex with women in his group was something he did without knowing the purpose of it, but that it allowed him to move deeper into "greater reality," where his purpose for "moving in this way" became clear to him, because it was greater reality telling him to do so! Like all of John's explanations for his behaviors, this is both circular and subjective to the point of meaninglessness. There is no way whatsoever to verify the truth of it because John is speaking of realms beyond mental understanding. One can examine his statements for coherence and deeper meaning, however, and doing so doesn't reveal much besides John's usual argument: "I did it because I felt like it, and it felt good (right, true)."

In his explanation on March 4 (around 81 mins), John extends his twilight language into a literal claim of trans-physical expression: "To move sexually with another woman, for me," he says, "is to move in the same way that we will all move after we have died, not being confined to our relationships, to our marriage... I am moving in that level of union that is of, if you could call it, the other side—here." In his prodigious display of linguistic gymnastics back in 1999, John softly assured his followers that he had not lied to Joyce or been adulterous when he slept with the von Sass sisters behind her back, because it was all unfolding at deeper levels of being. Now, in 2017, he gets to be a faithful husband on one level, while sleeping with anyone he can lure into his golden-hued basement room on another (though both levels are physical). He is: "Modeling union not based on marriage ... while at the same time, I am married," because these are two "different realities" that only look like one reality to those of us on the outside of John's interdimensional reality-consciousness. Later on in his epic obfuscation, spiritualization, and mystification of misdemeanors, John makes the bold claim that for him, having sex with women "precludes male-female interactivity."

When John is asked by the interviewer about all the secrecy involved in his "Calling," he resorts to the same tactic. (Essentially, it is the only one he has besides simply denying everything, which doesn't work when people are speaking out, as they were in 2014 and 1999, and as they are now.) First of all, he makes reference to "the personal, the private, and the sacred," indicating that whether something is secrecy depends on the context it is occurring in. He states (at 96 mins) that "absolute transparency is not relevant" and "not a well-thought-out ideal." There are "measures of transparency," he says (followed by a stream of standard John-speak about "knowing," "holding of meaning," etc., etc), and "so many different levels."

He then offers a more palatable term to secrecy, "containment," which he describes as "awareness being one with what you know even when the self is not like that." This "directly exposes the lack within the self" and, as one relaxes into the sheer discomfort of that, the heat increases and there is an "alchemy of change" that "makes manifest the entire self." It is unclear how this sort of containment (which seems to amount to a willingness not to express unpleasant feelings while experiencing internal conflict) relates to concealing and lying about his sexual practices (if containment is the opposite of transparency, does that make it opacity?). John deftly turns the whole question of his accountability around when he speaks about "duplicity" and "the split between conscious and subconscious self." He implies that suppressing the subconscious equals real duplicity, and that, since he expresses his subconscious desires through his sexual proclivities, he is not duplicitous, not divided. The reason he keeps all of this secret is apparently related to "containment," i.e., it is the necessary containment of information and of what is seen by others. But necessary to whom, and why?

John argues that the real duplicity is to suppress or deny one's subconscious desires, rather than to let them come up while keeping them "contained" (which in his case means merely hidden or secret). He is saying that, regardless of how honest our behaviors might be at a surface level, we are duplicitous whenever there is a split in us. Since by this definition everyone is duplicitous, he implies that no one can judge him for his actions ("who is without sin cast the first stone"). In contrast, while his actions might *appear* duplicitous, they are not, because there is no split within him. Yet, if this is the case, why the containment? By his own definitions, the purpose of the containment is for his conscious self to be alchemically reconfigured by the pressure of personal discomfort that comes from going against his conditioning. Is John acknowledging that his conscious self is in need of reconfiguration and that he is still trapped inside a conditioned self? If so, why is he taking the moral high ground and claiming there is no duplicity or secrecy in him, no split between his conscious and subconscious, and that it is all the "Calling"?

John's art is a persuasive art. It is highly dependent on obfuscation: the harder he is to understand, the more wiggle room he has to change tacks whenever he is in danger of being caught in a lie. As I am able to understand it, however, John's position on his own undeniable secrecy and duplicity (besides that it isn't what it looks like) is that he is mirroring people's own level of awareness, readiness, and integrity, and meeting them "where they are at." If this is really true, he would at best be "parenting" his followers. But even if we allow for this possibility, parenting implies children who eventually grow up, and at a certain point need to be treated like adults. This entails giving them all the information they need to make their own decisions. If this doesn't happen, parenting becomes overly protective and oppressive and the child will act out in anger and rebellion, as often as not via self-destructive behaviors. Biological parents generally don't know how to shift gears gracefully when their children are coming of age or how to relate to them as equals. John appears to be no exception to this rule—and this is only if we give him a massive amount of doubt-benefits here.

*

When it comes to the effects of his sexual opportunism, this is where the rubber of Johnny's cosmic rationalizing meets the road of human reality. John is somewhat clearer about this question, but also about the fact that he doesn't actually, really care either way. He describes the overall result of having sex with the women in broad terms: "the entire self goes through a fundamental destabilization," he says, without "any kind of held purpose." In other words, the women will undergo a crisis that will be incomprehensible to them, and that is also (at the level of their own awareness) pointless. He hammers the point home later on (1 hour 19 min) by saying: "What that brings up in anyone that is unintegrated is really, sweetly, besides the point. . . . It will bring up everything," he says (all the shadow material from the subconscious), but "how that manifests doesn't actually, really matter." Will he feel the same way when one of the cuckolded husbands comes at him with a baseball bat, I wonder?

One reason it doesn't actually, really matter to John is that all this destabilization comes with a purpose known only to him: his female "initiates" are on the "fast track of integration . . . very high pressure." So then, does it even actually, really matter if it kills them, since, in John's world, it's all one continuum anyway? The other reason it doesn't matter is that John is following the Calling and has "no fear of making mistakes," ever. When pressed, John admits he can make mistakes, but is quick to add that this is only at the level of self, mind, and "communication," and so does not impede or impair the Calling. Since all his mistakes occur at a surface level, he is not concerned with the risk. I was surprised John admitted to being able to make even a trivial mistake, but then I realized that it would be foolish for him to claim otherwise, since this would be far too easy to disprove. (What happens the next time he drops a fork? Blame the Calling?) Once again, John has it both ways: he is denying any kind of equivalency or congruence between levels, while claiming to be one at all the levels and embodying the truth of what he knows at all times.

On the March 6 disclosure talk (around 25 mins), John admits that there are inevitable casualties of what he is doing. He then assures his followers that such casualties are "not the responsibility of how the Calling moves but the responsibility of you as a person, dropping down to an appropriate level of knowledge that you can deal with what it is that's in question . . . so really it's your responsibility to go into what you actually know." John's frame of reference for being true to "the Calling" is one hundred percent non-dependent on all external consequences of his actions. No matter the number or the severity of casualties that may result from what he does, it is entirely *their* responsibility, not his. This is the very opposite of a parental instinct, and if this is really how John feels, why is he "protecting" his followers by keeping his activities secret until they are "ready" to know the truth? This seems like a policy designed to cause the maximum amount of damage to others, while ensuring the minimum degree of accountability for himself. Presumably it has something to do with John's idea of "high pressure," controlled destabilization, of "setting the nervous system afire" and the "alchemy of change." Or is it that his scorched earth, take-no-prisoners policy is simply the best cover for a decades-long sexual rampage?

Whether a person becomes a casualty of John's alchemy depends, as he sees it, on "a level of choice that isn't easily discernible" but that is "like a light switch." If his followers react badly to his influence, then they are, at a very subtle level, choosing to do so. They are choosing to align with their conditioned selves, with dishonesty, with the darkness of untruth, and thereby sullying his divine gift and turning it into something poisonous via the poisons of their own "insistence," their resistance to John's goodness. Almost unbelievably, he manages to turn himself into the exploited and innocent victim, the Lamb of God who gets to forgive those who know not what they do. But if John is able to discern this ultra-subtle light-switch in those he selects for his golden goosing, can't he also discern which way they are likely to go? John claims his responsibility is "making it clear to the other what's at stake," and that he is "not needing a yes" and "not asking for something." He is only "the person's deeper-self-advocate." His golden promise comes with a warning, etched in tiny print: "Anything that moves from the deep puts the accustomed self at risk." For the starstruck and truth-hooked John-ite, it's probably a small step from this to believing that anything that puts their accustomed selves at risk (as long as it is coming from John) must be coming also from "the deep." It's the college of disintegrating philosophy, complete with a placard over the door: "Whatever doesn't kill you, makes John (Truth) stronger."

*

Questions for Oasians: why is John's speech in the disclosure videos so halting and jerky? Why do the words stick in his throat so much? Why does he lack all spontaneity, to the point that he can't even smile or clear his throat without it seeming carefully modulated? What is John holding inside? What is he afraid of letting others see?

Towards the end of the March 6 meeting, John claims he is "completely dependent on you relating to what you know" in order to be able to move in (or in on) his followers. "Yes, I have powers that you don't have," he says, but he can only use them with the person's inner consent. He has "no power over you" but "a tiny little bit of power in you."

It's essential to keep in mind that "what you know" is really Oasis-speak for John's goodness, because this latter is the only thing Oasians are one hundred percent sure about. When John says he needs his followers to relate to what they know for him to be able to "move in them," what he's actually saying (I think) is that he is completely dependent on their love for him in order to influence them. To have power in/over them, he is dependent on securing their consent, and he secures their consent by instilling them with blind, undying love, trust, and loyalty. In the first public disclosure meeting, for example, the interviewer, Roger, makes a ridiculous (or coded?) analogy between John's sexually propositioning his female followers and an invitation to go hiking in the hills. You don't get mad if you don't want to go, Roger says, you just say No thanks. John then makes a "joke" to Roger: "Are you wanting to go hiking with me, Roger?" he croons. Once the laughter has died down, Roger says he would!

When Roger asks John about dissent within the group and whether it can be valuable, John replies: "Is there room for dissent here? Yes." But then he quickly adds, "It isn't really going to go anywhere, inasmuch as it's a posturing of the self." It may give "an experience of power," he says, but "it's not real power." If the dissent is "an embodiment of humanness and weakness" and there is "nothing adversarial in it," that's OK. But otherwise, it is only "importing the past to re-experience it" and there is "nothing real" there, only "a protracted experience of ourselves." A few minutes before this, Roger makes a comment (not a question) about the niggling fear some people have expressed that Oasis is becoming a cult. His tone of voice implies that such fears are foolish, as does his following comment about the idea that John's followers "sign off their critical faculties when they come into the room." This is greeted by a burst of laughter from the group.

One (female) follower who testified to her profound learning curve under John in 2012 writes of meeting "the challenge of learning to communicate without emotion and to reach beyond myself contrary to all my feelings." She winds up by affirming, "We are responsible for our own evolution. Not a victim of circumstances but gatekeepers to the reality we choose to create. I am grateful to John for meeting me in my hunger to develop in Truth. His teaching have [sic] and continue to satisfy me to the core. It has tipped the balance. All other wants and needs pale in comparison to fulfilling my purpose as a human on this earth." John has met this woman at her hungry core; he has taught her to express no emotions and given her a purpose that makes her wants and needs go pale, then instilled in her a "calling" to help create reality and serve as a loyal gatekeeper to it. This is scary stuff.[12]

John's empire is an empire of persuasion. Like all cults, it centers on the power of one man to cause people to fall in love with him. However he does it, John manipulates people—energetically, emotionally, neurolinguistically, or via unknown mesmeric powers—and reduces them to an infantile state of wonder. Once they are infantilized, he imprints them with blind love and trust for him, with the absolute belief ("knowing") in his goodness. Because his most devoted followers (those who move to Edmonton to be near him) are imprinted at this deep level, as he abuses their trust, their dependency does not diminish but increases. The more evidence they are faced with of John's lack of integrity, honesty, goodness, or simple human decency, the further they have to go from what their own senses are telling them in order to continue to believe in his goodness. Their sense of John's corruptness becomes further proof of their own "badness" (just as with a child who is abused), and so they become more and more dependent on him to lead them "out of themselves" and into his care (under his power). In this (admittedly stark) reading, John's aim would be to create lifeless, empty shells which he can then fill up and animate with his own psychic poisons, forging an army of golems programmed to love and worship their "Precious," and spread its glory far and wide.

*

Returning now to the "John-code," what surfaces time and again in a close inspection of his use of language is that John shifts levels according to his requirements in any given moment. He applies certain truths in a way that is convenient to his own goals, but that is inappropriate at the level the targeted listener is at. If his levels of meaning are "the personal, the private, and the sacred," it's fair to ask when and why he chooses to refer to a given level over another. From what I've seen, John ignores the personal when it comes to how people feel about or react to his actions (that is sweetly beside the point). He cites the private when he wants to enforce his own secrecy (it is "indelicate" to talk about these things). And he evokes the sacred when he wants to shirk all responsibility at the levels of the personal *or* the private. John does not embody truth (just the reverse, his actions consistently run contrary to what he preaches), he wields truth as a cloak and a weapon. Part of his goal appears to be to neutralize his followers' ability to trust their own "knowings" without referring to his own influence. He turns truth into lies by using truth as a means to conceal or disguise his own behavior (and when he can't do either, to rationalize it), and he embeds words with his own special, hidden meanings. This allows him to communicate two different levels of meaning, one for his larger flock of followers, the other for the inside circle who know (more about) the truth of his behaviors, possibly including some members who are entirely complicit with the deception, either because they believe it is integral to the Calling, or because they are cynically pursuing their own gain and don't give a damn.

In the process, in his plundering of the personal behind the screen of the private and under the auspices of the "Calling," John has co-opted just about everything that's sacred. This leaves his followers, should they choose to follow their gut-sense about him and abandon the Oasis nest, with next to nothing to hold onto or believe in. Since John's spirituality is a corruption of the highest spiritual values a person can conceive of, he leaves his followers—the ones able to wake up from the dream he has spun for them—with nothing untarnished by his touch. To leave John then becomes more or less synonymous with abandoning spirituality altogether and turning one's back on Truth. It becomes the ultimate test.

John leads (or leads on) the men and women (and children)[*] he targets for recruitment into his Truth army to believe they will have a special relationship with him if they "move towards him"—i.e., relocate to Edmonton or jump in the sack with him. Once they take the bait, he becomes unavailable to them and they realize they are just another brick in his Empire, as expendable as all the rest. By then, however, they have invested too much into his golden promise to turn back or admit defeat (it's only their conditioned selves that are disappointed, and Truth requires the ultimate sacrifice). And so they remain, the intensity of their hope inflamed by every disappointment and

---

[*] In 2017 John began holding meetings especially for teenagers.

betrayal, like hungry dogs waiting for stray crumbs at the court of the King. And of course, they can always tell themselves that their reward is not of this world anyway, that they are giving up everything in order to follow John's Calling all the way back to Original Meaning, Ancient Knowing, or whatever the latest de-Ruiter brand for the Ineffable is. I wonder if they have considered the possibility that the exact same thing is going to play out on the inner realms, and that hundreds of hopeful John-ites, trusting to meet their guru of goodness on the other side with open arms when they "cross over," will find themselves naked and alone, abandoned and betrayed, staring at a cold, flat, and dark wasteland, with no oasis in sight?

Notes for Part Five

[1] http://www.cbc.ca/news/canada/edmonton/disappearance-of-alberta-government-scientist-troubles-police-1.2585784

[2] http://collegeofintegratedphilosophy.com/dialogues/conclusions-and-clarity/

[3] http://www.climbing-high.com/hypothermia.html (Emphasis added.)

[4] KFNX How I Created a Cult — Alex Howard Meagen Gibson, House of Mystery Radio. https://www.youtube.com/watch?v=9dIBHQ5TfYc

[5] See: https://collegeofintegratedphilosophy.com/conversations-john-college-part-1-2-3-4/ See also: https://collegeofintegratedphilosophy.com/offtheshelf/

[6] http://mit.irr.org/joseph-smiths-changing-first-vision-accounts

[7] Chisholm, Hugh, ed. (1911). "Agapemonites," *Encyclopædia Britannica*. 1 (11th ed.). Cambridge University Press. pp. 365–366.

[8] Lucy Ballinger and Colin Fernandez (2010). Rapist "guru" in a Bentley cast his spell on hundreds of terrified young women. *Daily Mail*, 27 July, 2010. http://www.dailymail.co.uk/news/article-1297818/Rapist-guru-Michael-Lyons-cast-spell-hundreds-terrified-young-women.html

[9] "Independent Report on the Justice System in Romania–Cap. V. HUMAN RIGHTS IN ROMANIA." https://web.archive.org/web/20070801182012/http://www.sojust.ro/sistemul-juridic-din-romania-raport-independent/5-human-rights.html

[10] "The Cult of Tilak," by Stephen J. Dubner, *New York Times*, 22 June 1993 (p. 33-39).

[11] Matthew Jacobs, "Life Inside This Cult Was Beautiful, Until It Wasn't." *Huffington Post*, 27 May 2016. http://www.huffingtonpost.com/entry/holy-hell-cult-documentary_us_5744c96ae4b055bb11708e51

[12] Also scary is the fact that the original link for this quote was replaced (within hours of my posting this chapter online) by an entirely different text written by a man, with a title that didn't even match the url! I found a cached version of the original page but it was also removed. This suggests close monitoring of my blog and substantial technical expertise. Unfortunately, I neglected to take screenshots, though I copied and pasted the full piece here: https://auticulture.wordpress.com/2017/04/10/the-casualties-of-truth-deconstructing-john-de-ruiters-sexual-calling/#comment-9263

All links last accessed Nov 4, 2017.

Part Seven
End-Times at Oasis?

"The enigma of his face is in part the concentrated mask of a sociopath who is juggling countless balls of deceit. His vaudeville hides a darker burlesque. The gaze is searing, but he's not looking at you. The tragic devotee will say 'He's looking through me,' which carries the unconscious meaning of: 'I'm not really here.' There's a good chance he's never seen you. He doesn't want to see you. He probably can't remember your name. Narcissists cannot see you. Is it so hard to learn this because we are as fascinated with their image as they are?"
—Matthew Remski

"Thank god we can be human again because if you stay a student of John's you forgo your humanity."
—Former follower

A Wounded Choir/Injured Others

This would certainly be a suitable place to end this, but there are still some loose ends that need to be woven in here before I feel able to close the book. The reason this is finally getting released is that, by April 2017, there was a growing number of disturbed, disgruntled, and disillusioned ex-John-ites speaking out, albeit via a private forum. I participated in that conversation while preparing the manuscript for publication and as a result, ironically, the same impetus that was moving me to publish also opened up a potentially endless stream of new testimonies and evidence.

If I wanted to release the book (so people could have access to this information now it was becoming more and more needed), I might have to close it just as things were really opening up, with "to be continued . . ." in place of "the End." There is the option of revising the book at regular intervals, or of writing a follow up, or simply of continuing the exploration online within a group setting. But in the meantime, I think the best way to (try to) end it is with testimonies from people, like myself, who have come out the other end of the Oasis tunnel, into the light of a deeper "knowing" about John de Ruiter. Those who have seen the shadow side so long concealed are in the difficult but rewarding process of integrating a string of unpalatable truths about their former guru of goodness, and, by extension, our own tendency to be deceived.

What follows are *some* of the voices that are beginning to sound. There are not as many as I originally planned, however, as during the final stages of the book, several ex-followers decided they didn't want to be included after all. The reasons given were fairly consistent. In one case, it had to do with not wanting to be on John's "radar" or give any more energy to him. Another was afraid of becoming "re-entangled" with John's energy threads or grabbed by his "far-reaching tentacles." A third felt that their experiences with John were mostly positive so they wanted to maintain a respectful distance, even though they agreed there were "shadow" aspects to his behavior that people needed to be aware of. There was talk of being quoted anonymously or using false names but I didn't want to do this as it seemed to defeat the whole point of the exercise, which was to provide a space, in this book, for ex-followers to testify to their experience, openly and without fear.

I felt angry about these people's decision to withdraw, especially since their combined testimonials amounted to about a third of the material I had. Also, since much of it was a reproduction of an online conversation, removing it would disrupt the flow of the chapter. But the main reason I felt annoyed wasn't so much to do with the effect it would have on the book. I felt it showed a lack of solidarity or commitment to presenting the truth about John and to supporting me in my endeavor. Though fear of litigation wasn't mentioned, it's likely the imagined threat of John's "tentacles" was a legal as well as an energetic one. Whatever the case, once again I had the experience of being blocked by a wall of fear/loyalty to John de Ruiter by his ex-followers, who were—perhaps understandably—more concerned with extricating themselves fully from his grasp than they were with helping others to do so. The irony of this is apparent: their refusal to testify was in itself a powerful form of testimony.

At first, in my anger, I considered removing this entire chapter. Eventually I decided on a different approach that would potentially turn a distressing setback into an opportunity for a demonstration. Accordingly I have *redacted* all the quotes of these ex-followers, and included a brief summation of what has been removed whenever it seems important to do so. I am aware this might not meet with the complete satisfaction of these ex-followers, since, while it definitely eliminates any danger of litigation for them, it doesn't entirely place them beyond the reach of John's tentacles. But so be it, and *c'est la guerre*.

What follows are the voices of those who refused to be silenced, or to silence themselves.

Matt. (Matt types with many ellipses. I have left them in since it's his particular style, but I have corrected the typos.)

John spoke about "marrying your being"..... fidelity to truth.......monogamy.....often...it seemed he had finally resolved his past and was embodying a healthy human relationship in his marriage.......the things I tried to strengthen by being with John (devotion, fidelity and stability in relationships) I now find are issues that are not resolved in John's own private life...at all...he carries the same weaknesses I carry..... but is engaging them, like he does on stage, in an epic way......even the old blues musicians, low down and dirty......were clear enough to know "you don't mess around with a married woman".....it's not the morality that first bothers me....it is the practical reality of John's walk....... sexual lameness is in all of us......but to make obvious shallow and self-gratifying behavior into "virtue," and more so into a Calling.....that is beyond foolish in this day and age when we all actually know what doesn't work and never did work.......John's sexual life is messy, complex but more so ......completely unnecessary.......to say he is compelled by his commitment and devotion to Truth in these matters offends my own sensibilities.....my sexuality is lame, I can see this in my life .....I recognize it's not a virtue to satisfy myself at the expense of love, devotion and delicate natural boundaries...I can see the cost.......I don't blame John, I actually am astounded he could be blind to these realities, or blind himself to them so deeply.....I really don't find it sincere or honest.....because I know the difference in myself, I know the difference in John too.....regardless of his claims of being in a special category.....

It's like he immobilizes whatever he talks about.......he makes it into a "teaching" so it is externalized in the listener, and so, removed from the listener's natural sense.....when he speaks of "using common sense" he is taking that ability away from the listener....common sense becomes something John "taught" us...."brought" us......so when we really need it in regards to him, it is incomprehensible because our common sense says "untrue" but our "deeper sense" (which is John's illusion) says "Truth"...... Thank god we can be human again because if you stay a student of John's you forgo your humanity....and common sense. It's still bizarre to me that a man loved and revered as a leader and paternal figure could place himself between a husband and wife sexually......to me, that is breaking, not binding them.....it is not right

These men whose wives are involved with John.....there hasn't been much discussion yet regarding them.....but they are carrying the shadow of the men in the group in many ways.....emasculated.....and the sexuality, I see it, is a coping mechanism.....to be violated by John's will, that is like a sexual violation of the men involved, indirectly, through John's use of the women.....a root violation.......it creates suffering to be overpowered.... .....it's a strange form of sexual abuse by John towards the men.......sexual because it is about the Root center, the power center, free will.........being a possession.....without real choice....I think when I found this out, my own deeper power could not enjoy being humiliated or overpowered.....I saw it as a sickness and would rather die than surrender my existence that way.

In 2000 I found it terrifying that another human being could invade my consciousness in such a way.....it was abhorrent to me that I was subject to John's power.....and there was no escape.....John is not a therapist or a minister.....he is more of a scientist or explorer......experimenting with consciousness.....with his relationship to other human beings......and of course there have been casualties ....one woman said in a "session" she went into different realms and John exclaimed "OH!! sorry...I am not supposed to do that!!".....this was a one on one session......his ability to actually help individuals has diminished as his power has grown....he can "only awaken"......he is not responsible for the effect that has on others.......this awakening transcends all personal boundaries.....he becomes something bigger to the person than they are to themselves......not in all cases, but in the case of suicide we can see where the experiment failed......massive awakening yes.....but love? We cannot overlook the impact of the PHYSICAL awakening John intends for others.....his purpose being to do just that....massively awaken others.....this is where he is different than other teachers.....he actually talks about it....and teaches it....that he is here to transform consciousness.....to create massive upheaval.....he has always been prepared to hurt people....and go beyond their "limits"......he said recently "I know the effect I have on others"......but he sees himself as HAVING to hurt people.....it is inevitable that he is going to have to break some eggs to make his omelette.....

In relation to the cuckholding of male followers, Matt also quoted this passage from Wikipedia:

> The jus primae noctis was, in the European late medieval context, a widespread popular belief in an ancient privilege of the lord of the manor to share the wedding bed with his peasants' brides. Symbolic gestures, reflecting this belief, were developed by the lords and used as humiliating signs of superiority over the dependent peasants in the 15th century, a

time of diminishing status differences. Actual intercourse in the exercise of the alleged right is difficult to prove, and there is no hard evidence to suggest that it ever actually happened. However, the symbolic gestures can be best interpreted as a male power display with a basis in the psychology of coercive social dominance, male competition, and male desire for sexual variety.

[Ex-follower expresses how turning oneself into an "awakened guru" is similar to a kind of confidence trick, in John's case a trick of reinventing Christianity for New-Agers.]

Chris: People seem courageous enough to raise the issues with John, but then they give him complete control to set the terms for how they should think/feel/understand/perceive/relate to the situation and to him. . . . I learnt from a former flat-mate about a type of personality, or complex, which is cloaked in spiritual garb, but is egocentric and arrogant underneath. The point is, the guy is a WANNABE GURU, with a website and a published book, and offers seminars on spiritual awakening. I'm reminded of this when I listen to these conversations between John and his acolytes. Who is this guy, I wonder, who dares tell people how to think, about matters in which he is implicated, and in such a way that HE GETS OFF THE HOOK EVERY TIME.

What is an effective teacher, what is a genuine teaching of what we most deeply hanker for as vulnerable humans on this confusing planet and in this wonderful life? And then, if those things are known, assessing the John-phenomenon in the light of that knowledge. It's all well and good to be in a nice tight community with a warm glow, so that one mostly feels good and feels connected, but if that really turns out to have nothing whatsoever to do with the self-knowledge that liberates, then that might bring about a questioning of one's participation. Having said that, though, it has been very interesting to hear all the stories from the disaffected, and to read Jasun's material. It has disabused me of any lingering tendency to idealize John in any way. He may indeed have a great deal of light, as well as a deep shadow, but in the end, what if he just doesn't qualify as a teacher, nor possesses a valid teaching, if the one thing that sets us free is knowledge of who we fundamentally are as beings. All our "knowings" and "callings" and "warm okayness" or dying into the deep whatever the hell the latest catch-phrase is ends up being quite beside the point. In short, spiritual "experience" may not be where it's at. So is he qualified, what is he teaching, and how?

[Ex-follower discusses Oasians' refusal to see John's shadow side because of how good the energy *feels* at Oasis, and because John is like God to them.]

Gunhild: All these deep light- and stillness experiences was also what got me to follow John and stay there over years. It seems for me, that this couldn't be wrong. I saw it and sensed it myself, and I trusted my own deeper sense. Some of it, as I see it, is really goodness, but it can appear also with "fake Gurus" and when we "normal humans" meet each other deeply. I once got a very, very deep transmission from John. He called it a download. When I look back on it, it was really goodness. In the situation, I said that I was ready for more, so I invited him to do it. It was not an attack or something like that, and I went into a very clear "state" that went on [for] a month or so, and grounded me deeply. So . . . for me, the point of no return was when I lost my trust, when I so clearly saw, that he is lying with words and . . . sometimes use transmissions to manipulate.

Part Seven: End-Times at Oasis?

[Ex-followers wonders about the "creepy" phenomena that is occurring with some followers, about where John's spiritual power comes from, and about the purpose of his sexual "Calling." They describe the intense positive energy in the group and how it makes followers immune to questions or criticism.]

Manfred: It's an addiction.

Denyse: One thing that really struck me as I read what happened to you is how John and Leigh Ann work in tandem to validate, solidify, and encourage the absolute belief in his message. It's very frightening and manipulative to the heart, mind and emotions.

Gunhild: As I see it, John has a quite big lack of empathy, and because it has been so blissful to be with him, it is shocking to realize this cold side of him.

Denyse: But one aspect of this that I realized that people were really telling me is that once I'd talked to John I would see my (self-constructed) error and be back drinking the Kool-Aid like them. If I remain "at large" unconvinced about John's motives it's uncomfortable for them and if I just got back in line then their discomfort could be covered over (at least until the next bomb hits). The only other alternative is to pathologize me and that's not easy to do given I don't have a history or mental illness and I can discuss matters reasonably. So that then puts a friendship at risk. It's very very tricky.

Chris: It'll be a fine balance to honor the true and the good and be honest and unflinching about the bad and the ugly.

Perhaps the true and the good will always pull, but the craziness for me is how both sides can co-exist within the one being.

Beverley: He would be perfectly balanced. The light so brilliant and the shadow so dark.

Andreas: Mixed levels... as he has accused so many of us.

[Ex-follower discussing energetic sexual invasion of some followers, and women having spontaneous orgasms around John.]

Part Seven: End-Times at Oasis?

[Ex-follower wonders about the question of "informed consent" and describes their experience as an "invasion," and as being very similar to Anina's account.]

Jane: Someone who was here and left felt him inside her body the night he stayed in 1998 when she was coordinator. He's been doing this stuff all along. She shouted no at him. He said you invited it to her—a massive clue as to why he feels it's ok. It's all about technicalities with John.

Beverley: I agree that John had "sex" with Anina. Having read the long letter translated, I feel her family also knew this happened, and in the sorrow of the words, of the gentle pleading to understand. With John's lawyers' letter of threat to the family, John also knew what happened. This letter was the final straw for me, to give any grace at all to John.

Jane: Highly disturbing [Anina incident] and Oasis recovered well. Two years down the line John's had sex with god knows who and energetically too and god knows why. It's not for me. He's a manipulative man. He uses truth like a weapon...

[Ex-follower discusses John's obvious issues around sexuality and the heavy focus on sexual energy in the teachings;

suggests that normalizing his own issue is a way of reducing guilt.]

Jasun: If people who leave JdR are afraid to speak negatively about him, how much more so those who are still "in"? What's needed is people who know to go on record; but so far they are either too afraid, too ashamed, or too loyal to JdR (brainwashed); or maybe sometimes all three (fear & shame is great way to create "loyalty")

[Ex-follower discusses how a polarized view of John is not an effective way to understand him, and how direct contact with his energy is necessary to know why people stay with him as long as they do, despite all the negative aspects, as well as why they refuse to speak badly of him. This ex-follower asked to be removed from the book for precisely this reason.]

Jasun: I was there in 2010, so I know what it was like to feel part of something profound & extraordinary. Is there something qualitatively different there in 2017? As for why people would be afraid to speak about negative aspects of John's behavior because they are part of something profound & extraordinary, do you think they are afraid of losing access to those feelings of profound extraordinariness, so much so they don't want to risk the high by thinking about the less pleasant aspects? Is it similar to loving a drug or a food, or being in a romantic relationship, and not wanting to think about the negative aspects because then we have to consider whether this is really healthy behavior for us?

Trine: I think 2 major contributing factors to people not speaking out are:

1. Not fear of John as much as fear of losing his love and
2. Fear of being judged by the group, to become an outcast.

For many here John and the group is all their life so to be cast out of it is no small matter.

[Ex-follower suggests that people who follow John see him as a god and hence cannot say anything bad about him.]

Jasun: Self-condemnation is the punishment. And yet . . . many people who have left JdR and know he is not God are afraid to go on record. At least some of them are afraid of John himself.

Paula: Oasis is a cult. Its practices designed to evoke devotion to John and quell dissent. I have no doubt that there are many lovely people in the group. . . . But this doesn't detract from being left very uncomfortable with the love space format [described by another ex-follower, redacted]. Sharing disquiet into the silence generated by people who are heavily invested in John-love and keeping the cult status quo feels as unhealthy as counsellors within a cult counselling members who have been damaged by the cult.

Joyce: I just re-listened to the audio (Conclusions and clarity [about Anina]). This time around, I am more inclined to believe that John was actually having sex with Anina. Of course, it could also be very likely just a reference to the women with whom he was in fact sexual (i.e., the calling). He would know that the calling might come to light one day, and therefore need to pose the possibility. [But] It is the way he prods the woman to also consider allowing herself to be open should it be the case that truth called him to go there. I know this pattern of John. First suggesting things as hypothetical, as a way of testing, while in fact the situation is already occurring. I can't analyze it all here, but this time around, I hear more. I try so hard to rest with my issues with John, but they are bothering me more and more.

Beverley: I remember reading the full letter translated from a German article, and as I am reading it, time kind of slowed downed and I read "between" the lines. . . . I knew without a doubt that Anina would be alive now if not for John's intrusion into her life. . . . In reading that letter, it opened me, to stay involved at all cost to stand ground for Anina, and all others in her situation, past present and future. It has and does make me face a fear in me, of being "wrong," of "interfering," of being "hurt" or "destroyed on a psychic level" but that is okay.

Having just listened to this audio again, John is very pleased with himself because he led the group to his own desires. I can hear that no one wanted to truly believe what happened. The questions were unconsciously aimed at getting John to soothe and pamper and lead the group to being totally "okay" with this. He even added hints that this is true and good . . . the sex with Anina. Priming them for the future. He came back from Europe afraid and needing to cull the rumors and he succeeded. He is extremely clever and knows the flock and how to "move" them.

*

Paula's comment about counsellors is apropos, considering how many of de Ruiter's followers are licensed therapists. For example:

> Jerry Rothenberg BFA, Dip. Psych. A Psychotherapist and counselor since 1972, with over 40 years [sic] experience, Jerry has extensive training in Jungian Therapy, Reichian Body Analysis, Bio-Energetics, Gestalt, Encounter, Psychosynthesis, and couples counselling. He has studied eastern philosophy and has been a meditation practitioner for nearly 30 years. Jerry was known as the "psychotherapist's psychotherapist" in the UK, where he was a leading figure in bringing Humanistic Therapy into the mainstream mental health community. He has worked as Senior Clerical Supervisor for Tower Hamlets College Diploma Course Counselling in London, UK for the last 10 years. And is now supervising "Mindfulness and Counseling Diploma Course" London, UK. (http://jerryrothenberg.com/)

David Rolston: "Contract Therapist at Jewish Family Services. He worked as an Engineer at COM DEV International from 1989 – 1992. . . . My responsibilities included designing and supervising the development of multiplexing systems for space satellites."

Other Oasis therapists and counselors include:
Tina Kafka.
(http://www.jfse.org/about-us/staff-members/)
Mei Chi-Chan.
(http://www.coreprocesscounselling.ca/about_me.html)
Karin Praveeta Linschoten.
(http://www.newpathwaycounseling.com/)
Jack Lewis. (http://www.jacklewis.ca/)
Pearl Mindell, "M.S.W., Former Clinical Professor of Psychiatry at Albany Medical Center, Albany, New York."

Are these therapists recommending de Ruiter to any of their patients? At least one person I spoke to had been encouraged to see de Ruiter by her therapist. How many more formally trained psychotherapists are at Oasis, and what sort of capacity are they working in? Is it surprising for such a high number of psychologists to be working in a spiritual group? Or is it statistically normal? Wouldn't a trained psychologist be very discerning about joining a cult or following a guru, much less recommending others to do so? On the other hand, it is easy to see why a cult would want psychotherapists in its group.

Of course, there are many sorts of therapists, just as there are all types of people who become doctors. But a doctor who follows a guru or sends his clients to one isn't quite the same, since there isn't the obvious overlap of fields. A closer parallel would be if a doctor sent a client to a faith healer, which would be highly unusual.

There is a bond of trust that's essential to a working therapist-client relationship, and a therapist who follows John essentially has placed him in the position of their own primary therapist. Generally, trained psychotherapists have to be overseen by another therapist with more experience than they have. Presumably such an overseer would have concerns if a therapist they were advising was following a guru and seeing clients who were also following that same guru (and certainly if they were sending clients to him).

On the other hand, having a team of psychologists working with followers in a cult-like group is standard operating procedure, as happened in Jonestown. It's also possible some might have been assigned to a group like Oasis for observational purposes by other organizations (i.e., to learn about cult psychology).

So how many of John's followers are receiving support from therapists who are also in the group, and how exactly is this not a conflict of interest? If, for example, an Oasian is disturbed by John's secret sexual affairs with his followers, most therapists would agree that this is a valid reason for them to be disturbed. An Oasian therapist is more likely to tell the person under their care that the problem is with *them* and not in John's behaviors. I know a former Oasian who described exactly this. The Oasian method is essentially: "If you have an issue with John's behavior, the problem is in you and your resistance." This would constitute a serious breach of therapeutic etiquette.

And what about women who are being "called" by John, or who (like Anina?) are having visions of energetic visitations from him and struggling with it? Will an Oasian therapist tell them to trust John and open to his "Calling"? It seems more than likely. Aren't there laws against this sort of "therapy"?

The Perils of Matching "Perfection"

At my second ever meeting with de Ruiter, at the Center Point building in 2008, I spent the whole time "tuning into" him and "matching" (what I perceived to be) John's internal state of being. In practical terms, what that meant was keeping completely still and gazing fixedly at him (I even tried not to blink). This is pretty much the formula at a John meeting: the querent holds the microphone gently below their chin (I was instructed exactly how to hold it) and speaks in hushed, halting tones while gazing at John and doing everything they can to be "in their knowing" and not in their thoughts, feelings, or ego identities. It was my experience of matching John, as much as or more than our dialogue the day before (and maybe even as much as my apocalyptic dream abduction), that "hooked" me. What I saw—or imagined I saw—in John was something I desperately wanted for myself. Power.

Did this projection and desire relate to my belief at the time that John was an almost wholly "yin" being and that he was somehow lacking in a fully embodied "yang" or masculine side? (I saw him like a baby and wanted to take care of him! I wonder now how many others—especially women—have felt that way about him?) Certainly, I had spent many years trying to find— never mind embody—my own masculinity; and it may be that part of John's appeal for me was that he made me feel *more* masculine by contrast (as well as more accepting of my own feminine qualities). I even believed I had some tricks to show him!

I now think that John's masculine side is not under- but *over*developed and over-expressed, albeit covertly and not openly (at least until recently). Perhaps John's seemingly insatiable sexual appetite is related to this concealment, the fact that his sexuality has not been integrated into his public persona and teachings? Maybe, like a cancer, this has allowed it to metastasize in the darkness? Now, in 2017, due to unplanned admissions by at least one group member, John has begun to incorporate his "private" (i.e., secret) practices into his open philosophy. This is being done in the hope that the secrecy will be forgotten in all the excitement, and that his disingenuous explanations about "timing" will be accepted, like dodgy pharmaceuticals, without a look at the fine print.

All of this begs the question as to what, exactly, I was unconsciously tuning into, and taking on, when I "matched" John's *outwardly* feminine aspects. Would it also have included his hidden, seemingly aberrant, masculine proclivities? There is evidence in my life to suggest this. It relates to the period in which I was most heavily identified with John, which happened to also coincide with a period in which I was counseling people, for a small fee, via a private online group that included video one-to-ones. Over time, working with my clients (who were mostly but not exclusively male), I adopted an external manner—a way—that was in direct and conscious imitation of John. (I was also sharing audios of John meetings with my clients and quoting him constantly.) I spoke slowly and softly, using long pauses; I began each consultation with a period of silent gazing (made slightly awkward by the video feed). This wasn't entirely a pose; in fact at the time I didn't consider it a pose at all but only a faithful application (embodiment) of John's teachings. I was "going finer" and dropping into "the little bit that I knew," however long it took to do so, in order to let that tiny bit of knowing "move me from within" (etc., etc.). The point here is that I was convinced for a time (and was apparently able to convince others) that I was a kind of "Little John," embodying the same Truth that he was, at a less advanced level. I was my clients' connection to John, just as John was my connection to Truth.

There was one person I was unable to convince, however, and that was my wife. In my marriage, things were not improving as a result of applying John's teachings; far from it. It might not be quite fair to say that applying John's teachings was making things worse between my wife and I, however. While I do think this was the case, it's also true that, the harder things became between us, the more desperately I tried to apply John's teachings. Not listening to my thoughts and feelings, not giving in to want and need, letting the relationship be "impersonal," never trying to "get" anything for myself, dropping beneath the surface, and so on. All of this came down to a very unnatural and resentful submission to being "weaned" of all emotional needs within the relationship I most depended on to meet those needs. And of course, I was becoming needier with every self-imposed denial. The ignominy and despair this created in me led to an attempt to control the process by becoming more and more "John-like": to compensate for and cover up my increased distress by becoming more contained, aloof, emotionless, commanding, and, frankly, inhuman.

My wife had told me long before that John was her "orientation." Because of this, I thought John was what she wanted in a husband, and so, John-like was what I would be. Not the private John, of course, which I was still clueless about (despite there being clues everywhere). I emulated the soft, cool, gentle, distant, calm, passive, seemingly compassionate but emotionally absent, *public* John. Eventually (not all at once but in a series of actions), this assumed persona—my imitation of John—exploded into distraught, desperate, raging, and finally abusive behavior. This obviously intensified the estrangement between my wife and I, and my agony increased. By the time we both went to Edmonton for the October 2010 seminar, it was a marriage in name only. Discovering the truth about John a few weeks later—as recounted in this book—only accelerated our decline, and a few months later we separated. (We were later reunited and are together now, but this might never have happened if I hadn't had some spiritual guidance from other quarters.)

The point of all this summation is twofold. Appearing the way John appears in public (i.e., with relative strangers)—"embodying truth," convincing people through body language, vocal patterns, and some choice turns of phrase that they are in the presence of the divine—is *not really that difficult*. What's more, it is disturbingly easy to convince *oneself* of being in a state of "knowing" simply by "assuming the position" and adopting the right language. The more one believes it, the more others will believe it and the more convinced one will become that it is true. I only kept this act up for a few months, with at most two dozen people for followers (via the internet), before divine intervention burst my bubble and I fell back to earth with singed wings but limbs and sanity mercifully intact. Imagine keeping up the act for *thirty years* and gathering hundreds, even thousands, of followers who look to you as their one and only connection to truth, goodness, and purity! Is there anyone alive who wouldn't fall prey to the deceptive allure of such power and responsibility?

We all have a little messiah complex in us. It goes all the way back to infancy. Very few of us get to build a persuasive persona out of it. Of those that do, fewer still are ever able to recruit sufficient believers to construct an actual, worldly edifice and externalize their complex as a fully functioning physical "embodiment." These are the princes and princesses of this world. They are also, I suspect, the most wretched creatures on earth.

*

The second point is more difficult to write about, as it pertains to John's sexual proclivities and how they are, I think inextricably, entangled with his ongoing abuses of power. In my struggle to embody (John's) truth in my marriage, all my efforts towards wisdom, compassion, equanimity and all the rest, were essentially geared towards one goal: to get it on with my wife. It would take far too long to go into the hows and whys of sexual dysfunction within a long-term relationship, but anyone who has been married for more than a few years probably knows how things go (I am speaking specifically of heterosexual human marriage here; other kinds might be different). Cessation of sexual desire and the lack of sexual synchronization within a marriage relates to the deepening of intimacy and, conversely, the deadening effects of familiarity (which I suspect is really a reaction against deepening intimacy). The usual cliché is that the man continues to want sex while the woman loses interest, and that this is because men can enjoy sex without much emotional content (or real intimacy) while women generally can't. The man then winds up seeking sexual gratification outside the relationship, even if only via prostitutes, internet porn, or one-night stands, while the woman is more likely to have an emotional affair. This is the conventional viewpoint anyway.

When I first met my wife, I believed in the idea of polygamy (at least if it was one-sided, i.e., it would be OK for me to have multiple partners if things moved in that direction). I have never practiced this, but it was an idea I got from books, many of them "magical," and from the tradition of shamans having many wives, and so on. As the marriage progressed, and as the sexual part became more problematic, two things happened. I became increasingly determined to have extramarital sex, not only to reduce my own frustration but also as a form of revenge against my wife for withholding sex from me (i.e., as a way to show her how much she was causing me to suffer). I never acted on this desire (perhaps mostly due to a lack of opportunity), and as the painful process continued, something else began to dawn on me. I started to understand how essential the experience of "not getting" what I most wanted within the context of a marital relationship (which is supposed to be *all about* getting it) was to understanding my own unconscious drives and the deep wounds that lay beneath them.

The point is that, in 2017, after almost ten years of marriage, and having reached a point of relative equilibrium within it, I see that process (of reluctant sexual abstinence while intimacy and familiarity deepens) as the hardest, and maybe the most crucial, aspect of my "spiritual journey" so far. And while it is generally not helpful to compare, I can't help but wonder how John's core philosophy of "settling for less" squares with his own choice to have his very own hidden harem within his followership. Is this really a viable way for him—for *any* man—to integrate his sexuality? From my current perspective, it resembles the modus operandi of either a god or a predator, but definitely not a mortal who is reconciled to the natural limits of the flesh—or, perhaps more saliently (since spermatozoa really do have no limits), the human heart. Simply put, it looks like nothing so much as an elaborately spiritualized maneuver for avoiding the psychic distress of sustained intimacy.

In this version of the book (as compared to earlier ones), I have tried to avoid psychoanalyzing John de Ruiter, because to do so requires too much presumption—and too high a risk of projection—as well as a reliance on jargon and theory. All that leaves, then, is the juxtapositioning of my own experience with his, or what is known about it. Because if John and I are the same sex and species, at all, then he has chosen to take the very opposite route to the route my own life has taken. My path has been one of increased humility and the recognition, and acceptance, of my human limits, my ordinariness, and of the values of intimacy, honesty, and simplicity over those of desire, influence, and power.

While John was telling his subjects to settle for less—above all less sexual satisfaction in their marriages—he was sneaking around behind their backs and satisfying his own, seemingly preterhuman levels of desire. That which he was asking his followers to give up (specifically the men), he was taking for himself. Isn't that the oldest con of all? "Virtue is measured by sacrifice, and since I am true virtue, sacrifice unto me all that you have, and I will use your goods wisely."

My own experience of being "under" John was of being oppressed by his goodness and by my own corresponding shame, along with growing anger, resentment, and hostility. All of these feelings I was of course unable to direct at John (even in thought), because to do so would only have been proof of my unworthiness. Instead it ended up being directed against my wife, the ostensible *cause* of my sexual frustration, thereby driving her further and further from me. I wonder, is this a dynamic currently playing out in the homes of Edmontonians across Oasis?

It's a cliché that the sexually promiscuous male is secretly a misogynist and that all his conquests are a form of sublimated violence against women. Like most clichés, it points to a subtler and deeper truth. The desire to have sexual power over women (especially in large numbers) is the desire to never be under the power of *one* woman—to never be caught in the grip of a desire that cannot be satisfied. It's an infantile pattern—a pathology—sourced in an unhealthy child-mother attachment. While this may not be all there is to John's secret agent predations—*ahem*, I mean his sexual transformations—it's almost certainly a *part* of them; and since infantile imprints are the deepest ones there are, it's likely to be *the primary drive* of those behaviors. The only alternative I can think of is that it is the expression of a Godman who is self-created and complete, bestowing divine effluences on his flock, as Oasians currently believe.

Is John a wounded infant running rampage inside a man's body, or is he a self-created Godman? Hopefully this book makes it clear which I consider more likely. But I can only speculate and ruminate. What counts for more (since theories are a dime a dozen) are the testimonies of the women John has impacted directly with his holy/unholy seductions and trance-missions. These are testimonies which it would require a brutal sort of contempt to dismiss as nothing but the wailings of women spurned—even though that is exactly how John and his group have dismissed them. Candy, Joyce, Benita and Katrina, Anina, and all the other voices that have not been heard, whether because they have been silenced or because they have chosen to remain silent—or a combination of both.

*

For de Ruiter, the only life worth living is a life lived for Truth. Living for truth means putting what you know before wants and needs. Wants and needs are an expression of a lower level of awareness and of a life lived in untruth. You cannot serve what you know and give in to want or need. A "high level relationship," as de Ruiter calls it, does not allow for want and need to enter into it, because it is driven by a higher, more impersonal purpose, that of "Truth."

I tried to sustain a marriage based on those ideals—it didn't work. Naturally, I believed the fault lay with me. Eventually, I realized there was another reason it didn't work besides my own failings, which is that marriage is a *highly personal* affair, and that wants and needs do not go away for being denied. On the contrary. I suppose it *might* be possible the way de Ruiter tried it—the polygamy way—but judging by his own example (rather than his words), it seems unlikely. So if an impersonal approach to marriage doesn't work *even for de Ruiter*, why is he still preaching it? And why are his followers still trying to practice it? Is he getting his followers to practice what he preaches so that *he* doesn't have to?

It is an ironic fact that de Ruiter instills in his followers the deepest possible want and need, the want and need to be free from want and need so they can receive the approval and blessing of their loving father who art on a whole other level. Yet his embodying that inhuman role can only lead his followers into dependency, and to a constant, gnawing sense of their own inferiority and "uncleanness," feelings which, in extreme cases, end in madness or suicide. If de Ruiter is, as I suspect, preaching an inhuman ideal that is not a practical reality, this would explain both why he doesn't practice it, and why he is careful to conceal that fact. So what happens as those pretzeled husbands become more and more frustrated with themselves and with their John-adoring partners? From my own experience, chances are they become increasingly racked by a sense of inadequacy, impotence, and self-doubt. Eventually—unable to "bend" (or twist) to accommodate "Truth"—they "snap" and express all their disowned, suppressed want and need the only way they can—either by becoming abusive or, as de Ruiter had done, by seeking satisfaction outside the relationship. After having been kept sealed tight inside the plastic wrap of de Ruiter's truth for years, what happens when the seal finally breaks? Where does all that raging, primal, infant desire go?

If de Ruiter is the head of his Oasian church, then the congregation of followers are his body. Whatever he disowns has to go somewhere, and where better than into the hearts, minds, and bodies of his flock? Where once Bob was the demon-carrier, is it now the whole of Oasis?

Might de Ruiter's shadow side express itself through the angst and impotent rage of his male followers, on the one hand,

and through his own secret sexual predation of their wives, on the other? I do not wish to cast aspersions, but at the very least it's symmetrical. That would be a high level of enmeshment, all right: one big, incestuous ball of cobbler's wax. While "high level enmeshment" is perhaps the greatest danger of any guru-disciple relationship, it might also be built into it as *an inevitable side effect*. Transference is part of the psychological process, after all.

During the first year or two of our relationship, my wife quoted several times something de Ruiter had said: "If you want to really feel pain, try *not* feeling pain." One of the primary no-no's of de Ruiter's surrendered way of being is to seek pain relief. Pain is sanctioned by the teachings, and at times even seems to extend to, "If you aren't suffering, you aren't *getting* it."

If de Ruiter's "enlightenment" is incomplete—and if there's anything I am sure of, it's this—then presumably it came at the cost of disowning an aspect of his being which he was "not okay" with. One way to consolidate that quasi-enlightenment would be by becoming a teacher and guru to others and persuading them that he was "clean" to the core. His unconscious (and maybe primary) intention behind gathering a following would be as a means to continue disowning that undesired shadow aspect—his personal pain—by offloading it onto the group. Teaching opening and softening, unconditional surrender, and "warm okayness with never being okay again" would ensure that, no matter what his followers experienced as a result of energetic enmeshment with their master, they would continue to open, soften, and be okay with *absorbing all of de Ruiter's disowned personal trauma*.

Conversely, the most frequently described experience (besides physical discomfort and boredom) by those in proximity to de Ruiter is one of *bliss*. There is a "contact high" that keeps his followers coming back for more, regardless of how little their ordinary lives improve as a result (or how intolerable and pain-filled they become). Spiritual masochism is nothing new: it's a tried and true *Christian* tradition. De Ruiter's archetypal model is the (Piscean) "man of sorrows" of Isaiah 53; the logical extreme of asceticism and self-sacrifice is flagellation, self-blame that leads to self-castigation. Many people *are* addicted to pain, to "negative thoughts and feelings," just as I had admitted to in my first meeting with de Ruiter. Giving pain addicts a sound rationale for suffering and self-punishment (i.e., that it's the natural result of opening and softening) is like giving booze to a drunk. There's no drunk happier than the drunk who has found an airtight reason to drink. And yet, as the lives of his followers have continued to come apart at the seams, de Ruiter's empire has continued to expand, and his lifestyle (allegedly) to become ever more extravagant and hedonistic. The rationale? Since he has died, he gets to really live.

There are two likely responses to this teaching, at least that I have experienced. One is a feeling of inferiority, the corresponding reverence for de Ruiter and his superior goodness, and a fervent desire to *match* it. This gives rise to a super-egoic imitation of John and the corresponding satisfaction and sense of superiority (as displayed by so many Oasians, in my experience of them at least). The second likely response is a feeling of guilt and/or shame for not being as pure and clean and good as he is, and the corresponding resentment. If they indeed create guilt, then de Ruiter's teachings are a reinforcement of the very qualities being identified as undesirable. It is the same story with Christianity: two thousand years of preaching about sin and the evils of sex have not made for a less sinful or sex-obsessed world. Presenting the idea of living for truth and juxtaposing it with negative descriptions of "want and need," of "trying to *get*," of personal agendas, self-interest, and insistence, only make those ideas grow stronger in the hearts and minds of followers.

The only recourse left for a Christian, as the flames of desire creep higher and threaten to consume his soul for eternity, is unconditional submission to Church doctrine, no questions asked. For the Oasians it is much the same deal. Hearing de Ruiter speak of impossible ideals creates a belief that he is as awesome as what he talks about. The only possible conclusion is that he has to be *loved* to get his juice. All those who believe in him will be saved. His followers may see it as initiation; but is it really closer to seduction?

As this narrative describes, I went from believing de Ruiter was Christ to believing he was the Antichrist. Apparently this was, for a time, the only way to relieve the tension of cognitive dissonance that glimpsing his "human side" caused in me. And yet making John the Antichrist was like giving back to him with my left-hand the power I had only just managed to wrest free with my right. As I see it now, de Ruiter is an extremely messed up individual with some very impressive charismatic powers of persuasion. That's about it. His story is really the oldest and most persistent story there is: that power corrupts, and absolute power corrupts absolutely. And now he has stitched himself up inside his own Dogma because, at this point, for *anything* to be good or true about his behavior requires that he is Perfect Goodness and Truth, Purity, Innocence, and Infallibility; there's simply no middle way for him or his followers anymore. Even *one* of the countless disclosures about John's "private" activities destroys that illusion and shows him as either delusional or a deceiver, or both. The more the evidence racks up, the worse it looks and the less possible it is to believe there's *anything* innocent or pure about him, because *all of it* is being used as a means to exploit others and to conceal the abuses of power. So *everything* eventually gets tainted. This doesn't make John "all bad"; it just means that nothing he says can be believed, and no experience of his "divine goodness," however direct and personal, can be trusted. When John stands naked and alone, without a single believer or belief to lift him up, only then will we get to see what sort of man he is. Only then will *he* get to see.

Father & Son

What follows is a response to Nicolas de Ruiter's blog piece about his father, "Fire by the River"* (March 10, 2017) which I posted at my own blog on April 1, 2017. In his long ode to John, Nicolas rationalizes his emotional distress about his father's behavior in a "diplomatic" attempt to explain (justify) it to John's followers. He is like an ambassador between John's (imagined) inner world of Truth and the incomprehension (and probably in some cases mild trauma) of John's followers (the ones caught in doubt).

Reading between the lines of Nicolas' ponderous appeal, I ended up wondering who his primary audience was. He seems to be trying to convince himself that it is only cultural conditioning that prevents him, Nicolas, from seeing how wonderful John's being-in-truth is. Yet since he admits John's marriage-ending adultery caused him "a decade of turmoil," he is talking about more than just cultural conditioning coming undone. Nicolas was only eleven at the time of the break-up, and such early trauma has an impact at levels deeper than merely cultural. It goes into the body and is psychically formative. John's own spiritual philosophy (which is like a psychological re-conditioning program) is that emotions are "not of the highest" and are to be ignored, suppressed, disowned, in lieu of listening to "what one knows." Even so far as this may be true, it

---

* http://www.drumsandwords.com/fire-by-the-river/

doesn't address the question of affect, namely how powerful emotions that are encountered early in life imprint not the mind (the culturally conditioned self which is still forming) but the body.

Judging by Nicolas' own words, he never had time to fully recover from the messy break up of his parents. He left Holland as a teenager, to spend time with John and try and find his father again, and it was soon after this that John hurled him into a painful reenactment of that early trauma, letting Nicolas know about his, John's, continued adulterous practices. To add insult to injury, he gave Nicolas a heavy burden of secrecy to share: a secret so dire it was "liable to upset thousands of sensible people." (This is a calculated understatement on Nicolas' part: there has been at least one suicide among John's followers, Bryan Beard, attributed by some people to intense disillusionment at seeing the truth of John's secret life. Then there is the recent death of Anina, which may have been related to that secret life also.)

Nicolas' main argument in his piece is that his father's character is beyond reproach and belongs to a higher dimension, i.e., is not of this world. Yet in his most "human" (socially and culturally normal) anecdote of his father's parenting, he cites getting drunk with John as a teenager and being too inebriated to get himself into bed! If this is John's (or Nicolas') idea of father-son "bonding," it's hard to imagine a more culturally conventional (or unhealthy) example, short of maybe taking him to a prostitute. All the other tales of being fathered which Nicolas shares are about the shock, awe, and scorched earth of Nicolas' soul from standing too close to this Man of Truth on his mission to undermine all cultural norms and values in the name of spiritual liberation. (It pays to wonder if Nicolas really believes in such a spiritual process in light of the past few hundred years' history—or even the last fifty?) Boil it down and what Nicolas is saying seems to be something like: "My dad did some socially and morally dodgy things, and he caused me massive amounts of pain; but he also got me drunk as a kid and put me to bed, so he wasn't such a bad dad!" Add to that the fact that, you know, he's God, and Nicolas is reconciled to a few peccadilloes and a decade of turmoil.

According to one ex-follower I spoke to, John also hung his sons upside down off bridges when they were small, to help them to conquer their fears. In the process, perhaps he taught them to put their total trust in him. Is what he has been doing with Nicolas as an adult really any different? What choice does a young boy have, while hanging by his ankles over an abyss, except total submission and silent prayer that whoever has his life in their hands is trustworthy? Abuse works the same way: when there is no one to rescue the child (when the abuser is the parent), emotional dependency only deepens.

When John talked Nicolas into staying with Benita von Sass (one of the two sisters John slept with while married to Nicolas' mother), even after it became insufferable to Nicolas, Nicolas says he became the "last bridge left in their relationship." What was that all about? More pressure-testing and faith-building? Or did John need Nicolas there as his eyes and ears while that particular sexual experiment went bad? Nicolas writes of "the matrix outside of his [John's] own conscience," meaning that it is only the deceptive, enslaving world that sees John's actions as morally wrong or harmful, while in his own inner space (read mind), John knows he is spotless. "I was also able to hear the tone of John's voice," he writes, "and see his face as he spoke about what he was doing."

So Nicolas made regular checks of John's facial expressions and his tone of voice, could see he wasn't wrestling with doubt, and, big sigh of relief, knew everything was under control. Has Nicolas ever heard of a poker face—or that there are people who learn to modulate their tone of voice and facial expressions as a means to get what they want? Nicolas is testifying that his father is not a culturally normal human being, but does he recognize that this designation cuts both ways? His main justification of John's actions is that John is beyond moral criteria for judgment, and Nicolas knows this because he knows John's "character." But what is a man's character to be judged by if not his actions? Why do facial expressions and tone of voice count for more in Nicolas' eyes than "willed sexual deviance" (to use a phrase out of Benita von Sass' affidavit)? Are we supposed to believe that John feeling (or showing) no guilt over his actions means he is not guilty?

That said, I would be quite surprised at this point if Nicolas doesn't see John's inner struggle written all over his face, and that it has very little to do with "battling Satan," and everything to do with a heroically sustained delusion that is starting to come apart at the seams.

*

Nicolas writes his key line of psychic defense against the nay-sayers:

"His equanimity reminded me that the conflict was in myself, not in John's actions, which are a cultural and not an inherent issue. As I had learned to do when I was 12, being told about John's relationships with Benita and Katrina, I left the drama, and followed the voice of reason."

Nicolas is saying here that John's actions can only be judged according to cultural norms of morality and that this criteria is irrelevant. This means he is actually saying: "John's actions are not an issue," period. No matter what John does, Nicolas cannot judge those actions, because to do so would betray his cultural bias. He is giving his father carte blanche.

By voice of reason, I can only presume Nicolas means John's voice, installed in his head, a constantly running program reminding him not to trust his thoughts and feelings but only *what he knows.* Since Nicolas can't trust his thoughts or feelings, however, or even his intuition, essentially this means trusting John to tell him what is reasonable and then trusting *that.* And the voice of reason is an odd choice of words here, because Nicolas is talking about embracing behavior that lacks any moral, cultural or human justification, and that belongs only to unseen dimensions of being. Reason implies intellect, but intellectually speaking, Nicolas' arguments for his father's benevolence are all at sea and out to lunch.

"What John was doing was real and the repercussions weren't mitigated by ideology or philosophical ideas."

He gets that part right at least.

> On the one hand, I could hear directly how people were processing their involvement with John, in their difficulties, awakenings, and insights. These conversations opened inner eyes for me, and I saw the surface of reality peel away, levels of meaning cracking open; beings cohabiting our urban spaces. I saw an ache, cocooned in a man's heart, break open like a butterfly of realization. I saw the skin of the world removed, showing structures of meaning that move subsurface, where controversy and confusion become two-dimensional.

Nicolas uses self-consciously mystical language to describe countless people's pain, turmoil, confusion, and suffering as a result of John's actions—all of which are being committed in the moral vacuum of "John-space." This is an indication of how reluctant Nicolas, like his dad, is to look at or to feel the human dimensions, the actual, lived consequences, of John's ideology and philosophical ideas. All of Nicolas' flowery, turgid descriptions seemed designed to distance the events described from any coherent thoughts or feelings. They have a mythical, fairy tale flavor to them.

Nicolas has found a space of dissociation within which to come to terms with these events, and he is faithfully representing that state to the reader, as if to usher them into it. (I am sure many Johnnies gratefully submitted to be ushered). The accounts of soul-crunching confusion and despair in the face of John's many betrayals are all couched in John-isms about endless pressure as necessary to the overcoming of the conditioned self, pressure that can only be increased, exponentially, by the prescribed suppression of all emotion as being of the conditioned self and not "what you know is true" (i.e., what his father tells him to believe).

When Nicolas writes that "Over time, questions were to be answered and deepen my integration of the extreme," it's another example of how he uses unnecessarily complex, codified language to cover the more brutal aspects of his experience. Integration of the extreme = shocking, possibly traumatic experiences that caused him disorientation, anxiety, panic, and probably dissociation as a means to cope with overwhelming psychic content. In which case, deepening "*dis*integration" is just as likely to be the result of extremity. Certainly, the style, as well as content, of Nicolas' piece does nothing to reassure the reader. His reasoning sounds like someone being repeatedly dunked into a truth trough, mistaking momentary relief between dunkings for illumination.

Nicolas wants to believe John's behavior is magnifying Truth, helping him to overcome his cultural and moral conditioning, and that his feelings of horror are nothing but culturally conditioned reactions. But what if the real cause of his horror is John's shock and awe methods and his own deep aversion to them, his knowing that they are inherently, not just culturally, wrong? This would mean he is not going to find any relief except in the momentary gulps of air which his father allows him, during which John's storytelling skills (the Truth-program) come to the "rescue" in the form of a dark lullaby.

As anyone who has followed John for any time at all knows, John teaches his followers (maybe the correct term for them is "thralls") to be unemotional. Suppressing emotions might bring some relief, but if so it is only at a high cost. Where do the emotions go when they are suppressed, ignored, disowned, unacknowledged? Into the body, as toxins.

It's an ironic, even tragic, fact that people who leave John are still tied to him as long as they have unresolved feelings about him. And how can they not, when he never acknowledges their feelings as real? It's a powerful, devilish trick for keeping people waiting on the line indefinitely. Whether they are incensed, outraged, confused, bitter, angry, resentful, sad, or grieving, such seemingly unresolvable emotions (unresolvable because John is emotionally out of reach) will cause them to seek refuge in John's own advice not to listen to or take seriously their feelings. And so, the ex-Johnnie, having no way to resolve that tension, finds him or herself perennially back under the Master's influence.

This is the Oasis revolving door: even as we think we are leaving, we find ourselves back again. If we reject John, criticize or question him, most especially with strong feeling, that's just the proof of his power and purity, on the one hand, and, on the other, of the impurity of our "patterns" and our inability to appreciate the goodness of John or the goodness within us that only John, in his supreme virtue, can appreciate. This sort of "thinking" is built into the group's mindset—it's foundational to John-think—and it is designed to ensure there is no escape for the Birds of Being from the Nest John built. How can you escape from a mirage when it appears wherever your eyes fall, inside the desert of John's "teachings"?

I went through this horrendous process myself, and it took months, years even, to stop drinking sand and locate my own source of sustenance. Maybe I am still completing the process, and this is why I never released the book. In the worst of it, John seemed everywhere, like a parasitical organism that regenerated itself from a single cell whenever I thought I'd got it completely out of my system. But was it really John, or was it the internal image I had created of him that was endlessly regenerating?

*

Returning to the so-called "disclosures": Does Nicolas or anyone else not wonder why John's choice of "timed revelations" essentially equals only owning up to stuff when there's too much evidence to deny it? As the secrets are revealed, and he is inducted into the loop, Nicolas sees it (or wants us to see it) as all for his own spiritual edification. Couldn't it just as easily be seen as a way to make him complicit with his father's crimes and to corrupt and prepare him for worse to come? Such things as Nicolas may already be privy to, but which are not part of official disclosure because, so far, no one has blown the whistle on them?

So far as John naming names to Nicolas, were any of the women asked if they minded John sharing their info? Did he also share his private collection of racy emails, gathered from the many hopeful applicants to his harem? (John allegedly asked potential sexual recruits to describe their idea of moving unto him in much detail, via email.) Nicolas writes: "The reason for my inclusion in that information, as I understand it, is to create a third party for accountability and support." It's not clear if Nicolas is referring to the Accountability Committee here (a committee ostensibly set up to address the concerns of followers over the increasingly disturbing claims about John's hidden behaviors; I think it first came into being after the von Sasses took John to court). But reading between the lines again, the words suggest that, insofar as Nicolas was informed, he didn't really know why, so once again he was forced to speculate, ruminate, confabulate, and embellish (and above all, rationalize) John's actions to reduce the massive cognitive dissonance they were causing him.

What is clear throughout Nicolas' testimonial is that he cannot speak authoritatively. Nicolas may be the chosen heir to Oasis, but he is also only twenty-eight (or twenty-nine), and, from what I've seen, no one around John (not even a long-timer like Baba) has any kind of truth-authority or much of a clue about what John is actually doing or saying. The higher-ups seem more, not less, likely to fall back on blind trust in their Master, and on an admission of incomprehension backed by an avowed gladness to forgo the superficial comforts of intellectual thought, opinion, etc., all of which are not to be trusted because they are just part of conditioned self-defenses.

Since at Oasis, Ignorance is Strength, it seems reasonable to suppose that the so-called Accountability Committee has no power, no autonomy, and no clue about their purpose. It certainly isn't there to make anyone accountable, unless it's the whistle-blowers and victims of John's power abuses, who are seen as troublemakers, disruptors, gossipers, and potential enemies of Truth. So the Accountability Committee is a) all for show, to make it seem like something is being done to address the question of consequences; b) to cover up John's actions and protect his image by managing the dissident voices (making them accountable) and amplifying the party line, quashing doubts as fast as they can surface. Meanwhile, all support is directed exclusively towards John and his Oasian Empire of One.

*

In his film review of *American X*, Nicolas writes, in the same overwrought language, of redemption through death: "Returning to the Christian framework, 'righteousness' doesn't earn perfection. Perfection requires the blood of the lamb." So who is the lamb? John self-identifies as Jesus, the Lamb of God, forever making the ultimate sacrifice. He has even convinced Nicolas that having a harem of worshipful women is like being trapped under a mountain. But what does John actually sacrifice in this story? He is fabulously wealthy, has a bevy of ever-changing sexual partners (or concubines), is adored by hundreds, never has to admit he is wrong or apologize for anything he does, and effectively possesses absolute power within his day to day life. He eats, drinks, smokes, and fornicates to his conditioned heart's desire, because that is all just superficial or, if it's not, it's a movement of truth that is not for his "person." He charges for his time and gives nothing of himself emotionally to his followers. Where exactly is the sacrifice in all this?

On the other hand, by presenting himself as the supreme martyr whose every act is an act of self-sacrifice, John coerces everyone who is in thrall to his "goodness" to sacrifice themselves before him. In the current context, this means defending him no matter what he does or what the consequences of his actions are. It means lying in public. It means keeping silent about his abuses of power and then writing long, impassioned defenses of him that can only serve to silence others by throwing them into guilt and self-doubt for ever having questioned John's goodness. It means joining an army of spin whose primary aim is the suppression of truth wherever it threatens to surface, and the continued crazy-making of promoting willed delusion, insanity, and self-indulgence as a devotion to Truth at any cost.

Meanwhile, his actions, as they become revealed (due above all to an inability to keep them hidden), are provoking more and more confusion, distress, despair, and anger in his followers, all feelings to be suppressed or concealed, thereby making them all the more oppressive and consuming. For now, this "negativity" is likely to be mostly directed at other people in the Oasis group; but sooner or later, it is going to be directed at the Leader himself. What's his contingency plan for that day? Is that why he bought Rottweilers and had security cameras installed in his home "complex"? Is John preparing his secret getaway for when the trumpet sounds, or is he going to make his stand, face the music, and risk losing everything?

So far, nothing about John de Ruiter indicates that he is the sort of man to take responsibility for *anything*—and certainly not for the consequences of his actions, for all the emotional, mental, and energetic harm he may have caused to so many of those who stumbled or staggered hopefully into his line of "friendly" fire, their hearts and palms extended. John's four-by-four does not brake for pedestrians. He is on a mission from Truth, and everyone else is expendable. His real mission may be just that: to secure his own survival at any cost, the truth will out, taking no prisoners. And since John seems to believe his mission as Truth-Embodiment is worth more than life itself, when push comes to shove, where will he draw the line?

Reaching Out to Nicolas

On April 12, 2017, I sent this email to Nicolas de Ruiter:

> As you know, I am writing a book about my experiences with John, and am currently revising and expanding the MS to include recent developments at Oasis. While writing for me is a powerful means of getting to the truth, I am aware of how it can also be used to misrepresent, obscure, and distort. I am especially aware of this danger with this current project because of the obvious consequences it can have in people's lives, beginning (but by no means ending) with John's close family.
>
> Like yourself, I consider honesty a fundamental virtue, and I do my utmost to practice it regardless of how much inconvenience or discomfort it can cause me. As a writer, I try to be as fair, accurate, and compassionate as I can be towards my subject(s), and to see from all possible perspectives, both for ethical and aesthetic reasons.
>
> Though we have never met, I feel as though our paths are destined to intersect at some point, so I'm preempting that by writing to you now. I started out passionately devoted to John but over time have come to believe he is only a man, and quite a devious one at that. Your own trajectory seems to have been the exact opposite. While our points of view are currently opposed and it would be easy for us to fall into adversarial roles, we also both understand how much perceptions can change, even reverse, over time. Maybe there is a way for us to meet on a common ground, if only the ground of shared curiosity and desire to get to the truth, in the midst of so much confusion?

Besides the obvious, it does seem like we have more in common than differences: an interest in film, writing, and getting to the truth; troubled family histories unfolding in the public eye (my brother was a celebrity who died in 2010); an ongoing struggle to understand our past, which has fueled my writing for a decade now. One thing I have had to fully face up to through knowing (or "knowing") John is just how wrong I can be; ironically, this means I have to allow that I am still wrong about him. All I can do is continue to sift through the evidence in search of an increasingly coherent and meaningful picture. This current book is a central part of that effort, the continuation of a lifelong effort to make sense out of my experience.

I would be grateful to hear more from you on how to improve the book before publication. We may find it difficult to agree, but I am willing to try, and am available to talk, off the record or on, whenever suits you. I might also be able to put [sic] you to understand why so many of John's followers are leaving now, perhaps even clarify your own position, which I can only imagine must be an incredibly difficult one.

Knowing John and some of those close to him has been one of the richest experiences of my life so far, and not just as a writer. There is a great deal of sadness and pain, but there is also excitement and the joy of discovery. I have noticed a remarkable sense of awakening around those who have found the courage to leave John, so much so that I can't help but wonder if this isn't part of John's secret intent. Anything is possible!

If you're interested in talking, let me know and we can arrange a time and place. You can find out more about me via my website, where you will discover I am transparent to an almost neurotic degree. I am not a keeper of secrets (just the reverse), and I will always strive to be upfront and honest with you.

Nicolas replied five days later with three lines, saying he was pleasantly surprised to hear from me and would be happy to meet up, after the seminar. I replied that I wasn't likely to be in Edmonton anytime soon and suggested a virtual meet-up. Nicolas responded that he was only interested in a flesh and blood meeting. I made an argument for the positive benefits of online communication, and this time he wrote a longer reply, mentioning that he had read *Paper Tiger*, questioning the accuracy of my portrait of my brother, and of my motives in writing about John. He suggested that my relationship with and perception of his father was all in my imagination, all "projection."

I responded:

> dear Nicolas,
> Happy to hear you read and appreciated *Paper Tiger*. I am guessing that was the copy I sent to John back in 2010?
> The question of projection is a recurring one, of course. An ongoing concern for any self-examining person. In a way the whole spiritual path comes down to how to separate our projections from reality, and I have wrestled for years with this. This includes specifically what you address, the concern that all my attempts to discover and demonstrate abuses of power might be compromised by an unconscious compulsion in myself, making them worthless, and worse, self-defeating. What if it were so? An awful prospect, right? I would certainly be glad to hear any

specific ways you think I may be projecting onto John.

The process for me has been a purging one, recognizing over time with growing peace and clarity that it's not an either/or question (which is very much the point). It is not either projection or reality; it is not even that projections obscure reality, because nothing can do that, finally. Reality is a mirror for our internal state, and this includes those projections which reflect our own internal patterns or "veil" and so obscure reality from us. In other words, examining the actions of others, for me, has proved to be a valid way of identifying my own patterns (projections) and getting to the truth. In fact, John said it himself: our patterns are our way home.

When I write about John (or my brother, or Whitley Strieber, or myself), it begins with a search for and an examination of the simple facts. It's really detective work. Since I am aware that the self that is doing the examining is unreliable, then this awareness always factors into the examination process. The facts point back to the self that is examining them. They indicate the ways in which it, the self, needs to be examined, and why.

You suggest that my own projections make my view of John unreliable. My response to you is that using John as a mirror to see my own distortions more clearly is the primary goal of examining John. It is also precisely what allows me to confirm that what I am seeing in John is accurate: by confirming it within my own "knowing." Irony abounds! What it does not allow for is moral judgment of the other being investigated, because my capacity to see these flaws is always accompanied by, in fact is only possible through, a deep empathic understanding of them. Without that empathy I would be lost. It is, along with the "mere facts," the very ground of all the research.

And of course it is the matching patterns (the psychology [sic] wounds and accompanying proclivities to abuse power) that drew me to John in the first place.

It is true that I never managed to have a personal relationship with John. This is because he always resisted it and maintained a safe distance between us, despite all my attempts to bridge that gulf (such as sending him a copy of *Paper Tiger*!) But of course, this itself says a lot about John and his need to keep people at a distance, something that characterizes his methods as a teacher and also as a human being (judging by what I have been able to gather from those who do know him well). In my view, John's need to remain distant, aloof, and emotionally unavailable is central to his maintenance of control and to wielding power over others. There's nothing especially spiritual, or unusual, about that. As you know, it did trigger my own patterns (having had a similarly distant father) and stir up a vast well of unmet need in me. Being able to address that has helped me to heal (from) my own power abuses, both potential and actual.

Bridging the symbolic gulf between John & I corresponds with bridging an actual gulf within myself. It entails connecting to those who have been most profoundly affected by John, which now includes yourself (an opportunity I am grateful for). Via these connections I am slowly uncovering a reliable, accurate picture, both of John, the man, and John the spiritual "awakener" ~ which means the nature of the effect he has had on others.

A medicine can only be judged by the people it has healed; there is no other criteria. I am afraid that

John's disregard for the simple, human, personal dimension of "awakening" and of spiritual guidance has had tragic consequences, not only for those who have put their unquestioning trust in him, but for John himself.

Personally, I can testify that John's impact on myself was fairly balanced overall, in terms of positive and negative. But this is only insofar as I have recognized just how misguided my original perception of him was, and have been able to move past that projected idealization, and then again, past the negative inversion of it that helped to cancel out the first. I now feel I have a relative "clean slate" with John. I feel neither admiration nor condemnation, but only warm engagement and interest. I believe this is how and why it was finally time to revisit, complete, and release the book.

This is only happening via the inclusion of other testimonies, people's lived experience of the impact John has had on them, not so much in terms of awakening but those of confusion, trauma, pain, distress, fragmentation, and anguish. This is a reality that no amount of spiritual jargon or clever re-contextualization can change. Or is John going to say that this [is] all those people's "projections"? Certainly he has persuaded many, including yourself, that this is all merely a rather painful means to a wonderful end. But so far I have [seen] a whole lot of means, with no end in sight. Isn't it fair to question a medicine that's only guarantee of efficacy, in the end, seems to be what's printed on the packaging?

Thank you for your well wishes. Today the sun is indeed shining ~ and is it happens it's my father's birthday too!

Nicolas did not reply.

Oasis Strikes Back

Two weeks later, on May 7, 2017, I sent an email to 73 members of the Birds of Being Google group, as follows:

> First off, please excuse the impersonal nature of this collective email. Most of you won't know who I am (though I posted on BoB for a while in 2010-11). Some of you may know I have written a book about John, which I began in 2010 and have been working on, on and off, ever since. John knows about the book (I told him about it at Oasis in 2011), and as far as I know he has seen a copy of an earlier draft. I have also been in touch with Nicolas about the book.
>
> The book is above all a sincere attempt to understand the ongoing phenomenon that is John. I am currently updating it to include the latest disclosures and revelations, some of which you will know about, others you may not. In attempting to understand John and his teachings, I have relied principally on three things: John's own words; my own direct experience of him; the testimonies of others, both those who have known him personally and his followers. I have heard many testimonials, but I would like the book to be as balanced as possible and want to avoid speculation as much as I can. The wider the spectrum of experiences I can draw upon, the more I can do justice to the subject.
>
> If you would like to contribute to this project ~ by sharing your understanding of John, anonymously or not, on or off the record ~ I would be very grateful to hear from you. I will respect all requests for confidentiality, 100%. Specifically, I am seeking clarity around the disclosures about John's sexual Calling, but also more generally, in terms of how

> people understand, experience, and apply John's teaching-transmission.
>
> What is the integrated philosophy of the CoIP? What's your understanding about the nature, purpose, and meaning of John's sexual Calling and why it was kept secret for so long? Do you have any reservations or doubts, and if so, how do you deal with them? I am also open to hearing whatever else you may wish to say about John and your experiences of him.
>
> I'm currently serializing parts of the book at my blog, and if you are interested, you can read the first few chapters here:
>
> With warmest wishes

Over the next 36 hours, I received three responses, ranging from critical to hostile. I didn't know it until the next day, but on May 8 Nicolas de Ruiter posted the following at BoB, with the subject line of "Birdsong solicitation....I recommend flying away from that":

> Hi everyone, sorry to bring a notification of this tone. It's just worth it, and important to be aware. An email has been sent to an unknown group of people asking for contributions to a book about John. The email has the subject, "Soliciting bird songs." The writer claims that John is aware of the book and that I have been in discussion with the writer about his book. It's true that John is aware, and that I have been in contact with the writer, but the writer and his book haven't really considered John and I have not suggested to the writer that I support his book at all. I have read the manuscript and would say that the contents are far more narrow and negative than the writer's email suggests. If you expect a balanced, fair, or kind

> perspective from this writer, I suggest giving no information at all to him. The level of this writer's reliability is low.

There were several responses to this post, two from the same people who had emailed me. William T wrote: "I second that. He claims to want testimony for a balanced perspective, but he clearly has an agenda, and that is to denigrate John. His graphics and words about John make that obvious, and he is trawling for more grist for his debunking mill." Marina M wrote:

> Hello dears, It's also worth remembering that anyone clicking on a link on-line pushes it up the web rankings, effectively giving "credence" that it's worth reading. Not just to members of the group but to the public at large. Also anyone contributing to the request for information provides validity that the work is 'balanced'. "Journalism" is based on the idea that balance is a combination of "opposing views," i.e. [sic] if "He says this" and "She says the opposite," that's balance. But anything can be twisted positively or negatively to back up the author's perspective, thereby posing as journalism within what is usually a very narrow paradigm. The author's agenda is always the most important thing to consider, and to me if someone is sincerely exploring the ongoing phenomenon that John is, that person would be here in Edmonton, part of its ongoing unfoldment and evolution. Making conclusions, third hand, from a distance does not sound sincere to me. Anything called the Messiah Complex sets off major warning bells and a sense of foreboding. However nicely the request is written.

Barbara wrote: "Hear, hear! Thanks for these strong, good and appropriate words."

Shortly after Nicolas' post at BoB, the College of Integrated Philosophy released a newsletter warning recipients not to talk to outsiders about John and announcing the "re-introduction" of the Accountability Committee. From that post (with emphasis added):

> In 2009 there was quite a stir in the group caused by the departure of Benita and Katrina and John's marriage to Leigh Ann. In response John formed the Accountability Committee to increase communication, and for him to open, share and discuss concerns with a high level of detail and personal relevance.
>
> John continued to meet with the Committee on a regular basis, drawing from what its members brought to the discussion. We started out dealing with specific issues stemming from questions amongst the community, and widened the scope over the years to include other community concerns and interests. Examples of topics have been, how can we answer deeply held concerns that are not often voiced in the chair? How can we as a group support people whose difficulties are less in view? How can we support people who feel left out? Or what can we do to support deeper and constructive thinking and enquiry around difficult topics?
>
> When John told the Committee about the movement of the calling through sexuality we spoke for many meetings about the nature of this movement through John and how it affected individuals and the group. Through John's opening this up in a deep, delicate, sensitive, discreet and forthcoming manner over many meetings, we were able to reach new

understandings, but more than anything we reached a depth of restedness, the same quality of knowing that opens in the regular meetings. We were settled by John's transparent manner of communicating and our sense that his nature remained consistent even as circumstances were becoming more complex. To reach this level of settledness without bypassing anything is what each Committee member owes the community.

There has been criticism that John put together a committee of people who would agree with him. It is essential that the Committee is rigorous and honest in any discussion, and that we bring forward our clarity, and the clarity of community members who speak to us.

Our lives in relation to meetings will continue to be rich and complex, and we're in it together. Where we can support the connection between us and to what we know, we are available. We are also available regarding the representation of meetings and John to the public or the media. *With increased interest from journalists and other interested writers, we need to take care in what we say and how. A recent message, for example, has gone around requesting information. Our words can easily be taken out of context and also misused by researchers, reporters and other writers. If you are approached in this way, we recommend checking in with a Committee member or The College.*

The Committee members are available for your thoughts and concerns, although you may only hear in return that your thoughts are received and will definitely be brought to John and the Committee. *It is not part of the purpose of the Committee to report back to the community.* Everything does contribute to a greater understanding, and can lead to

> developments like the Cohesion and Off the Shelf events. The members of the Committee have seen that *what comes from John has always been good*, and we continue to meet every month or two, looking at what is moving in the community and how we can all take care in the best way possible.
>
> You can contact us about anything concerning or inspiring to you, in person or by email:
> With kind regards and respect,
> Pearl, Ernst, Zaba, Nicolas, Guy, Leilah, Leigh Ann and John

I composed what I planned to be an open letter to Nicolas that included a series of logical arguments and a selection of quotes from people who had left John. I shared it with the people quoted (as well as Joyce), and was planning to have Phil Stretch post it to Birds of Being as soon as possible. It was confusing and a little upsetting to be met by John-ites with such a negative response to my invitation, and by the assumption that I could only have devious intentions. The position they took effectively nullified any possibility that, regardless of my feelings or opinion about John, I might be trying to get to the truth. The assumption was that, by questioning John and wishing to examine his behaviors, I must have a selfish agenda. (By implication, those who wished to defend John and to prevent such questioning from happening, had no agenda!)

Obviously I hadn't expected a flurry of interest or enthusiasm; I had expected mostly silence, possibly some distrustful responses, and a lot of poetic outpourings of love and devotion for John without much logical analysis to back it up. Would I have quoted those people to show how "brainwashed" John's followers are? That would have depended entirely on how brainwashed they sounded. My impression of the College's response was of a group going into lockdown. It read to me as controlling and cult-like, soulless and mechanical and deadening to read. It also suggested a panic response. Why have such a reaction if there is nothing to hide? Rather than allowing people to speak for themselves and risk their eulogies being used as grist for my "satanic" mill, Nicolas and the Accountability Committee chose to act to discourage people from communicating with me at all. They tried to paint me as an unreliable journalist (leaving out the fact that I was also an ex-follower), a lone wolf howling at the gates, representing nothing but my own baser (anti-Truth) interests. In fact, I was just one particularly insistent voice among many, one that was willing to be identified and who only *appeared* to stand alone. I represented many other voices not yet ready to be identified, expressing a collective concern—or maybe despair—for John, for Nicolas, for his followers, and above all for those that have been unjustly silenced, that had never been heard.

These were the voices of John's followers and ex-followers, some of whom had been with John for decades. If Nicolas, John, or the A.C. didn't care what they had to say, what exactly *did* they care about?

*

I wound up my letter with the following:

> When Joyce left John in 1999, she tried to warn him and the group that her husband had lost his way. No one listened. She was seen as being unable to handle the truth or to surrender to John's goodness and her testimony was deemed irrelevant. Nicolas and his brother, Nathaniel—also now working with John—believe she brainwashed them to turn them against him.
>
> When John dumped Benita, he testified in court that she had never been his wife and pushed her out

of the business without recompense. Having helped to build Oasis, Benita became *persona non grata* there, and her testimony was seen as malicious slander, unfit for the delicate ears of the Birdies. She too was silenced.

When Anina died in 2014 under mysterious circumstances, her family tried to find out the truth of John's involvement, and ascertain whether he might have been in any way responsible for her death. They were served with a SLAPP (written threat of legal action) by John's lawyers and frightened into silence. Some people at Oasis questioned this and wanted to know more. They were discouraged from asking questions in the group and referred to the Accountability Committee.

Now anyone who is approached by me, or by any other researcher seeking clarification (besides John's licensed hagiographer Guy, a member of the AC, like Nicolas), is being referred to the newly unveiled AC, where they can be advised who to talk to and what is acceptable for them to say. So who exactly is the AC set up to protect?

In the introduction to my book, I write that no one who is in a cult believes they are in a cult. This is built into the organizational framework from the ground up, for how else would a spiritual organization become a cult? There is simply no way for people on the inside to see this, and no way for the people outside who *can* see it to enlighten them. It is a seemingly unbridgeable abyss. What can be talked about, however, is the harm being inflicted on those inside the organization. This can be testified to by those who have made it out. Yet tragically, these people are no longer seen as trustworthy by those on the inside, precisely because they no longer belong to the organization. They are seen as traitors who have turned away from "the Truth."

The inability to listen, receive, and take on the full implications of what those who have left the group have to say—because their accounts are negative and because they come from outsiders—ironically, is itself the most compelling evidence that cult mechanics are in play, and of the harm being done by them.

I don't think you [Nicolas] are afraid of what John's followers might tell those of us on the outside of his influence. I think you are afraid of what they might learn from us.

Open Letter to Nicolas

Due to a number of factors, I delayed sending. That night, after some time mulling it over in bed, I decided that logical argumentation was almost certainly futile in a case like this, possibly even counter-productive. I had the sense that Nicolas, the AC, and Oasis were laying a trap for me, and that to respond with rationally measured argumentation would only be falling into it. At the very least, I would be falling back on my usual way of dealing with things, and if ever there was a time for dropping habitual defense reactions, it was now. I wrote another letter, which I sent the following day.

Dear Nic,

On May 7 of this year, I sent an email to 73 of John's followers who subscribe to the Birds of Being Google Group, inviting them to share their experiences with John for my book. On May 8, you posted at BoB, warning people not to engage with me and telling them: "The level of this writer's reliability is low."

As you know, we shared a brief email correspondence in April, during which you expressed warmth and a willingness to meet up in Edmonton if I ever visited. My last email to you addressed some of your concerns about the book, in as direct and as honest a way as I was able. I invited you to tell me more about how I might be "projecting" my issues onto John, as you believe I am. You didn't reply, and so our brief correspondence ended. When I read your words about me at BoB, I was both surprised and hurt. Was this really what you believed, or was it only what you wanted others to believe about me? Of course I was aware that the gulf between our perspectives was potentially unbridgeable—how could I not be? Yet while it lasted, I felt there was at least some mutual respect between us, and a shared interest in having an honest dialogue. Maybe I was mistaken.

FYI, the email I sent John's followers wasn't seeking information about John (as the recent College newsletter implied). I know his dedicated followers would never say anything negative about him, and you know it too. I was inviting those people to testify, to share their experiences with John, and if possible to help clarify what, in their view, he is doing and why there is such a sharp contrast between his teaching and his private behaviors. You presented me as misguided and ill-motivated for wanting to shed light on John's shadow side. But is this really so terribly wrong?

John represents to me not just a puzzle but the greatest challenge I have ever faced as a writer—that any writer has ever faced—the challenge to reconcile the tension between "good" and "evil," relying only on the evidence of the senses, inner and outer. I think John presents this challenge—knowingly or not—to all of his followers, and to all those who care about him. I also think that very few of them are bold enough to meet this challenge and to take the proverbial Minotaur by the horns. Does anyone know how consciously John is embodying this archetypal conflict of light and dark? I doubt if anyone but John can ever know for sure, but then, I don't need to know to meet the challenge.

John offers his followers an image of goodness, purity, power, and perfection, and he offers words to match that image. He provides an incredible, blissful "high" through proximity to his presence—by literally being where he is at—and it's a high that (I can testify) is addictive. There's a conundrum in this, as there is with every spiritual teacher. A spiritual teacher cannot teach self-reliance. He or she cannot lead a student to autonomy. Have you ever wondered why there are no graduates in the College of Integrated Philosophy? (You are a smart guy, I am sure you have.) The reason in my view is that no one can embody or integrate the love of what one knows by going to a college. The title of COIP is a joke, intended or not. (Who knows? I know John loved to pull pranks as a kid and a teenager, and I sometimes wonder if his entire Ministry is a prank.)

You may ask, what's a spiritual teacher to do, when the one thing worth learning can't be taught, when we can only rely on ourselves to determine the difference between good and evil, truth and falsehood? Worse still, when the creation of an externalized image of goodness, to worship or even to emulate, is the source of the greatest confusion and error that exists in this world?

There is an answer to this question, and I believe I have found it via my experience of John, and that the answer is the skeleton key that unlocks the shadowy labyrinth in which the Minotaur dwells. It is to present a contradictory image, one possessed of the very opposite qualities, a shadow image, and then to conceal it in plain sight, like a purloined letter. By superimposing the negative image on top of the image of goodness, it becomes invisible. Over time, that shadow image—the exact inverse of the image of the perfected spiritual Master—slowly becomes visible to the followers, bringing about a steady erosion of belief in the positive image, and the corresponding disillusionment. This invites the follower-student to reject the father-teacher image they have created—out of their own wants and needs—and to "slay the Buddha." Only when we see the shadow clearly do we realize we are facing in the wrong direction—looking outward and not inward—and change our orientation, away from other, back to self.

You are John's oldest son. No one can know better than you do how there is always an element of rebellion and defiance in such a shift, away from transference and dependency and towards integration, autonomy, and wholeness. There is always some experience of betrayal. What has betrayed us is not the father or the teacher—who was always only human—but our own projected image of them. It betrayed us because an image cannot ever give us what we need—as children or as spiritual followers—a living, loving, tactile, full-body connection to the other. John is not there for any of his followers, and I suspect he was not there for his children or his wives either. But then, no one is there for him, either. Communication is only possible between equals, and John's whole way of being precludes the possibility of equality.

John's shadow side is real. As you of all people must know, it is exactly as deep and wide as his light side, and correspondingly dark. The brighter the light, the darker the shadow cast by the object, and the object here is John's "person," his human side. The more luminous he has to be for his followers, the shadier he has become behind the scenes. Everything strives towards wholeness and balance, and so slowly, inexorably, the dark, hidden aspect of both the man and the teachings is being disclosed. Who among John's followers is ready for "full disclosure"? This is what we are getting to see now. Can you really blame me for wanting to help draw back the curtain?

Is all this "lovely and good"? That depends on your perspective. As long as we are perceiving dualistically, nothing we perceive is ever only lovely and good. Of course this applies to John too, and only a fool could ever think otherwise. But John has built an empire on the backs of fools; you know it, he knows it, and I know it. However painful admitting that might be to those of us whose backs have been co-opted for John's ascension, it can be lovely and good to let ourselves see this, to see all that is unlovely and bad—craven, corrupt, mean and manipulative—not only in John but in ourselves. Seeing changes everything, and the alternative is denial and self-rejection, a condition that prevents wholeness from happening. Like everything that lives and is fragmented, John wants to become whole. Who knows, maybe he even wants us to become whole too? Or maybe he wants to prevent that from happening with all his being? And maybe his very determination to prevent us from becoming whole is what provides us with the most golden opportunity?

My question to you is this: are you and John's followers willing to know the whole truth about John the man, regardless of your investment in the image of goodness which you have created? Can your idea of him, your belief, and your "knowing," withstand every last revealed truth about his worldly (and otherworldly) behaviors? If not, then what? Which is more precious to you: to know the truth, whatever the cost in belief; or to hold onto an idealized image, regardless of how unreal?

As his oldest son and heir, I have no doubt at all that you carry John's secrets—his shadow—in a way no one else alive does—not even John. I came from a family of dark secrets; some of them may be almost too dark to imagine. I can easily imagine how heavy this burden must weigh on you—the knowledge that so few of John's followers could ever bear even a portion of those secrets the way you have had to. I also know—or imagine I know—that you feel it's your duty to carry and keep those secrets, that it is essential to serving John and supporting him in his work. No doubt that's true, but I wonder if you are aware just how heavy the cost is—not only for you but for those you love, and who love you?

John wants people to believe that transparency is a flawed concept because truth is relative, that it is only as appropriate as the circumstances merit, that letting it all hang out is fine at a nudist beach but not-OK at an Oasis board meeting. Unfortunately, this has become a justification, not merely for discretion but for opacity, obfuscation, and lies—and for the sorts of interactions that I suspect most of John's followers, however loyal, would see as sexually inappropriate, if not shocking, and shady backroom (or basement) deals.

This creates a problem. When concealment is seen to be serving self-interest, then all the lofty spiritual explanations become not a way out of that trap, but a still deeper layer of the labyrinth. If John is using truth as a means to conceal, goodness as a cloak for evil, then not just you but any of us who have ever supported John in what he does become complicit in that deception. We who have had our trust abused become abusers of trust.

The book I am writing is my way of owning up to this, of absolving myself of past sins, for supporting John and offering his mixed bag of good and evil, truth and lies, to the world. It is not a question of pointing an accusatory finger at John but of recognizing my affinity with the same power abuses and betrayals which John appears to be guilty of, and of owning and integrating my own shadow side. This is very far from a painless process. I don't volunteer for it lightly.

I can only imagine how much more painful and challenging—but also vital and potentially liberating—the process must be for you, as his son. It would be patronizing of me to think I could help with that process, especially since you obviously don't want my help. And yet, it would be remiss if I didn't admit that this is my deepest, truest reason for writing to you. Because what else has value in this world if not two souls connecting across an abyss, at a level of deepest vulnerability, and having the courage to share the things they are most afraid to own up to? What else is even real, if not this uncertainty and unsafeness of ever meeting, and the willingness to try?

With love,

Jasun

P.S. Since the scope of this letter extends beyond the two of us, I have made it an open letter, to be posted at various places on the Net. You can respond in whichever way feels most comfortable to you.

*

The first response was from a man named Manfred: "'A pen went scribbling along. When it tried to write love, it broke.' Jalaluddin Rumi." The second was from Nicolas:

> Dear Jasun,
>
> Thank you for writing about what you see. My impression is that your reply has filled out what I wrote on Birds of Being, as now each person can read your approach in your own words. To reply to your first comment, my enjoyment of our dialogue is the same as always, even though I recommend that people not send in their commentary for your book. So far I have chosen not to give my words to your book, and I recommend the same to others because I expect that my thoughts and theirs have more clarity

and value inside of us than represented through your writing. That's just my view, and I thought it was worth sharing whether or not anybody agrees.

That being said, the gulf between you and I is easily bridged. I think it's fine that we see things differently. The dialogue and the connection will continue, no doubt, and I would still be happy to meet in person if the opportunity comes up.

Warmly, Nicolas de Ruiter

The third, from Robert W:

> Jasun, I must say, as a long time knower of who and what John is, your letter did a most excellent job of making Nicholas's case for him. Your letter is so full of projection, lack of self awareness [sic] and dishonesty that the task of assisting you to approach your subject with the kind of depth that those of us who get it know is required, it is clearly not worth the time and effort it would take. This work is the responsibility of you and only you, as all of us who have taken the time and exquisite care to do so are fully aware and can so easily see that you are in need of doing before you could realistically approach your subject with the respect and care that it truly deserves. This is exactly the task that John is uniquely qualified to do and the difficulty of which is the reason why it is taking so long to accomplish. You would do well to join us in this effort as there remains much to and time is short.

After that, one from Dina said simply: "You could write a book Nicolas. I would buy it. Your words land like music in me :)"

I'm not sure what to add to that. Perhaps needless to say, I didn't find Nicolas' response warm or friendly. I didn't feel as though he was even addressing me, much less responding to my letter. What I read was a form of perception management meant primarily for John's followers and having two main aims: firstly, to show BoB-ites how "open" he was to me, even though he didn't bother to respond to any of my points (including my admission of feeling hurt by his dismissal of me; which was true, I was). Secondly, his response conveyed the idea that my letter was *confirmation of my unreliability*, without backing it up with a single shred of evidence.

Intended or not, Nicolas' "spin" *was* picked up by subsequent posters. My pen was broken but Nicolas' words landed like music (i.e., *he* was the one who should be writing a book about John). The one from "Bob" obediently echoed Nicolas' words and then added some extra barb, revealing the iron hand inside Oasis' velvet glove. What Nicolas implies, his lackeys make explicit: I am dishonest, lacking self-awareness, and not worth the time or trouble "assisting" when it comes to understanding how good John is. The only hope for me is to bring me over to the other side, work me over, subject me to committee analysis, make me accountable for my sins, and strip me of all independent thought. Only then will my opinions be worth listening to.

Nicolas wrote that it is fine for us to disagree, but he wasn't interested in addressing any of my concerns, including being dissed by him while he pretends to be warm and friendly. He doesn't see our disagreement as a gulf because he can simply dismiss me as unreliable without showing how or why (and there's the gulf!). He doesn't *have* to address any of my points, because I have only confirmed my unreliability with them. My impression of Nicolas after these exchanges is that he is very much his father's son: uninterested in having a dialogue if it means relinquishing even a little bit of control of the situation. In other words, the very opposite of open.

Selling Sand: Guru Worship, Reality Distortion & the Question of Harm

During the seven years (on and off) I have worked on this book, there has been a seemingly endless back and forth going on in my mind regarding John de Ruiter. No matter how much evidence I find, no matter how many times I reach a point of *knowing* that he is a destructive personality and influence, there always remains a tiny, niggling doubt, like a virus that's so deep inside my system that no amount of colonics and enemas can completely flush it out.

Many people feel they have benefited from their time with John, including some of the people who have left him. Others feel they have been damaged by him and that they know of other people who feel the same way. Some of those who have left John may also feel that the people who are still with him are *observably damaged*, to the extent that they seem to be impaired in their capacity to reason or make choices. I certainly think this, and in fact, the most persistently persuasive evidence I have found for de Ruiter as a harmful influence has come from interacting with those people who most fiercely defend him. (To some extent also with those who have little good to say about him but who still seem to be somehow in thrall to him.) It is for these people—and the part of myself that still aligns with them—that I have most fervently searched for some final straw to break the Wizard's spell, once and for all, some piece of evidence or testimony that is so disturbing and conclusive that, after hearing it, no one could possibly still believe in John's goodness.

I know this to be a futile wish, and probably a neurotic one, too. It is like the conspiracy hunter's dream of a smoking gun. Mysteries of the sort that surround John de Ruiter are not so easily solved by such profane methods. The toxic effects of a spiritual guru and his teachings are slow, subtle, and insidious, and therefore the evidence must be painstakingly accumulated, over time, and carefully arranged in such a way as to be conclusive. When I reached out to the Birds of Being for testimonials, I was sincere in my request: I wanted to be able to present the evidence that de Ruiter's people *do* benefit from his teachings, and how, and then judge for myself how convincing this evidence was. Because let's face it, so far very little of it has been more than, "John is pure goodness and only by being with him and being totally committed to him will you be able to see that." Either that, or claims that he has brought sweetness and loveliness into their lives by his mere presence, with little or nothing about the lives as lived outside of John's influence.

Certainly there is no one, not a single person, to testify to the benefits of John's teachings who has now left him and the group behind.* There is no question at all in Oasis that "following what you know is true" means following *John*, which means staying with him (attending meetings) permanently, continuing to tithe to him, to refer to his wisdom and rely on his teachings. Autonomy is not on offer at Oasis, and wholeness is not part of the de Ruiter package. Rather, he offers a seemingly never-ending process of dis-integration, disempowerment, and (for the lucky ones) disillusionment.

*

---

* My wife might be the closest, since I think she would still say she benefited from her time with John. But she also agrees that his behavior in recent years is highly suspect and would probably admit that, with hindsight, there were indications she missed regarding his lack of trustworthiness.

The question as to whether John de Ruiter is committing harm via his teaching and his behaviors is perhaps the most important one to be raised. One of the best defenses of John and his teachings is the one he himself uses, which is that you cannot make an omelet without breaking eggs. Spiritual growth requires destabilization, for the soul-being to emerge into awareness, the constructed identity must be cracked, and arguments of this sort. With so many followers, it can also be argued that there are simply bound to be *some* casualties when the goal is fast-track transformation via high-pressure exposure to undiluted Truth. This is logical enough, but is it worth the cost?

One of the women John and Leigh Ann singled out for John's "Calling"—i.e., propositioned sexually—who accepted, gave me a full account of her experience and the effect it had upon her. Of the encounter itself, she said that her experience was that John had not considered her feelings and that she had not felt any kindness or tenderness from him throughout. She said that she was in shock afterwards, that she felt numb, confused, traumatized by the event. She couldn't understand what the purpose of the encounter had been and was unable to get any answers out of John, who ignored her many emails. She began to have suicidal urges and to experience high levels of distress, derangement, and a feeling of contamination—as if her innocence had been "imposed upon" by John's sexuality. She received counselling from one of the members of Oasis and was told that they, her counselor, saw nothing wrong with John's actions. She has since left the group. I transcribed her testimony for this book, but she later decided she didn't want to make her experience public, not even anonymously. In October 2017 she told me she is still healing from John's "psychic interference," which went on for over two years. "I was in complete despair and had liver failure when I asked John to remove the connection, which he did very recently. Recuperation continues since then." She also told me:

> I have been watching programs about cults and I recognize the fragility of the people involved. I cannot trust anything in my interior, my thoughts, feelings, anything. I am also having difficulty trusting others on the outside.

It's the responsibility of any spiritual teacher (just as it is of a therapist or any other professional) to be aware of the risks and to always be on the lookout for ways in which his or her methods might not be working. More crucially still, they need to be on the alert for ways they might be actively backfiring, either through premature meltdowns (as in the case of the woman I spoke to, and Anina), or, less dramatically, by causing unhealthy behaviors, fixations, and "spiritual neuroses" to occur. Has anyone really been improved by John's teachings? If so, does this compensate for those who have been hindered by them, inappropriately counselled, misled, or given the wrong tools for life? I would say this latter is true in my case, and that it had quite disastrous results. This doesn't mean I blame John (I take full responsibility); but it does mean I would consider his teachings—his influence—to be potentially harmful.

Oasis is currently under scrutiny from more eyes than my own, however. Even at the very first fly over, we have two suicides and one death from unknown causes, as well as many testimonies of psychic violations, strange apparitions, energetic disturbances, suicidal urges, many of which can be traced back to John. Then there is also the sort of harm the victims themselves may not be aware of, which in many ways may be even more pernicious, ways in which their cognitive faculties have been impaired, for example. Some of the evidence I encountered suggesting a seriously toxic element to John's behaviors and teachings has not been included, for various reasons. Of the allegations made in 2017 by "God," which appeared briefly at Birds of Being, some were confirmed (by Joyce and others); others were not. Of those that were confirmed, no one was willing to go on record and so I have been unable to include them here.

Others are less actionable while still being significant. I heard accounts from several people who have left the group that John encourages his wife Leigh Ann to drink heavily at social events, or at least does nothing to discourage it. This struck me as an extremely damning fact in more ways than one. If being around John is nothing but pure truth and goodness, why does his wife need to get drunk? If—as ex-Oasians also told me—John is so tightly controlling of Leigh Ann's behaviors, to the point of criticizing her facial expressions in public (for showing tiredness or irritation, say), why is he so laissez-faire when it comes to a potentially self-destructive habit? Something doesn't add up in Demontown, but apparently this is the sort of detail Oasians can ignore, under the advice of their Master: "Let the shallow be shallow, let the deep be deep." (Getting drunk is just a shallow activity and has no bearing on the deep—never mind the harm it does to Leigh Ann's body.)

Allegedly it's not only Leigh Ann, either. One correspondent who contacted me anonymously (I never found out who they were) told me that Benita's son, Alexander, and Nicolas used to go to bars with John, watch him get drunk, and then bring him home, silently body-guarding for him. One long-tome follower (now ex-) relayed a tale he heard from Baba—of a time when Baba was with John and they were sitting next to an ashtray. John nodded towards it and said, "If you love me, you'll eat that cigarette butt." Baba obediently swallowed it, after which John laughed or gave some sign that he was "only kidding."

Apparently, Baba relayed this as a funny story, and definitely not as a criticism of John. And as grotesque as it sounds, this does seem like de Ruiter's style of "pranking": getting people to do perverse and self-harming things as a means to exercise his power over them (and have a good laugh). To Baba and other roughneck Edmontonians, it might seem like a bawdy little story showing John's playful side. But in what it reveals about John's fundamental lack of care, it is like the shimmering tip of a dark and ominous iceberg.

*

I think much of this book shows, though Oasians might disagree, that de Ruiter does not really "do" personal relationships. He keeps people at a distance and doesn't let them know him. Judging by their testimonies, even his wives weren't able to get close to him. We know from their testimonies that the women John was closest to not only feel like he shut them out and kept them in the dark (deceived them), but that they were in some sense harmed by their relationship with him, and that the negative effects linger on. If John is causing harm to his nearest and dearest—while persuading those he keeps at a safe distance that he is pure goodness—isn't it logical to suppose that his "goodness" is not so pure, after all?

If John is involved in deceit, sexual exploitation, substance abuse, family-splitting, bullying, threats, manipulation and psychic violations, can such dysfunctional and unhealthy behaviors be separated from the question of what is harmful? If we think about the sort of self-deceptive, logic-twisting doublethink which Oasians have to inflict on themselves, and upon others, just to remain faithful to him, does this itself indicate that they are being harmed, or that they are harming themselves? Personally, I can think of nothing more harmful than the distortion of reality and the recruitment of others into an ongoing project of the same—even without the literal imbibing of toxins. I would even say this kind of crazy-making is the *sine qua non* of harm, as what unmoors us from the ground of our being and strips us of autonomy, wholeness, and well-being. It's also what we've come to recognize as the most basic characteristic of cults: the psychological sabotaging of people's capacity to discern truth from fantasy.

It's been seven years since I began to extricate myself from the influence of John de Ruiter, seven years since I first began this book-length study. From time to time, I still find myself referring back to something John said or was quoted as saying and being struck by the profound truth of it. Many of the most meaningful realizations—"knowings"—that I am settling into in middle age are similar or identical to things John has taught over the years. The notion of enjoying being in one's body and letting that enjoyment move you, for example; or of tuning into the awareness that nothing needs to be done and then acting from *that* awareness. There are so many benign statements he has made that are not just harmless but wise and tender and full to the brim with meaning. *And yet*, I didn't come to embody these truths as a result of hearing them from John. On the contrary, it is only in the years since I "left" de Ruiter that I began to discover for myself (with some help from other spiritual quarters) some of these fundamental principles and values, and only as they have become real for me through the process of living.

From this, I deduce that for all the wisdom and knowledge that John de Ruiter appears to have access to and share (for a price) with his followers, it does not (generally, there may be exceptions) lead to any kind of freedom, wholeness, or spiritual autonomy. It's my hope that this book shows, via countless testimonies and examples, that the *seemingly* benevolent nature of John's teachings, and the profound psychic-energetic impact of being part of the Oasis group, are inherently deceptive. They are means, yes, but means to a very different end than that which they appear to be offering. To use a very obvious example, like a magnificent horse built by Trojans, the aim of de Ruiter's wisdom is to dazzle and impress and make it past the gates, into the kingdom—the kingdom of the individual psyche. The aim, I believe, is to gain access to our interior spaces as a means of plundering our resources.

In my thirties (well before I met John), I once had a dream about floating through a realm of cosmic bliss. As I floated, I gradually began to realize—or at least suspect—that the bliss-effect was generated by invisible predators in order to make whoever passed through it docile, passive, and easy to pick off. In a word, to turn them into prey.

One of if not *the* primary explanations (qualifiers) for de Ruiter's behaviors has been consistent throughout this account, and throughout his "career" as a living embodiment of truth. In the words of the AC, it is simply this: "*what comes from John has always been good.*" Always been good means no exceptions. Any perception of not-good things coming through John is in the (distorted) eye of the beholder. Implicit in this bold claim (which is also a disclaimer) is that John has always been operating at a higher level of being than can be understood by rational, moral, cultural, mental or emotional standards. In other words, before casting judgment on John, due reverence must first be paid. If you don't revere what-John-is, you haven't understood him; so how can you cast judgment on his actions?

There is no possible answer to this line of reasoning because it preempts all attempts at logical argumentation. At the same time, fortunately, it also exposes the very mechanics it is attempting to conceal. It is the very call for reverence, worship, and for the suspension of rational or emotional judgment in lieu of complete trust that, in my opinion, most persuasively demonstrates the emperor's nakedness, and the corresponding necessity for constant dissembling and thought control among his followers.

Just as independent thought is nullified by a state of blind devotion and religious (or spiritual) awe, so a worshipful attitude towards another human being is only possible via a suspension of independent thought. The dark side of Oasis is therefore an exact match for the cautionary child's tale of the emperor's new clothes. To create a mirage in the desert in which the spiritual seeker finds him- or herself requires hijacking the seeker's capacity to differentiate between truth and fantasy, between sand and water, between a hope-generated mirage of deliverance and a true oasis. Simply put, if there is one thing I have learned unequivocally from John de Ruiter, one thing that has significant practical value in life it is this: Those who inspire reverence are not to be trusted.

Appendices

Appendix One: The Things Bob Had to Swallow

"To return back to this picture of John and who he was: for me personally, that became more and more clearly the picture that I would know him, there was an issue for myself with trust. . . . There could be situations that would enter into that for me . . . it could be harmful on the surface, or appear negative . . . . It would be like being a guinea pig, in a sense, in that John would do anything with me . . . For me then, the issue [was] of how much it would cost me, could I trust John to cause me to lose everything if he blew it?"
—Bob Emmerzael

The subject of Emmerzael and the entities is one of the more obscure areas of de Ruiter's history, and despite my best efforts I was unable to uncover much about it. Barrie Reeder, the elder who asked de Ruiter to leave Bethlehem church, told me (in 2011) that Emmerzael was known as "the burden-bearer": "He'd take other people's sins upon himself and then John would deal with Bob!" Hal Dallmann, who witnessed de Ruiter and Emmerzael working together, believed that "Bob was acting as a medium: he would take whatever the pain or hurt or disease was into himself and then John would lay his hands on Bob and do the healing that way." Dallmann found the use of a medium questionable from a Christian perspective, as the Bible specifically forbids working with mediums as "sorcery." At the 1998 meeting already cited, Emmerzael described the process:

> There would be stuff dealing with entities and people having entities and then John would make them go into me. . . . I would actually mirror, show, and manifest these entities that were in others. . . . We would spend until early in the mornings with that

> kind of stuff. It was part of what was being shaped, what was being formed with John . . . there would be things that would be shown that were hidden, secrets, stuff that they wouldn't have told anybody. These types of things would come up. There was one instance of a girl hearing what was taking place and then she just ran out of the room, I don't know if she was screaming. It was the most frightful thing that ever happened to her. . . . It would be like a connection with these people, as well, in that they would be given a picture of the truth, and in working with the truth, their hearts were also able to just soften and open with that kind of stuff.

I was aware that "opening and softening" had become one of the lynchpins of de Ruiter's teachings, an "absolute," universal truth to be practiced at all times, even—or especially—in the case of negative forces. I had even heard a tape on which de Ruiter used the example of the Antichrist as the ultimate opportunity, and necessity, for opening and softening. From what I gleaned from Bob's account, his entity-channeling allowed people to perceive the negative forces within them and provided an opportunity to soften and open to those forces, canceling out their influence. What Emmerzael was describing regarding "entities," however, wasn't a method I was familiar with, despite being well-versed in occult, and some Christian, lore. I could only guess at the metaphysical dynamics (or rationale) involved. Apparently, by using Bob as a medium (occultists often use young boys for this purpose), de Ruiter was "scrying"—bringing to light the presence of "demonic" entities dwelling within the members of the congregation. Emmerzael then either took the entities (temporarily) into himself or mirrored them via his bodily expressions, often writhing about on the floor and groaning "orgasmically" (Joyce's word) for the duration of the ritual. From a Christian point of view, at least, what de Ruiter and Emmerzael were up to was at the very least playing with fire, at worst "sorcery."*

Paul remembered that Bob and John spoke about "times they would go park in the van and witness demonic activity." This was "presented as a positive thing because it proved they were in the middle of 'Spiritual warfare.'" Paul told me that although he "never heard the term exorcism, entities might have been a term used for 'Demons.' It did seem to me that [John] would expose himself to demonic things but never take action to protect and exorcise them."

I was already familiar with de Ruiter's beliefs about demonic entities from a notorious Oasis tape called "What is Evil?" Although the tape was no longer available at that time (copies had been asked to be returned by Oasis), I had obtained a copy and found it fascinating. Many years after leaving his Christian roots behind, de Ruiter discussed satanic beings "mining" the planet for energy. I also knew that, in the early days at the *satsang* meetings, people writhing about and making guttural sounds—as at a Pentecostal meeting—were not uncommon. (I had heard such grunts and groans—usually belonging to one of de Ruiter's key cohorts, Baba—on many of those early tapes.) None of that really answered the question of what sorts of phenomena were occurring around de Ruiter, however, or whether they were deliberately caused by him. It was all largely inconclusive. The one thing that was clear to me was that Emmerzael acted not merely as de Ruiter's "guinea pig" but, in some more obscure manner, as a receptacle for forces—demonic or not—which de Ruiter was stirring up at that time. In Joyce's

---

* Bob Emmerzael developed cancer sometime after this.

words, Bob was "the carrier of demons." It seemed a curious role for the beloved disciple to be given.

Emmerzael eventually left de Ruiter's company and I knew from speaking to him—and from what Joyce had told me—that the two men had not been in touch for the better part of a decade. When I checked with Joyce to confirm the time Emmerzael had left, she admitted she didn't know, because his leaving had been gradual and never formally announced. "In that sense," she wrote me in an email "he never did 'leave.' His 'leaving' was a very, very gradual, scarcely noticed process." In the same email, she described how, sometime after de Ruiter moved out of her house and in with the von Sass sisters, Bob stopped hanging out with de Ruiter after the evening meetings and began going home directly. Initially it was just Bob and John, she said, but in the years from 1998 to 2000, Benita was also included. Benita and de Ruiter then began meeting at her house, and once de Ruiter moved in with the sisters, Emmerzael opted out of the post-meeting encounters.

Sometime after that, between six months and a year later, Bob began missing some of the meetings. It was always for what seemed like valid reasons, Joyce said, but it happened more and more often. After Joyce moved to Holland in 2003, she remembered her sister, Bob's wife, mentioning how long it had been since Bob had been to a meeting. Emmerzael allegedly never spoke about it, he simply stopped showing up. When people asked him about it, he avoided answering. As a rule, Joyce said, he was always vague and evasive. Initially he did say he expected he would begin attending meetings again at some point in the future, but later he said that "it would take a major shift for him to go back." He still spoke well of John, Joyce said. He had not disowned him but he did suggest there was "more going on than mere truth."

By his own account, Emmerzael invested just about everything he had in de Ruiter; his trust in him was total and unquestioning. In the end, was that trust betrayed? There were two obvious developments in the years leading up to Bob's departure: Emmerzael got cancer, and de Ruiter began his clandestine affair with the von Sass sisters. It was years before Joyce finally asked Emmerzael if her husband had already started sleeping with Benita during the post-meeting encounters, in 1998. She said Bob was vague at first, claiming that he often fell asleep and wasn't always sure what went on.

Eventually, he admitted that on occasion he would wake up from a nap to see de Ruiter and Benita coming down the stairs from Benita's bedroom. Bob claimed he hadn't known what was going on up there, and when Joyce replied that she doubted they went into Benita's bedroom to pray, Emmerzael's face remained a blank. Joyce was certain Bob knew what was going on at the time, but guessed that he had a "degree of denial" around the subject. "He was doing his best to be evasive and hide behind the argument that he could not know what happened behind closed doors." Since Emmerzael's wife was in the room while he and Joyce were having their discussion, it was likely Bob didn't want her to know how complicit he had been. Bob, like all of the others, came from a very moral, traditional background, and the situation, as Joyce said, would have been "a very hard one for him to swallow. But somehow he did."

Postscript: The allegations made by "God" previously mentioned concerned (among other things) Bob and other male disciples from the early days, and the claim that de Ruiter obliged or coerced them to perform certain sexual actions, possibly as a form of punishment. I called Bob a second time in 2017, partially to ask him about this. He hung up on me before I could even say why I had called.

Appendix Two: The Bully Type

The following is taken from Tim Fields' website, www.bullyonline.org/ I italicized those parts that most obviously match de Ruiter's behavior, public or private.

* *Jekyll & Hyde nature*—vicious and vindictive in private, but innocent and charming in front of witnesses; no-one can (or wants to) believe this individual has a vindictive nature—only the current target sees both sides

* *is a convincing, practiced liar and when called to account, will make up anything spontaneously to fit their needs at that moment*

* *is possessed of an exceptional verbal facility and will outmaneuver most people in verbal interaction, especially at times of conflict*

* *is unusually skilled in being able to anticipate what people want to hear and then saying it plausibly*

* is emotionally retarded with an arrested level of emotional development; whilst language and intellect may appear to be that of an adult, the bully displays the emotional age of a five-year-old

* in a relationship, is incapable of initiating or sustaining intimacy

* holds deep prejudices (e.g. against the opposite gender, people of a different sexual orientation, other cultures and religious beliefs, foreigners, etc.—prejudiced people are unvaryingly unimaginative) but goes to great lengths to keep this prejudicial aspect of their personality secret

* *is self-opinionated and displays arrogance, audacity, a superior sense of entitlement and sense of invulnerability and untouchability*

* has a deep-seated contempt of clients in contrast to his or her professed compassion

* is a control freak and has a compulsive need to control everyone and everything

* *shows a lack of joined-up thinking with conversation that doesn't flow and arguments that don't hold water*

* *refuses to be specific and never gives a straight answer*

* *is evasive and has a Houdini-like ability to escape accountability* [!]

* undermines and destroys anyone who the bully perceives to be an adversary, a potential threat, or who can see through the bully's mask

* is adept at creating conflict between those who would otherwise collate incriminating information about them

* is quick to discredit and neutralize anyone who can talk knowledgeably about antisocial or sociopathic behaviors

* may pursue a vindictive vendetta against anyone who dares to hold them accountable, perhaps using others' resources and contemptuous of the damage caused to other people and organizations in pursuance of the vendetta

* is also quick to belittle, undermine, denigrate and discredit anyone who calls, attempts to call, or might call the bully to account

* *gains gratification from denying people what they are entitled to*

* *is highly manipulative, especially of people's perceptions and emotions (e.g. guilt)*

* *poisons people's minds by manipulating their perceptions*

* *is arrogant, haughty, high-handed, and a know-all* [!]

* *often has an overwhelming, unhealthy and narcissistic attention-seeking need to portray themselves as a wonderful, kind, caring and compassionate person, in contrast to their* *behavior and treatment of others; the bully sees nothing wrong with their behavior and chooses to remain oblivious to the discrepancy between how they like to be seen and how they are seen by others*

* is spiritually dead although may loudly profess some religious belief or affiliation
* is mean-spirited, officious, and often unbelievably petty
* *is mean, stingy, and financially untrustworthy*
* is greedy, selfish, a parasite and an emotional vampire
* is always a taker and never a giver
* *is convinced of their superiority and has an overbearing belief in their qualities of leadership* but cannot distinguish between leadership (maturity, decisiveness, assertiveness, co-operation, trust, integrity) and bullying (immaturity, impulsiveness, aggression, manipulation, distrust, deceitfulness)
* *is constantly imposing on others a* false *reality made up of distortion and fabrication*
* *sometimes displays a seemingly limitless demonic energy especially when engaged in attention-seeking activities*
* *uses lots of charm and is always plausible and convincing when peers, superiors or others are present;* the motive of the charm is deception and its purpose is to compensate for lack of empathy
* *relies on mimicry to convince others that they are a "normal" human being* but their words, writing and deeds are hollow, superficial and glib
* *displays a great deal of certitude and self-assuredness* to mask their insecurity
* *excels at deception*
* *exhibits unusual inappropriate attitudes to sexual matters or sexual behavior;* underneath the charming exterior there are often suspicions or intimations of sexual harassment,

sex discrimination or sexual abuse (sometimes racial prejudice as well)

* displays a compulsive need to criticize whilst simultaneously refusing to acknowledge, value and praise others
* is also . . . aggressive, devious, manipulative, spiteful, vengeful, doesn't listen, can't sustain mature adult conversation, *lacks a conscience, shows no remorse, is drawn to power, emotionally cold and flat,* humorless, joyless, ungrateful, dysfunctional, disruptive, divisive, *rigid and inflexible,* selfish, insincere, insecure, immature and deeply inadequate, *especially in interpersonal skills*

I estimate one person in thirty has this behavior profile. I describe them as having a disordered personality: an aggressive but intelligent individual who expresses their violence psychologically (constant criticism etc.) rather than physically (assault).

Appendix Three: Man of Sorrows, Hidden Christian Roots

"You need no protection to being pained. With protection, boundaries are put on goodness, boundaries are put on meeting, all on your terms. And of goodness . . . please, not too much. Let her *pain* you. Let whatever she is at present, reach you. It doesn't matter what she is in reaching you. It *will* pain you."
—John de Ruiter, 2011

De Ruiter talks a lot about "giving up one's life" to truth. The Gospel's Jesus said, "Whoever loses his life shall save it" (Matthew 6:25). De Ruiter speaks of living for truth, Christians talk of serving the Lord. De Ruiter teaches people to "do what they know is true"; Christians preach doing "the will of God." De Ruiter talks of "untruth," which—if truth is synonymous with God—equates with sin or Satan. De Ruiter uses the terms "clean" and "unclean," identical in meaning to pure and impure and equivalent to the Christian ideas of sin and grace. His term "okayness" seems to correspond with Christian grace, while he talks of "insistence" as the inverse of that. For a "non-dualistic" teacher, his teachings are rife with dualisms. De Ruiter admonishes against living for "want and need," while Christians are wary of giving in to "lusts of the flesh." "Settling for less," another cornerstone of de Ruiter's teachings, is equivalent to one of the supreme Christian virtues, humility.

One of the biggest no-no's for de Ruiter and his followers is trying to get something for yourself; any kind of "agenda" or self-interest is an instant disqualifier when it comes to "living for truth." That is the equivalent of the Christian idea of sin, of "going against God's will." De Ruiter talked for many years of "home," a state of rest inside "the tiny bit which one knows is true"; this is similar to the Christian ideas of grace and heaven.

More abstractly, a "movement of being" is de Ruiter's term for an impeccable happening that comes from truth itself; the Holy Spirit has a similar meaning for Christians. The foundation and supreme value of de Ruiter's teachings is "absolute surrender," which corresponds with the Christian idea of "salvation." And so on.

I came up with the above correlations in less than half an hour, via a cursory comparison of de Ruiter's teachings with the Gospels. I am pretty sure a closer examination would reveal plenty more correspondences. I am also struck by an interesting similarity between de Ruiter's spiritual evolution and that of St. Paul (arguably the man most responsible for Christian doctrine, including Jesus). Paul began as Saul, the persecutor of Christians. According to Joyce, before he became a Christian, de Ruiter was a bully. Saul had his awakening on the road to Damascus when Jesus came to him, and he converted to Christianity with the same zeal with which he had persecuted the early Christians. De Ruiter had his own awakening and conversion, and later claimed to have received a personal visitation from Jesus. Paul taught the law then discovered grace, and his teachings were a curious philosophical juxtaposition of law, sin, and grace. He argued that without law there would be no sin, but without sin, there could be no grace. The final result of that theological equation was, "Under grace, there is no law." De Ruiter also began as a fierce adherent of Christian law ("Pharisee-ism" was the term Joyce used, oddly) and suffered from a corresponding sense of sin (around his own sexuality) followed by an experience of grace. I am pretty sure the same pattern played out in his later sexual "awakening" also, with the von Sasses, when de Ruiter became adulterous but experienced (or at least described) the affair in terms of having attained a new kind of grace. Like St. Paul, de Ruiter became exempt from law, and therefore from sin. He had been absolved of both by the intervention of grace/Jesus Christ/the Truth.

As with all systems of control which enforce a correct way of being, de Ruiter's "absolute truth" is founded on a system of *morality*. The morality isn't obviously Christian, or even obviously moral, because it is unique to de Ruiter. It is *his* moral code because he alone has come to embody "the living truth" that is "the only true way of being." It is a totalitarian truth system, and rather like Christian doctrine, de Ruiter's moral system of "Truth" exacts a heavy price in suffering. Despite presenting it as the supreme virtue and the one living truth, de Ruiter has said that opening and softening "looks really terrible." (When a person is opening and softening, he has said, they will feel *really bad*.) For that reason, depression is sanctioned by the teachings. "When you feel worthless," de Ruiter has said, "you have the right information." (It is a phrase I have used repeatedly with others.) Depression relates to "disintegration of internal structures," and is considered necessary to clear up a space for "the innermost" (the Holy Spirit) to move into. That opens the way for a constant series of breakdowns, and for a whole lot of people feeling *really bad* as they undergo a continuing loss of meaning in their lives—outside of the meaning which Truth (de Ruiter) is providing.

In Christianity, Christ is the way, the truth, the light; belief in him is all that is required for salvation. De Ruiter taught a "way of being," which he claimed to embody, and assured his followers that it was not necessary for anyone to be awakened, enlightened, or to receive the truth. Such desires, he claimed, were sourced in the personal self and could never lead to the truth, because they could never be "clean." The good news was that it was enough to know that someone, somewhere, *was* receiving the truth. Christians likewise are encouraged to see themselves as sinful and recognize that only Christ is perfect.

*

"Jack, I may be going out on a limb here, but you don't seem like a happy camper."
—Parry, *The Fisher King*

There is a well-known western myth about a Fisher King. The Fisher King is the guardian of the Holy Grail who is inflicted with a wound that never heals, a wound which he received as an adolescent young man. In one version of the story, told by Robin Williams' character in Terry Gilliam's *The Fisher King* (which came out in 1991, and which de Ruiter the movie buff probably saw), the young prince has a vision of a fire with the Holy Grail in it. He hears a woman's voice telling him that he is to be the keeper of the Grail and will grow up to heal the hearts of men. The prince, overcome by the promise of destiny, reaches in to grab the cup. The Grail disappears and the prince's hand is burned by the fire.

In the Irish equivalent, Finn Mac Cumhail (pronounced "McCool"), a young man, catches "the salmon of wisdom," just as was foretold. He is told by an elder to cook it but not to taste it. While cooking it, he burns his thumb and puts it in his mouth to cool it, tasting the forbidden flesh. He is stricken with a wound that never heals. In a third version of the story, the young fisher king—also entrusted with the keeping of the holy lance—is wounded in the testicles during a ruckus when the spear is being stolen. This version makes the sexual nature of the wounding explicit, though even in the sanitized movie version, the adolescent boy reaching for the "cup" (feminine) is burned by fire (lust); the symbols shift and morph but the meaning remains constant. (In the Mac Cumhail version, the thumb is an obvious phallic symbol.)

The main point about the wound—besides its sexual nature—is that it never heals. In all the versions of the story, the wound grows deeper as the years pass. The prince grows up to be a King, but because of his wounding he is afflicted with anhedonia, the inability to experience pleasure or joy. Being "too ill to live but not ill enough to die," his life is a continuous ailing and sorrow, and as a result, his kingdom falls into apathy and disorder. The land becomes a wasteland, and the people lose all hope. "The fisher king wound," writes Robert A. Johnson, "is in the male, generative, creative part of a man's being. It is a wound intimately connected with his feeling function and affects every sense of value in his psychological structure." Johnson adds that it is "probably the most common and painful wound which occurs in our Western world." In his review of the Terry Gilliam film, Eivind Figenschau Skjellum (a young spiritual seeker, who also reviewed *Braveheart*), writes:

> So how does the wound appear? The playful, active boy who is told to sit down and be quiet receives a shock (wound) to a nervous system that only seconds ago was so alive. The mother who shames her son's sexuality "shoots an arrow through his testicles" and wounds his sexual feeling function. A son who requests his father's blessing and receives only his aloofness and temper ends up distrusting men and his own masculinity and a deep wound cuts through his psyche (Robert Bly refers to this as the father's axe blow).[*]

The wound relates both to the young hero's premature "grab" for the Grail—the desire to claim the sacred feminine for

---

[*] http://www.masculinity-movies.com/movie-database/the-fisher-king

his own glory—and to the (perhaps resultant) loss of the spear, symbolizing impotence.

> The spear represents the masculine integrity and feeling aspect which has been stolen and without it there is no protection, no "holding" for the Holy Grail to re-emerge. In psychology, author Robert Johnson has observed that "the Fisher King's wound is symbolic of men's difficulties in directly intimate and sexual matters."[*]

I have speculated that de Ruiter suffered some deep early wounding related to his father, and that it led to an abuse of power and to bullying behavior. As a young man, during or immediately following his first "awakening," I have suggested that he may have entered into a period of sexual confusion that eventually led to a "fall from grace" and the assumption of *strict Christian values and morals.*

In the myth, the Grail Castle falls upon hard times after the spear is stolen, an act which coincides with the Fisher King's wounding. In some versions, the Grail Castle falls into chaos, as the knights resort to "trickery, temptations and illusions to corrupt specifically the Fisher King and ultimately the Holy Grail (the unity with God).... As myth had it, many knights had tried to win back the spear but were all corrupted by the forces of the 'dark side.')" Doesn't that sound a little like de Ruiter's shenanigans at the Bethlehem church leading to the creation of the Oasis Empire? Like de Ruiter, the Fisher King didn't speak much. His wound was the most basic thing about him: his one,

---

[*] This and following two quotes, Richard A. Sanderson, "Wounded Masculinity, Parsifal and The Fisher King Wound," http://howellgroup.org/parsifal.html

inescapable reality, and whatever words came out of his mouth were sourced in that bottomless well of suffering. De Ruiter might *talk* of "core joy," but the echo from his own "Cor" sounds a different song. It is a song of isolation, because the King "only gets relief from his pain when he is fishing, meaning, doing reflective work on himself."

> With the coronation of the wounded King, the kingdom seemed to pass into some other dimension. It seemed insubstantial, the castle seeming to float, mist-like above the land, disconnected from the Earth. Eventually, traders would set out for the kingdom, following the same roads as before, and find themselves arriving in some other region of the land. It seemed that the kingdom no longer existed within normal time or place, as though the Earth itself had given up the kingdom and her wounded King to heaven or hell.*

De Ruiter even has a thing about fish: when I visited in 2010, there was a tank full of them in the entrance to the Oasis building (a tank Joyce told me he built himself). He named his company Oasis—a body of water. If yesterday's god is today's demon, is it possible de Ruiter is embodying the Christ of yesterday? In the Aquarian Age, worship and sacrifice, secrecy and denial, are no longer the order of the day. Characteristics of Aquarius are freedom, individuality, eccentricity, rebellion, directness of communication, intellectual analysis, transparency, an absence of hierarchy, and collective community endeavors. Since Aquarius signifies the collective consciousness of humanity, the return of Christ, if it coincides with the Age of

---

* http://mythicperspectives.blogspot.com/2006/03/monomyth-legend-of-fisher-king.html

Aquarius, would be—contrary to popular Christian belief—*a collective event, not a one-man show.*

If de Ruiter is living in the past (tuning into an obsolete archetype, that wound that cannot heal), it would explain why he claimed to be the Messiah predicted in Isaiah, even though that Messiah had already been and gone long before he was born. It is as if de Ruiter is caught up in a rerun of a show that aired two thousand years ago. The edifice he built around him has all the trappings of a Roman (Piscean) empire—complete with fish tanks, churchlike lecture halls, and a stage and throne for Caesar. It is a palatial space for the emperor to hold court in and for his many subjects to sit at his feet and drink from the sweet nectar that he provides, the living truth fountain at the center of the Oasis-womb.

How often does an oasis turn out to be a mirage?

Appendix Four: Ministered by Truth: Cult Mechanics in Action

(Brian:) "Look, you've got it all wrong! You don't NEED to follow ME, You don't NEED to follow ANYBODY! You've got to think for your selves! You're ALL individuals!"
"Yes! We're all individuals!"
—*Life of Brian*

After I returned from my 2011 trip to Edmonton (the Oasis auction event), as an experiment, and as part of "tying things up," I started a new discussion at the Birds of Being group. To my surprise, it was neither ignored nor shut down at once. I began by dipping my toe in the "group mind" with a tentative post about my doubts about de Ruiter, asking if it was okay to discuss them. I was told that focusing on doubt was generally discouraged—as it didn't "gentle the heart"—but that there was no rule against it. Because of my first post, the focus initially centered on the question of doubt, a bit of a red herring because I'd only used that as a way to ease my way in. Once I began to openly express my opinions about de Ruiter and the teachings, there commenced an attempt to "help" me to get back to "what I know" and, by definition, return to the fold. Most people who posted once did not post again. My experience was a bit like being in the ring as one contender after another climbed in for a round: Apostate versus Oasis.

There was some fruit, however. During the course of the "debate," I received a couple of private messages from people who didn't want to air their doubts at BoB, including an Englishman named Phil Stretch (who eventually posted there). Phil had been a devotee of de Ruiter for eleven years, having met him in Glastonbury. He had read my book *The Lucid View*, and had been surprised that such "a discerning mind" had been taken in by de Ruiter. He admitted that he had "felt the grace around John for years, the stillness, the light, the truth, the silence," but over time he realized that "what I felt was my real self, and my projection of it on to John was false." He believed that, despite the fact that de Ruiter "has surrendered and refined much hence that incredible energy . . . his ego is untouched, his need to be special is untouched, his need to be the most enlightened ever is untouched [and] has created unconsciously a cult of personality."

He also had some gossip: he knew "for a fact" that de Ruiter had started to see Leigh Ann before he had officially broken up with Benita, and that he took Leigh Ann on holiday to Egypt while "Benita thought he had gone with Katrina and Katrina thought he'd gone with Benita." "A combination of facts," he said, "revealing indisputable lack of integrity and my own seeing, that John's teachings kept people on a merry go round of utter dependence and that no one was ever going to be recognized as realizing what he had, led to my split from him." He considered de Ruiter to be "an incredible man," and honored how much he had surrendered, but was convinced that the ego that was left was "so concentrated and potent as to be almost invulnerable." He used the phrase "an enlightened ego": "the ego's last and most powerful stand." He cited a scene from the movie *Little Buddha* where "Mara appears in Buddha's image and says, 'You who has gone where no one else will dare, will you be my God?' To that John said yes, foregoing actual total ego death."

This was an entirely separate (and private) discussion, however, because Phil only posted a couple of times at BoB (and deleted one of his posts very quickly). So far as vocal allies went, I was pretty much on my own. My intention wasn't to change anyone's mind or win an argument, however, but to clarify my own thoughts and find out if the Oasis community really did function as a cult, as I suspected it did.

I posted at BoB that meeting John had been a wonderfully transformative experience for me, but that it was only complete once I was ready to turn away from him, that this was my "coming of age." Perhaps what disturbed me most about Oasis, I said, was that turning away from John was considered the equivalent of turning away from truth, when for me it had been the opposite. Without John, I might not have emptied my cup as quickly as I did; my mistake was trying to use him to fill it up again, when the filling had to come from within. It seemed to me as though John encouraged people to "fill themselves up" with *him*. (He was "living truth," after all.)

What I most often heard from people in the group—I had heard it from myself also, though I didn't realize it at the time—was declarations of faith posing as statements of fact—"knowings." There might be nothing wrong with having faith that John was a Master of Truth; but wasn't there something wrong with claiming an article of faith as fact? Most people around John could be defined as believers or non-believers, those who were "in" and those who were "out." The assumption of the believers seemed to be that anyone who had left had turned away from truth, hence was mistaken and deluded. Was it (as someone contended) a trap to question a Master's relationship patterns? Or was the trap having blind faith in a Master *as* a Master, so that whatever he did privately was both beyond our capacity to judge and none of our business?

The amount of concealment I had encountered around John's private activities, and around Oasis in general, was disturbing to me. There was no possible way for me to reconcile a message of truth and honesty with all of the concealment and dissembling. A proponent of truth needed to be an open book, I argued, but the book of John was not only closed, it was sealed tight with cobbler's glue and buried somewhere deep in the forest. Being told there was nothing to know about a Master because "there was nothing there" was the oldest trick in the book!

During the course of this discussion, I was informed that "doubt is a hindrance" and that it was not wise to listen to it since it took us away from "Knowing/Truth." The insidious thing about doubt, apparently, was that "it can wear a mask of 'goodness'" and convince us that it is worthwhile to listen to, when in fact it is always a lie, because "only Truth tells us what is true." I was encouraged to focus on whatever I found nurturing about John or his teachings, instead of my doubts or "issues." I was admonished that a sharp, incisive, critical mind was positive only when it served truth, otherwise it was a way to "maintain untrue ground in one self [sic]." I was accused of using intelligence to serve my own purposes and turning "every well-meant message" into a means to strengthen my position in the debate. I was told that there were lots of people who "don't realize John as a master of Truth."

I was assured that de Ruiter lived "an impeccable life." When I questioned how they could know this if his private life was off-limits, I received no response. The people of Oasis, I was told, had "beaten their self-horses to death" and wanted some of "the more" now! The implication was clear: I was still high on my self-horse, venting emotions and bearing a childish grudge, "avoiding the deep lonely within the self." Someone had a realization while reading a book that I couldn't "be helped," that trying to reason with me would only cause my "deepest level of awareness to hold on tighter to the old patterns it put in place." This would hurt both my "Beingness" and my "self/person."

It was around the point when someone suggested I was beyond helping that Norman, the board's moderator, thanked everyone for their contributions and announced that "any value this thread had is now exhausted." A couple of members spoke up in defense of the thread, and it continued for a few more days.

There were even a couple of people, Phil and someone named Bertram, who dared to express their own doubts about de Ruiter. I was stirring up the nest.* It was then that Baba posted a separate thread, exactly as he had done months earlier in response to my Truth Movies thread and for the same apparent purpose. He addressed his post to "BOB Managers," saying that, although Norman had stated recently "that certain thread had run its course . . . some individuals want to keep talking about their issues endlessly." He then proposed that "contributors who really don't have a whole lot to contribute should get a warning and/or be blocked," ending with the emphatic statement: "It is getting fucking tiresome!" One woman replied approvingly and called Baba "dear straightness." Another, who had approved Norman's decision to end the thread earlier, posted a definition of *hubris*: "Hubris often indicates a loss of contact with reality and an overestimation of one's own . . . etc. etc."

Norman piped up by saying that they didn't have any hard rules on how the forum was moderated, and that for the most part it "self-policed very well." There were exceptions, however, and Norman considered the current thread to be one. In the absence of any hard rules (and since his co-moderator, Kesh, was away), he had decided to end the thread and any spinoffs it had spawned. "Enforcement is more difficult," he wrote, because as moderators they had few tools for the job. One option was to ban someone, another to change their settings so their posts needed moderator approval. Although Norman considered

---

* Phil emailed me about his experiences at BoB: "I have expressed questioning in the lightest and kindest way and met with confrontation at times . . . Once I posted a poem expressing my own seeing, totally unrelated to John and was chided because it wasn't eulogizing John. Your own actual realization is not encouraged unless you put yourself below John and praise his, praising him *is* realization in the group in actual fact, though they would deny the idea of this."

neither option desirable, he was implementing the latter for anyone who did not respect his request. He added that he would be happy to discuss his reasoning with anyone "one on one," but "to do so here just prolongs and feeds the discussion." If anyone found his approach inappropriate, he invited suggestions on how to better regulate this forum "for the enjoyment of all its members," adding that "careful consideration could lead to something better than the policing options we have now."

I posted one last time and was advised by Norman that any further posts would be moderated. Before I left I pointed out that an unpopular thread did not need terminating because it died out all by itself. To curtail a thread because certain people didn't like it or found it "tiresome" was simply censorship. The fact that Norman wanted suggestions or questions to be sent privately was a way of isolating any dissenters and preventing further group discussion. (Before that, a couple of people had emailed me privately, wishing to take the discussion outside the public domain; I could see no good reason to do so.*) Almost none of the points or questions I raised during the debate were addressed (I am fairly sure not one of my questions was answered). Norman's behavior as a moderator was at best incompetent. If he and/or Kesh owned the list and single-handedly created the rules, it was their responsibility to make them clear to everyone, or to modify them when a supposed transgression took place. Baba meanwhile acted like a bully once again and his abrasive remarks were praised as "straightness." That Baba's bullying carried the day suggests a hidden hierarchy within the Oasis community, since Baba's word clearly carried

---

* Baba also sent me a private email, after all the dust had settled, saying that he hoped we could be friends. I replied in an open (though also challenging) fashion, but received no response.

more weight than other people's, and his aggressive and censoring comments went unquestioned, even applauded.

BoB is careful to include a disclaimer that it is not representative of Oasis, John de Ruiter, or his teachings. Like most disclaimers, it was based on a technicality. I have heard from more than one source that the longest-standing members of de Ruiter's community are among the most rigid, narrow-minded, and fanatical. As with Benita, long-term proximity to de Ruiter apparently hasn't given these people soft or surrendered hearts. If this is evidence of a trickle-down effect, then the behavior of the disciples gives an idea of the headman's true nature. BoB might not officially represent Oasis, and Oasis might not officially represent de Ruiter; but the same individuals are implicated, so what exactly is the difference? And if the highest ranking and the most outspoken members of BoB—the Oasis inner circle—are narrow-minded fanatics and bureaucrats, how is that *not* representative of the community and de Ruiter? If they are not representative, where are the voices of those who disagree with them? If a few blowhards and bullies misrepresent the group so badly, why allow them to? For that matter, where was de Ruiter in all this? If he was genuinely interested in truth and honesty, shouldn't he want to correct the culture of thought-policing that has grown around him, both at Oasis and at the BoB forum? He is reputedly *extremely* controlling about where and how his image is used; so allowing BoB to use it is tantamount to an endorsement.

The fact de Ruiter creates a subtle (or not-so-subtle) form of psychic servitude in his followers is surely beyond question. Whether there is a deeper purpose behind that is something perhaps no one but John can say for sure. For me there was, but I was grateful not to de Ruiter but to another who helped open my eyes, and above all to my own discernment. The party line which the BoBites used on me (an idea I was already partly sold on before I'd ever heard of de Ruiter) was that reason is a limited tool that, at a certain point, has to be relinquished to enter a deeper experience of truth. For a while, I let that argument sway me. Over time, I realized that what I saw around de Ruiter wasn't an ability to relinquish reason when it was time to move beyond it; it was an inability to reason clearly whenever it became threatening to strongly held beliefs.

With the affidavit, I didn't hear a single explanation (besides that Benita was making it all up) that made rational sense. It invariably came down to, "John's just a guy with problems like any other so we should mind our own business and focus on the good he is doing." As "reasoning," this is both illogical and irrational. How surrendered is it to have security cameras and Rottweilers? Such basic evidence of a fundamental contradiction between what de Ruiter preaches and what he practices can't simply be dismissed with the argument that "John's not perfect" or "He's only human"—nor with the exact opposite, that he is a master of truth who is beyond questioning; and certainly not with both arguments simultaneously!

A spiritual teacher's imperfections—and above all his attempts to conceal them—give vital clues to the ways in which his teachings—and his energy—might be polluted or misleading. The Oasian logic is that, since de Ruiter is a living embodiment of truth when his followers need him to be, it doesn't matter what might be going on in his private life. It would be easy to dismiss such an argument as moronic, except that some very intelligent people are resorting to that same line of "reasoning." Since they aren't morons, the only logical conclusion is that their thinking processes have been scrambled.

When Charlie began to question me about de Ruiter, and put forward some alternative points of view and anecdotes suggesting that he might be less than straight or trustworthy, my initial response was: "Why are you questioning John when I already know he is Truth?" I was irritated and defensive, feigned incomprehension, and assumed a mildly outraged and unsympathetic position. I know exactly how this kind of scrambled, logic-free thinking works because I once practiced it. Now I have descrambled my own brains, I continue to encounter people around de Ruiter who are defending "knowings" that haven't "transcended" logic but that have simply ignored and defied it, like a willful child refusing to face facts.

Simply stated: I have never seen so many people come so far out of "what they know" as I have seen at Oasis, in the rush to defend John de Ruiter.

Appendix Five: How to Spot a Cult

Warning Signs that You are in a Cult

Courtesy of the Edmonton Society Against Mind Abuse:
http://www.esama.ca/warning-signs-that-you-are-in-a-cult
(Link last checked Nov 5 2017.)

If you suspect the group you are in is harmful, but are not sure, ask yourself these questions:

- do they claim to have a special corner on the truth, something no other groups has?
- are you told to not question what is being taught, as the leadership are godly, honest, have divine authority and you must trust them?
- are you discouraged from asking questions as to why members have left, and expected to accept the reasons the group leadership gives you?
- do they put down other churches, groups, etc, while pointing out their faults and errors to build themselves up? do they use peoples faults and sins as examples of what to do and what not to do?
- are you made to feel your failures, as though your performance is not up to par to their righteous standards?
- do they recommend for you to be around their people, expecting you to attend all group activities? if you do not, are you are questioned about your spirituality or dedication?
- do they stop you from reading anything negative about themselves?

- do they call those who fall away enemies, dogs, or cancer, even using examples from the Bible or other such materials?
- do they place an emphasis on evil and the devil, declaring that the world outside is a threat to the group?
- do they defend themselves in every area?
- do they give importance to a spiritual goal, such as enlightenment, godliness, salvation, that has no real tangible way of being measured?
- do they operate in humility, or seem arrogant, and make demands on you to obey, using such statements such as "real believers obey without question or if you really were a devoted follower you would do such and such"?

Be aware of:

- an instant bonding or friendship without even knowing you
- being told you have a special calling or potential and that if you join you will move further ahead; flattery is used often in cults
- when you ask questions about the history of the group, the answers are vague or avoided altogether
- feeling that something is being hidden from you

Cults will always divide the family unit instead of bringing them together. They will make you choose between God and their church. They use scriptures such as: "Jesus came to bring a sword, not peace" or "one must give up brothers, sisters, wife, and house for the kingdom and be a true follower." Children often become the most hurt because of strict rules enforced on them. They lose their childhood and are deeply affected, being unable to adjust later on in life. Religious systems that are not balanced can be socially and psychologically disastrous for innocent children.

*

Cult Danger Evaluation Frame, by P.E.I. Bonewits

1. INTERNAL CONTROL. Amount of internal political power exercised by leader(s) over members.
2. WISDOM CLAMED claimed by leader(s); amount of infallibility declared about decisions.
3. WISDOM CREDITED to leader(s) by members; amount of trust in decisions made by leader(s).
4. DOGMA. Rigidity of reality concepts taught; amount of doctrinal inflexibility.
5. RECRUITING. Emphasis put on attracting new members; amount of proselytizing.
6. FRONT GROUPS. Number of subsidiary groups using different names from that of main group.
7. WEALTH. Amount of money/property desired or obtained; emphasis on members' donations.
8. POLITICAL POWER. Amount of external political influence desired or obtained.
9. SEXUAL MANIPULATION of members by leader(s); amount of control over sex lives of members.
10. CENSORSHIP. Amount of control over members' access to outside opinions on group, its doctrines, or leader(s).
11. DROPOUT CONTROL. Intensity of efforts directed at preventing or returning dropouts.

12. ENDORSEMENT OF VIOLENCE when used by or for the group or its leader(s).
13. PARANOIA. Amount of fear concerning real or imagined enemies; perceived power of opponents.
14. GRIMNESS. Amount of disapproval concerning jokes about the group, its doctrines, or leader(s).
15. SURRENDER OF WILL. Emphasis on members not having to be responsible for personal decisions.

http://www.religioustolerance.org/bonewits-cult-danger-evaluation-frame.htm
(Link last checked Nov 5 2017.)

About the Author

Jasun Horsley is a writer, artist, podcaster, and researcher-explorer of anomalies. He has written books (under various names) on movies, popular culture, paranoid awareness, psychology, spirituality, autism, organized child abuse, mind control, and social engineering. His website is http://auticulture.com

A many-times-published author, he makes an average of $100 royalties per annum.

He works at a thrift store in Canada and has no sizeable assets.